Geology
off the
beaten track

exploring South Africa's hidden treasures

Nick Norman

The Richtersveld offers geologists rich and varied rock outcrop.

Published by Struik Nature
(an imprint of Penguin Random House South Africa (Pty) Ltd)
Reg. No. 1953/000441/07
The Estuaries No 4, Oxbow Crescent,
Century Avenue, Century City, 7441
PO Box 1144, Cape Town, 8000 South Africa

Visit **www.penguinrandomhouse.co.za** and join the Struik Nature Club
for updates, news, events and special offers.

First published in 2013 by Struik Nature
3 5 7 9 10 8 6 4

Publisher: Pippa Parker
Editor: Helen de Villiers
Designer: Janice Evans
Illustrator & cartographer: Elmi Pretorius
Proofreader & indexer: Emsie du Plessis

Reproduction by Hirt & Carter Cape (Pty) Ltd
Printed and bound in China by 1010 Printing International Ltd., Hong Kong

ISBN 978 1 43170 082 0
E-pub: 978 1 77584 070 1
E-pdf: 978 1 77584 071 8

FRONT COVER: *Experience South Africa's austere and beautiful Karoo from Graaff-Reinet's magnificent Valley of Desolation viewsite.*

BACK COVER: *White cliffs overlook the limestone quarry where the fossilized skull of the 'Taung child' was found, for which the name* Australopithecus *was first coined.*

Struik Nature thanks the Council for Geoscience, De Beers and E Oppenheimer & Son
for their generous sponsorship towards the production of this book.

All the data for the maps in this book were supplied at no charge by the Council for Geoscience.

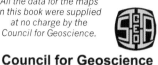

E OPPENHEIMER & SON

E Oppenheimer & Son is the investment holding company of the Oppenheimer Family interests, founders of the global mining company Anglo American, and managing shareholders of De Beers (the world's leading diamond company), until its recent acquisition by Anglo American.

The Oppenheimer Family has a rich history and association with conservation work in South Africa, having long been supporters of biodiversity conservation and research in natural sciences and wildlife administration.

These conservation efforts are inspired by the Oppenheimer Family's passion for the preservation of South Africa's natural heritage: Nicky and Strilli Oppenheimer were joint recipients of the World Wildlife Fund's Lonmin Award for environmental conservation in 2007, in recognition of their outstanding contribution to conservation. One of the projects highlighted in the award is the 'Diamond Route', which links together all the conservation initiatives of De Beers and the Oppenheimer Family.

The Diamond Route was established as a partnership between E Oppenheimer & Son, Ponahalo Investments and De Beers, subsequently launched at the World Summit on Sustainable Development in 2002. Today, the Diamond Route coordinates meaningful research geared towards conservation and sustainable land use. The project has interests in Namaqualand, Kimberley, Tswalu (Kalahari), Brenthurst Gardens (Johannesburg), Ezemvelo Nature Reserve and Limpopo. Over 250 000 hectares of ecologically diverse protected areas have been opened up to eco-tourism as part of the project.

Through initiatives such as these, E Oppenheimer & Son remains a dedicated custodian of South Africa's unique ecological heritage.

DUNCAN MACFADYEN
MANAGER: RESEARCH & CONSERVATION

Contents

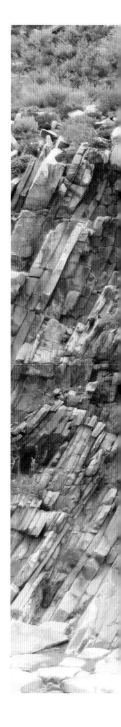

Flaggy sandstone of the Lekkersing Formation in the Richersveld.

Acknowledgements

First and foremost, my thanks go to Sue. Once again she has supported a husband often verging on insupportable, mostly with a smile and undeserved grace. I could not have done the book without her.

The book would not have been possible without the generous sponsorship of De Beers, through the good offices of CEO Philip Barton; E Oppemheimer & Son, in the person of Duncan MacFadyen; and the Council for Geoscience, whose Spatial Data Manager, Ken Wilkinson, arranged supply of map data at no cost.

Struik Nature's publishing manager, Pippa Parker, supported the project enthusiastically throughout, and rallied the team to do the impossible; editor Helen de Villiers never wavered in her dedication to understanding every sentence of sometimes obscure text; designer Janice Evans pulled together disparate elements of text, photographs, drawings and maps; and Elmi Pretorius created simple, clear maps from a wealth of data under difficult circumstances. Freelancer Emsie du Plessis checked chapters and proofread and indexed the book enthusiastically and competently.

In each of three areas with particularly challenging geology I was able to count on the best technical input available. There would be no Richtersveld chapter had it not been for the area's champion Paul Macey of the Council for Geoscience (CGS), who found time for meeting after meeting in his hectically busy schedule of input into projects both local and international. The 'Syntaxis Zone' of the Cape Fold Belt was opened up by Coenie de Beer, also of CGS, who took me into a part of the field he understands better than anyone. Also in Chapter 2, the Tankwa Karoo and Roggeveld Escarpment region were expertly laid bare during a two-day excursion led by De Ville Wickens and Prof. Izak Rust, both authorities on these areas. The former was on hand frequently to answer questions and review sections of text on the Tankwa Karoo and the latter reviewed an early draft of the whole book for glaring omissions and errors. In Barberton I was guided for two days by the area's champion and avid amateur geologist, Tony Ferrar. To both Tony and his wife, Sandy, I owe thanks for friendship, and for housing and feeding me.

For the fieldwork in the Richtersveld I was accompanied by my son, Christopher, who was delightful and stimulating company. Jim Rushby, an old friend from Botswana exploration, took time away from his drilling business to drive me through the Baviaanskloof in his bakkie, and his penetrating questions were useful in formulating that chapter.

Carl Anhaeusser, doyen of South African geology, helped me with a number of photographs and answers to questions on various aspects of South African geology. Dr Hannes Theron, former Director of the Bellville office of the Geological Survey (now CGS), gave generously of his time to answer questions on the geology of the Cape. Nick Baglow, Director of the Polokwane office of the CGS, answered questions on Limpopo geology, and from the same office Günther Brandl made a special trip to photograph the Blouberg unconformity for me, as well as answering questions about Mapungubwe. At the CGS office in Upington Hendrik Minnaar shed light on the geology of the Namaqua-Natal Belt in that area, which would otherwise have posed problems. Nigel Hicks of the Pietermaritzburg bureau of the CGS gave me his recommendations of what to see on the KwaZulu-Natal route, without which a number of worthwhile sites just off the road would have been missed. The Eastern Cape chapters were enriched by the input of local expert Marc Goedhart, recently of CGS.

Most of the people listed above gave of their time to review parts of early drafts of the manuscript. I cannot thank them enough.

In the assembly of visual material, mainly in the form of artist's impressions, thanks are due to geo-artist Maggie Newman for coming on board with enthusiasm; as well as to Roger Smith of Iziko Museum in Cape Town, Billy de Klerk of the Albany Museum in Grahamstown, Bruce Rubidge of Wits University's Bernard Price Institute, and Jennifer Botha-Brink and Lloyd Rossouw of the National Museum in Bloemfontein. Their help in sourcing visual material on our palaeontological and anthropological legacy was of utmost value. Sian Tiley-Nel, Curator of the Mapungubwe Collection of the library at the University of Pretoria, was extraordinarily helpful in supplying visual material relating to that site. Mike Johnson, who made the time to delve deep into the CGS archives for a photograph he had taken for another book, is thanked for going the extra mile, as is Ayanda Kheswa of Elitheni Coal, for text and photographs from their mine in the Eastern Cape. Johan Hattingh of Creo Design generously provided images of the evolution of Algoa Bay and of river development in the Eastern Cape.

Steve Richardson, head of UCT's Earth Science Department, loaned me specimens of kimberlite to photograph; Peter Booth of Nelson Mandela Metropolitan University and Vinnie Mitha of the CGS in Port Elizabeth, gave insights into Eastern Cape geology; and Chris Rippon in Barberton provided valuable information on the geology of those parts. Mike Denny supplied archival information on the Denny Dalton gold mine, Wikus Venter at the Kalgold mine, between Mahikeng and Vryburg, enabled access to imagery of the mine, and Prof Nic Beukes and Michiel de Kock elucidated aspects of Northern Cape geology. Peter Habberton kindly accommodated me at Tiger Kloof near Vryburg and showed me the stromatolites near the school as well as sharing the school's extraordinarily rich history with me.

Nearer to home, Fairview's Vineyard Manager Donald Mouton took me to two of the vineyards where grapes are harvested for their Solitude and Beacon shiraz wines, to show me two startlingly different terroirs. Hugo de Villiers opened his display cabinet of Stone Age implements at the family's Landskroon Estate so they could be photographed, and he provided useful background. Photographer Peter Kemp made time to take a selection of photographs of the tools, apart from over several days showing me how to use my new digital camera.

Heartfelt thanks are due to all the people listed above, as well as to many others unnamed who made contacts, sourced photographs, accessed maps electronically and gave much needed encouragement.

From beginning to end I have been aware that I could have done none of this without the blessing of the creator of it – and us – all, almighty God. I thank Him for amazing stories and the words to tell them.

NICK NORMAN

'*Water in the rivers of the Tankwa Karoo is a rarity.*'

When reading the geological maps accompanying each section of the journey, refer to the key on the inside back cover flap for an understanding of the geological units shown.

The siliceous tidalites in the Fig Tree creek near Barberton are a classic example of tidal sedimentation in some of Earth's oldest sediments. They are easily accessed, and worth a visit.

Preface

In the seven years since *Geological Journeys* was published windows have been opened into the Earth at a steady rate, and wider ones too. Reconstruction of environments that existed millions of years ago is becoming a more exact science than ever before. The theme of this book is that although our understanding of geology is increasingly more detailed, what we see is nothing new. Plate tectonics as the driving mechanism of geological change, deeply rooted in earliest times, is securely in place: we just know more about it and understand it better.

I need to pay tribute to the geological map as the basis of what we know. Without the published maps produced by the Council for Geoscience, formerly the Geological Survey of South Africa, there would have been no book. They are the framework; all the sights you see and marvel at make up the flesh on the bones.

Homage needs to be paid to the people who made the maps in the first place. A hundred years ago pioneer geologists set out with ox wagons or donkey carts, with bicycles and tents, their basis of work the most rudimentary maps showing the important rivers, mountains, roads and villages. Onto them they marked the formations they observed, slowly starting to make sense of it all.

After that, but still before the age of high technology, young graduates were sent out into the field with a bakkie, a caravan, an assistant, aerial photographs and maps showing topography and any infrastructure as might have existed, the expectation being that they would not be seen again until they had the beginnings of a geological map. From the many thousands of man-hours thus spent came the maps without which preparation of a book like this would not be possible.

A mapper of this generation commented to me, as we drove through the area he had mapped, how privileged we are, as geologists, to be able to see the world around us and to start to understand it. There was no questioning it, but then I remarked that we were equally lucky to live in a part of the world of such immense geological diversity and largesse. And it is that thought that pervaded my experience as I drove around: how blessed we are.

NICK NORMAN

Introduction

This book is a companion to *Geological Journeys: A traveller's guide to South Africa's rocks and landforms*, which discusses geological features along all the major routes across South Africa. In this later guide you leave the well-beaten track, with its traffic and familiarity, and take the road less travelled. You'll see fewer cars; you'll be freer to slow to a crawl, to pull off the road and stop and look. Whether or not you see new parts of the country, unexpected birds and animals or unfamiliar veld types, one thing is certain – that you'll see and get to understand geology you had never even noticed before.

'You'll see fewer cars; you'll be freer to slow to a crawl, to pull off the road and stop and look.'

Thinking big

The study of geology requires enormous elasticity of imagination. First, there is the stretch required to think in terms of millions, even billions, of years. And second, we need to regard the Earth's coastlines and landforms as they exist today as being relatively new – and constantly changing as a result of the composition of the Earth.

The matrix and siliceous cement bonding these cobbles is barely evident, yet the near-vertical face in this magnificent cutting in Enon conglomerate between the Baviaanskloof and Patensie stands year after year without appearing to lose a single stone.

Below the rigid crust and upper mantle (together known as the lithosphere), the lower mantle (or asthenosphere) is mobile: convection currents in the asthenosphere churn over and over, but ever so slowly. The currents are a response to the vast difference in temperature between the white-hot core and, thousands of kilometres above it, the atmosphere-cooled surface, where we live in comfort.

Massive convection currents drive the tectonic plates at the surface, pushing up linear fold mountains where plates collide. The Himalayas and the Alps are examples of such folding: the imposing peaks of the Himalayas were pushed up as the Indian subcontinent crashed into the Asian mainland; and, more or less along the same suture, the north-moving African Plate buckled the southern edge of its northern neighbour, Europe, shifting coastal plains into mountains high enough to be home to premier ski resorts.

Added to this are scattered, randomly located and deeply sourced plumes of hotter mantle material, located roughly midway under the moving plates, which cause volcanic eruptions at a distance from plate margins – Hawaii and Iceland are resulting examples.

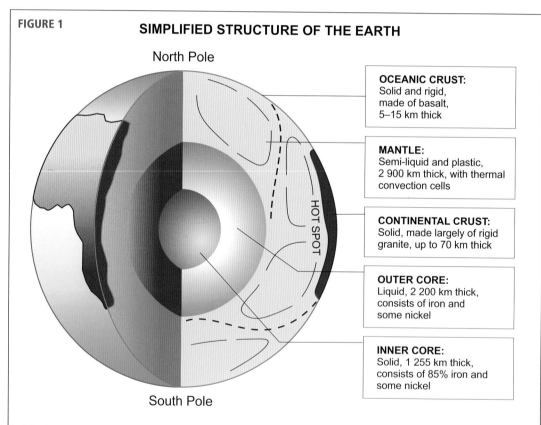

FIGURE 1

SIMPLIFIED STRUCTURE OF THE EARTH

North Pole

OCEANIC CRUST:
Solid and rigid,
made of basalt,
5–15 km thick

MANTLE:
Semi-liquid and plastic,
2 900 km thick, with thermal
convection cells

CONTINENTAL CRUST:
Solid, made largely of rigid
granite, up to 70 km thick

OUTER CORE:
Liquid, 2 200 km thick,
consists of iron and
some nickel

INNER CORE:
Solid, 1 255 km thick,
consists of 85% iron and
some nickel

HOT SPOT

South Pole

The Earth is roughly concentrically layered, like an onion, and has four basic layers. These are the outer 'skin' or crust, the mantle, the outer core, and the inner core. The crust beneath Africa is particularly thick and very stable. The hot core generates extremely large-scale convection currents within the mantle causing the movement and deep subduction of crustal plates, and generation of magma hot spots, shown here diagrammatically.

Southern Africa: a geological phenomenon

Southern Africa stands proudly in the global geological landscape: an extraordinary range of geological exposures are concentrated in what is a relatively small region, and rock formations covering the full span of Earth's history are all well represented here.

Two important rock 'labels' have their origins in southern Africa. The most silica-poor (ultramafic) primeval volcanic rocks, common around the world, are called komatiite, from the nKomati area in the southeast corner of Mpumalanga; and the primary ore of nearly all the diamonds mined in any hemisphere is named kimberlite after the tented mining town that sprang up in the Cape Colony in the 1870s. The first rock type is as ancient (more than three billion years old) as the second is young (about 60 million years). Of more universal relevance, the glacial rock tillite, originally thought to be of volcanic origin, was first correctly identified in South Africa. The ice-borne sediment called till, deposited during the last Ice Age, had been well known for decades in the high latitudes of Europe, Asia and North America. It was many years, though, before the mysterious rock, which occurs widely across South Africa, was identified as lithified till, and the name 'tillite' coined. Now tillites are recognized around the world.

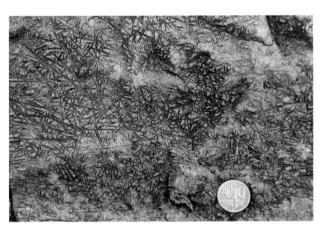

LEFT: *Weathered surface of komatiitic lava from close to the nKomati River near Barberton, showing characteristic spinifex texture.*

BELOW LEFT: *Kimberlite showing (a) a garnet crystal, rounded in its ascent from the depths; (b) an olivine crystal; and (c) a small xenolith of crustal rock.*

BELOW: *Dwyka tillite at Denny Dalton showing very large ice-transported boulders.*

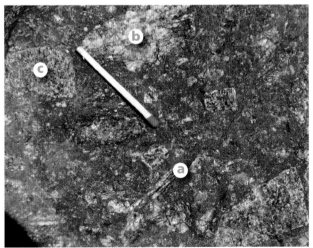

Principles of geological change

It is important to remember some key geological tenets: that geological timescales span billions of years and that the processes are cyclical, repeating endlessly through time; that robust, rigid beds of hard sandstone can be folded as though they were Plasticine; that minerals can be changed from what they were into something completely new – just as dough becomes bread in the oven; and that sediments once laid down deep in the ocean can now be seen high on a hillside, and fossil seashells can be dug out of a road cutting far inland.

An important principle underpinning the cyclicity of geological processes is uniformitarianism, defined as 'the doctrine that all geologic changes may be explained by existing physical and chemical processes, as erosion, deposition, volcanic action, etc., that have operated in essentially the same way throughout geologic time'. The present is the key to the past.

Change may happen by imperceptible increments, cumulatively, until a 'tipping point' is reached. Deep below the surface old fault lines can accommodate stress from movement in the asthenosphere for millions of years before something gives; the fault is reactivated for a moment to relieve the accumulated stress – and seismic devastation results. In 1883 the explosive destruction of the volcanic island of Krakatoa in the Sunda Straits between Java and Sumatra happened without warning, and was over in a matter of hours. In a short space of time, over 36 000 people lost their lives, as volcanic pressure that had built over countless millennia was given vent. Much more recently, tens of thousands died in northeast Japan as a shallow earthquake of unprecedented scale and close offshore gave rise to a tsunami: the giant wave upended ocean-going ships as though they were children's toys, and flattened multi-story buildings. Be they earthquakes, tsunamis or volcanic eruptions, none of this is new or unprecedented: all have happened countless times before.

Geology at work: the tsunami from the 2011 Tohoku earthquake reaches the coast of Japan.

A corollary to the principle of cyclicity, or recycling, is that geological evidence is constantly lost as later processes overwrite them. Because our planet, including its atmosphere, is essentially a closed system, nothing is added or subtracted: constituent elements are merely changed, in the same way as dough is transformed into bread; or they are moved about, as a diamond that is carried from its volcanic crater in Lesotho to the mouth of the Orange River and up the Atlantic coast. Geological raw material is endlessly recycled. Over billions of years, mountains have been pushed up and flattened; deep canyons have been cut, only to disappear as their walls slowly eroded away; lakes have been created before filling with sediment and drying up. In chronicling Earth's history we have to be thankful for the shreds of evidence that are left, and for the geological detectives that have built detailed scenarios from those scraps.

Interpreting the clues

As we go deeper into prehistory, the task of reconstructing palaeo-environments in less favourable hunting grounds is steadily more difficult, requiring increasing reliance on our imagination to piece together scraps of information into a realistic picture. As factual fragments come to light, each jigsaw piece serves to fill in the picture. Thanks to the technological age we live in, our understanding of the geological past is increasingly comprehensive and detailed. Carefully applying the principle of uniformitarianism, we can transport ourselves back millions, even billions of years and reconstruct the environments we find recorded in the rocks. We can plot the positions of the tectonic plates that converged to push mountains to their lofty heights. We can reverse the cooking of minerals till we've got the sedimentary particles that settled on primeval sea beds, or along coastlines, or on swampy coastal flats or flood-filled rivers. We can track sedimentary loads back to their sources, to highlands of which barely a trace remains. It's this fundamental detective work that makes geology such an exciting and rewarding field of research.

The more things change ...

... the more they stay the same. There was, to be sure, one single moment 13.7 billion years ago when it all began. As the first seconds and years and then aeons slipped by, the universe, its suns and new planets evolved; and among its planets the Earth changed from something scarcely comprehensible, to a landscape that would have been barely recognizable to us, and slowly to an increasingly familiar scene.

An alien landing his spacecraft in the Karoo 200 million years ago would have found it not very different from the scene that would have greeted his forefathers 200 million years before that, and quite similar to the scene his descendants would step into today. A billion years ago it would have been significantly different and two billion years before that, unrecognizable.

If uniformitarianism is a valid principle today – and applicable to most of geological time – it wasn't always so. In the beginning, the newly formed planet developed at a relatively dramatic rate: now that our planet has matured, change is almost imperceptible. As an analogy, we might recognize George Clooney or Julia Roberts in photographs as teenagers, but not as toddlers and certainly not as babes in arms.

Next time you drive through the Karoo, stop, stand, and look around you. Half-close your eyes and turn the clock back, say, 260 million years. Imagine you are on an island of higher ground in a vast, swampy flood plain, with lakes, pools and cut-off meanders all around. To the south are rugged foothills and, beyond them, towering snow-capped mountains.

Although through half-shut eyes the scene in front of you is not completely unfamiliar, you don't recognize any plants such as you might see today in any part of Africa. Nor do you recognize any of the animals – not surprisingly, considering that you have travelled back four times longer than the 65 million years since the dinosaurs died out. Another difference strikes you as you lift your eyes: the sky is empty. There are no birds, no flighted creatures of any description.

The animals you do see are mostly squat and heavy-limbed: they lack the elegance of antelopes or the grace of large modern felines. Few of the creatures roaming these Palaeozoic plains are furry: their skins are mostly hairless and scaly. They are reptiles – or, more precisely, mammal-like reptiles, both large and small, some carnivorous, others vegetarian. Some are aquatic, some terrestrial, some amphibious. They are precursors to the dinosaurs, themselves precursors to mammals, whose time still lies far over a future horizon. It is these mammal-like reptiles that form a crucial fragment of the evolutionary story. Their discovery has made the Karoo a celebrated source of fossilized relics of creatures that bridged the gap between the ancient quadrupeds and the new major Class of animals, the mammals. Fossil-hunters from far and wide continue to be drawn to the dry plains of the Cape.

An artist's impression of what the landscape in the Karoo might have looked like 254 million years ago.

A palaeontological wonderland

Certain factors have favoured the southern Karoo as a fertile hunting ground for palaeontologists. The relatively slow, tranquil sedimentary environment meant dead animals were entombed largely intact, and the enclosing sediments were left undisturbed, for the most part, in their original horizontal state. Hundreds of millions of years after its formation, this great package of strata, much of it fossiliferous, would be exposed as Gondwana broke up, forming a new southern escarpment with a new coastline; this exposure tells a wonderful story of adaptation and evolution. And, finally, the semi-desert climate prevailing in the region today has not been conducive to the formation of a soil cover that would obscure the tell-tale signs of exhumable fossils. South African geology can be thankful for the legacy of the Karoo sediments, which offer a unique snapshot of local conditions around 260 million years ago.

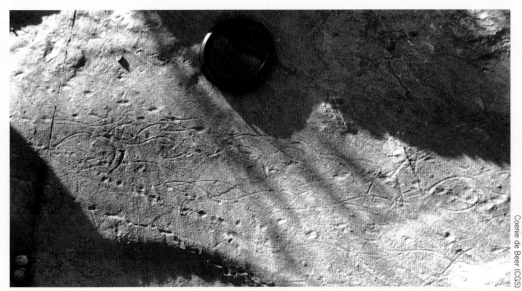

Coenie de Beer (CGS)

Fish-fin traces and footprints of small reptiles left in drying mud some 260 million years ago near Fraserburg in the Cape.

An unstable world

We know that we live on an unstable planet, even if in South Africa the reminders are fewer than, say, in Chile or New Zealand or Japan, where earthquakes are not a rarity, and smouldering, snow-capped volcanoes are a legacy of the red-hot lava that built them.

Today, the notion of plate tectonics, or continental drift, whereby landmasses continuously change their shape and position on the surface of the planet, is well established. We recognize that Madagascar was once joined to Africa and that just as it split off from the mainland, so, one day, will East Africa break away along the ever-deepening Rift Valley, leaving the mother continent that much smaller.

We're familiar with the idea of Gondwana as parent to the southern continents and India, and of a northern supercontinent called Laurasia that existed before the North Atlantic opened up. There is clear evidence of even earlier landmasses, like Pangaea and Rodinia.

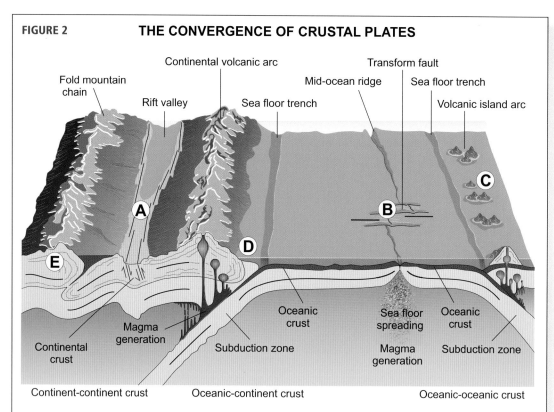

FIGURE 2   **THE CONVERGENCE OF CRUSTAL PLATES**

Continent-continent crust   Oceanic-continent crust   Oceanic-oceanic crust

A. On **continental crusts**, spreading margins create rift valleys. In the Rift Valley of East Africa there is substantial crustal thinning, not shown above, accompanied by the well-known volcanism.

B. By the process of sea floor spreading, **thin oceanic crust** moves apart creating new crust and forming mid-ocean ridges, cut by numerous transform or cross-faults, such as seen along the Mid-Atlantic Ridge.

C. **Oceanic to oceanic:** converging margins create subduction zones as one crustal plate is forced beneath the other, forming volcanoes, deep ocean trenches, earthquake zones and strings of volcanic islands, such as the Indonesian archipelago.

D. **Oceanic to continental:** converging margins also create subduction zones and form continental volcanic arcs, such as the Andes of South America.

E. **Continental to continental:** converging margins are marked by the formation of fold mountain ranges like the Himalayas or, closer to home, the Cape Fold mountains, themselves probably of Himalayan proportions when first formed.

We know that all the continents except Africa are drifting into the Pacific, whose floor is being consumed under the continents; and that a converse process is taking place in the Atlantic, which is getting wider as new basaltic magma wells up along the mid-oceanic ridge through global-scale fissures that are constantly pushing their edges apart. Plate tectonics, in which a series of rigid plates float on a viscous substrate, has been a formative process since the beginning of time.

The first land appears

The geological environment has changed beyond recognition. Around Barberton 3 600 million years ago, for instance, there was no land. Underwater rifts, similar to the mid-oceanic rifts of today, had started to open up, although the komatiitic lava that oozed up through them was quite different – it was hotter and more primitive (chemically speaking) than the basalt that spills out of the giant cracks running the length of the North and South Atlantic today. Sediment formed intermittently, though with no land to shed detritus into the ocean, the chemical precipitates were rich in iron and silica. The welling up of komatiite expanded the tectonic plates, forcing their outer edges beneath neighbouring plates, which were pushed up above the surface of the earliest oceans. There was volcanic activity, too, pushing up cones that stood high and dry above the sea surface. With significant magmatic activity, the Earth's crust was thickening and the first proto-continents were forming. Because the lava comprising a large part of the new crust was greenish, these most ancient remnants of Earth's evolution are called 'greenstone belts'; and they occur on every continent.

Greenstsone belts float like sailboat keels in a sea of granite, and are sought out by mining companies because even in those earliest geological times the igneous systems were generously endowed with gold. Terrain where greenstone belt keels are plentiful, such as Barberton, Zimbabwe and the Kalgoorlie area in Western Australia, are all historic gold-producing districts of note. (We will dig deeper into the auriferous ground around Barberton in a later chapter.)

These pillow lavas in basalt are from near Barberton, though they may be seen in greenstone belts around the world (see text box on p. 188).

The effects of climate change

We cannot escape the fact that, regardless of the causes, climate does change; it always has. As the main – but not the only – agency of change, Earth's axis of rotation alters relative to its path around the sun, only by a few degrees in every cycle, but enough to change climate and bring about ice ages and 'interglacials'.

During the interglacials, melting polar ice caps shed billions of cubic metres of icy water into the oceans, and the sea level rises around the globe. This happens regardless of processes in the mantle, which themselves cause the land to rise or subside. As the continents also warm up, hot air currents that ascend for most of the seasonal year repel rain-bearing cold fronts, keeping them offshore. Centimetre by centimetre, year by year, millennium by millennium, deserts and semi-deserts claim former crop lands, and rivers dry up and become choked with sand washed off bare hill slopes in rare and violent storms.

The pendulum always swings back, though. As the Earth cools again, the ice caps send frozen fingers and fronts out into polar oceans. Rainy seasons are longer and more intense; deserts shrink and forests spread. Muddy rivers are reborn, taking millions of tonnes of sediment to the sea, all the while lowering land surfaces. In southern Africa, the Lesotho Highlands erode steadily; as a complementary process, far from these heights, the sediment disgorged from river mouths builds wedges in the sea. Ultimately these form deltas at and just above sea level, which are colonized by mangroves and other coastal trees along their seaward fringes. Between river mouths, dunes form behind the beaches, waiting to be vegetated during the next interglacial. On and on it goes.

Sand dunes in formation near Woody Cape, east of the Sundays River in the Eastern Cape, are an ongoing element of Cape coastal geology; fossilized examples are evident from Langebaan in the west to between Ncanara and Grahamstown in the east.

The shaping of southern Africa

By 3 100 million years ago the basic foundation of southern Africa's geology, the so-called Kaapvaal Craton, was in place, itself an amalgamation of early smaller cratons or mini-continents. It occupies the northeastern quarter of modern South Africa, and all of the rest of southern Africa was subsequently added to it or overlaid on it.

The remainder of the landmass that we know as southern Africa was built on to the western and southern edges of the Kaapvaal Craton, in so-called mobile belts between it and adjoining cratons. In these belts, starting as sinking troughs, sediments were deposited, supplemented by minor flows of lava. With none of the rigid foundation that a craton would offer, the belts were subjected to forces from below and from the sides as the cratons moved relative to one another. The sediments and lavas in the troughs became folded, and in Bushmanland and Namaqualand and along the southern rim of the craton, extending to beyond KwaZulu-Natal (the so-called Namaqua-Natal Province), where the process was prolonged and attended by elevated temperatures, they became highly metamorphosed.

Meanwhile, on the craton itself, subsiding basins such as the Witwatersrand and the Pongola accumulated great thicknesses of a variety of sediments. Lavas of the Ventersdorp Supergroup poured out to build vast plateaus kilometres thick. Over millions of years these subsided and above and alongside them a new, very extensive basin formed to accommodate the dolomites and other sediments of the Transvaal Supergroup. Endless alternating uplift and subsidence, which happens over a vast span of time and unfolds without drama, led to the formation of new mountain ranges and new basins into which rivers would deliver their loads of sediment from the hinterlands.

These metamorphosed and distorted sediments of the Vaalkoppies Group in the Namaqua-Natal Province are part of the crust that was accreted (or plastered) onto the Kaapvaal Craton as a result of tectonic forces.

Basalt eruptions terminated the Karoo sedimentary era, the feeders remaining as dolerite dykes, such as shown here.

Finally, the subcontinent was almost stable, but for the dying phases of building the towering Cape Fold mountains, and forming the last major sedimentary basin, the Karoo Basin. This latter feature spanned a large part of Gondwana, first collecting glacial outwash and melt from huge polar ice sheets, and subsequently a varied range of sediments, aggregating many thousands of metres.

Gondwana moved from the southern part of the planet to straddle the equator. As mantle currents prepared to split the supercontinent asunder and great cracks formed in the crust, basaltic lava forced its way to the surface, capping large parts of the sedimentary pile. This basalt is preserved in the Drakensberg and Maluti highlands, and in the north-south Lebombo range, where it was draped over the edge of the continent as the Indian Ocean prepared to open up. Where it failed to reach the surface, the lava squeezed between layers to form sills or into vertical cracks as dykes.

As Gondwana divided and the peripheral fragments drifted away, new coastlines formed, closely akin to those we know today. Along them, both on the coastal plains and off the coast – on the shelf – new sediment settled. In the centre of the subcontinent, the Kalahari Depression accumulated extensive wind-blown sand, much of which is still a feature of the Northern Cape.

Southern Africa has risen since Gondwana broke up. In this case the uplift has continued for tens of millions of years, so that low-lying plains have been elevated to prodigious heights: the Lesotho Highlands, snow-capped for months during cold winters, are eloquent testimony to that.

The thousand-metre-high Table Mountain owes its origins both to the initial elevation during formation of the Cape Fold Belt and, later, the slow regional uplift with the rest of southern Africa.

In the time it took for the Himalayan mountain chain to form (around 70 million years), changes to the architecture of the southern African landscape have, by comparison, been superficial. The drainage patterns across its western part have meandered substantially as rivers have readjusted their banks – a cosmetic change, perhaps, but one with far-reaching consequences for the country's topographic evolution. Major tributaries have become choked with sediment and all but disappeared, while elsewhere, new valleys have been cut and steadily deepened. Table Mountain has at times been cut off by the sea from the mainland; what is now False Bay has sometimes been dry land.

And there, in a few pages, is a telescoped geological history of southern Africa. We will expand on individual aspects of it in the route and area descriptions, for which it should provide a useful context.

On the road: understanding geology

Geology, including geomorphology – the study and configuration and evolution of landforms – is the main, but not the only discipline covered in this book. The route-by-route treatment also lends itself to brief descriptions of the vegetation you will see and, where applicable, agriculture and even history. As you drive the country's provincial and regional roads, you will be introduced to geological maps and cross-sections. Geological maps, constructed from detailed mapping of rock outcrops, show an interpretation of the underlying geological formations as if all soil and overburden had been removed. Generally, the maps in this book show geological formations at the 'group' level to avoid unduly complicated images. Geological cross-sections are idealised pictures of what the underlying rock formations would look like if you could see them side-on, and this adds the third dimension to the geological picture. A selection (but by no means all) of places or sites of geological importance or interest, called 'geosites' ❷, are also shown on the maps and referred to in the relevant text, and are often accompanied by photographs.

Along nearly all national and some lesser roads, blue kilometre marker plates or beacons, located every 200 m, have been put in place by the South African National Roads Agency (SANRAL). They are clearly visible and comprise valuable markers to pinpoint sites referred to in the text. Where useful, GPS co-ordinates are given.

You will find as you travel with this guide that your experience of what is at your feet and around you is immeasurably enriched. If you complete every journey described in this book, plus those in the earlier volume, *Geological Journeys: A traveller's guide to South Africa's rocks and landforms* – you will have seen the most ancient algal remains visible to the naked eye, and lava erupted at temperatures far in excess of any today, over three billion years ago. You will have crossed Karoo and grassland where the fossil record is so complete that specialists travel from around the world to see the carefully exposed remains. You will have been to the quarry where the skull was found that gave rise to the name *Australopithecus*, a pre-human whose forbears and cousins would be found far and wide in Africa. Armed with this guide, each new cross-country trip will be not only an adventure, but an exercise in time travel too!

RIGHT: *Blue kilometre marker plates have been put in place by the National Roads Agency every 200 m along nearly all national and some regional roads.*

FAR RIGHT: *Key to the maps.*

| tarred | untarred | Freeway and national road |
| Main road |
| Secondary road |

🛡 ◆R30 R717   Route markers

– – – – – International boundary
——————— Railway

▢ Capital or city
◉ Chief administrative town
◎ Major town

○ Secondary town
⊙ Other town
○ Settlement

Ⓣ Toll route
❷ Geosite
▲ Mountain peak
■ Place of interest

1 Cape Winelands

GEOLOGICAL OVERVIEW

This drive incorporates four key wine-route destinations: Durbanville, Paarl, Franschhoek and Stellenbosch. Easily accessible from Cape Town and ranking high on the list of South African tourist destinations, the Cape wine route is full of geological interest. All three basic categories of rock type, namely igneous, metamorphic and sedimentary, are well exposed, and the scenery is spectacular.

Although you're in the Cape Fold Belt, with its high mountain ranges and wonderful geological exposure, you won't see much folding. That's because we're in

The view from the Durbanville Hills tasting room over newly planted vines and onto the Ciolli Brothers' quarry is a reminder of the interconnectedness of rock, soil and the fruits thereof.

the Syntaxis Zone, where the north-south ranges and fold systems to the north of Cape Town give way to the east-west elongation, which stretches eastward from here to beyond Port Elizabeth. In this region, comprising a tectonic domain of its own, instead of folds you'll see lots of very broken rock and some good faults.

Even though you're in the winelands we're going to touch only briefly on the subject of terroir and the extent to which geology might influence the style of wine. Feel free, though, to play the game based on what you read in these pages and the wine you taste!

Geology of the route

Cape Town to Durbanville

Leave the northern suburbs of Cape Town on the M13, which is not difficult to find. Ahead of you and to your right is the whaleback of Tygerberg, part of a group of hills called, informally, Durbanville Hills. The western and southern slopes of the hills are close enough to the west coast to enjoy cool onshore winds throughout the year. Together with the Mediterranean climate of the area, with its winter rainfall and dry summers, these slopes have the capacity to produce high-quality wine.

You may wonder about the gently rolling hills, quite unusual in this region of rugged, craggy mountains that rise straight out of the low-lying plains. The answer lies in the geology, and it applies to other areas of low relief in the winelands closest to Cape Town. These hills are all formed by sediments of the Malmesbury Group; they comprise mainly greywacke and phyllite, rocks made of clay minerals that easily erode (unlike the hard quartz of the range-forming Table Mountain Group).

Another thing you'll notice about these hills is their contrast with the bare granite slopes of Paarl Mountain. The slopes you'll cross as you enter Durbanville are covered by soil, which, where not under vines, supports a vigorous growth of grasses and indigenous fynbos – the natural cover of the area.

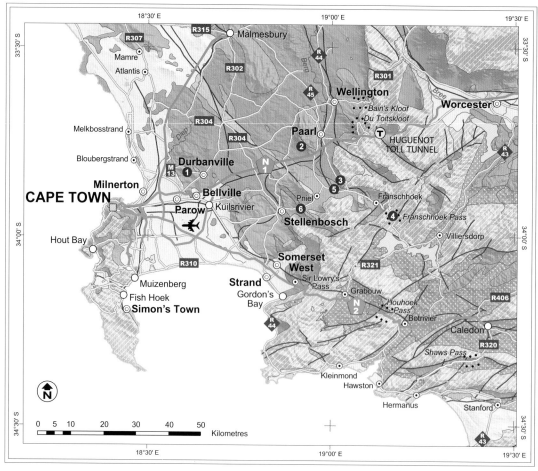

MAP 1

Ripple-marked Malmesbury Group siltstone in Lafarge's Durbanville quarry shows how delicate primary structures can survive several phases of deformation in a history of more than 500 million years.

The Malmesbury sediments were folded long before the sediments of the Table Mountain Group were laid down. These sediments were lightly metamorphosed by the folding, as well as by the heat of intrusion of the igneous Cape Granite as it formed plutons – bodies of rock that solidify below the surface of the Earth. During intrusion, the sediments immediately above and around the plutons were 'baked' to form a hard rock we know as hornfels (German for 'hornstone', after the characteristic 'horn' peaks it makes in the Alps). Both the heating (during granite intrusion) and the metamorphism (during folding of the sediments) have resulted in rocks that are brittle; this, added to their hardness, makes the Malmesbury sediments ideal road-building material. As you drive between northernmost Cape Town and Durbanville, you'll see a number of quarries **(geosite 1, map 1)** (GPS S 33° 46.33', E 18° 55.417') that excavate the hornfels to meet the endless demand for construction stone.

The flats you've just left, extending on towards the coastline on your left, are a relic from when the sea level was higher than today, and are blanketed by sand blown off the beaches. Looking further, on a clear day you can easily see Robben Island, formed partly of the same Malmesbury sediments that make the Durbanville hills, and partly by much younger cream-coloured limestone that Nelson Mandela got to know more closely than he might have liked. The limestone rocks are hard enough for the Robben Island prisoners to have carved a cavern out of the cliff, and the vertical quarry faces maintain their form long after their excavation. This is because the rock is held together by lime derived from minute seashells in the sand, dissolved and recemented, until firm enough to have required hard blows from local prisoners' hammers to break it.

Building aggregate

You pass two quarries as you edge past Durbanville. In both, stone is mined that is particularly suitable as aggregate, whether it's for road-making or for mixing into concrete. Such stone should be hard, durable, should crush easily and should be located close to where it is needed. Granite is hard, in most cases too hard. Shale on the other hand, although it is well bedded and often closely jointed, is too soft even when fresh. Worse still, on contact with air and water, it quickly decomposes to ultrasoft clay minerals, making it completely unsuitable.

The irony is that interaction between too-hard granite and too-soft shale – as happened when the Cape Granite intruded into the Malmesbury Group shales – gives us an ideal material. We call it hornfels or baked shale or slate. The cooking was barely enough to change the appearance of the shales, but sufficient to turn them into good, hard slate, which, unlike its progenitor, resists breakdown when exposed to the elements. So even if we don't see granite in the Durbanville hills, it is close enough to the overlying sedimentary rock to have been converted to near-perfect aggregate material.

An excellent example of 'dressed slate' can be seen in the Castle in Cape Town. Slate for the outside walls came from the Strand Street Quarry and other smaller quarries on Signal Hill, and similar material from Robben Island was used to construct the gateway.

These Malmesbury Group sediments have been 'cooked' to just the right consistency – by granite that ascended to not far below them – to be well suited to civil engineers' needs.

The array of Stone Age tools displayed in a cabinet on the outside wall of the Landskroon Wine Estate cellar reflects the evolution of human skills and lifestyles over the millennia.

Durbanville to Paarl and around Paarl

With a good map or GPS you'll easily find your way through Durbanville onto the R302. After about 9 km, turn right onto the R312. This will take you through farmlands to the western slopes of Paarl 'Mountain'. The countryside undulates gently as you continue to cross soft and fractured sedimentary rocks of the Malmesbury Group, which yield easily to processes of weathering and erosion.

There are so many options for tasting or buying wine that we will leave you to get on with that, reconnecting with you at the Landskroon Wine Estate on the southwest slope of Paarl Mountain **(geosite 2, map 1)** (GPS S 33° 45.634', E 18° 54.988'). Not only is this an excellent, long-established family farming enterprise, but there's an interesting collection of Stone Age artifacts on show (see text box on p. 32).

At this point, as you look at the cabinet of artifacts, you are standing on Cape Granite – the Paarl Pluton, to be specific. First, let's look at its context. Towards the end of the Precambrian Era sediments were shed off the Kaapvaal Craton into an elongate basin being formed around its western and southern margins. The unstable oceanic crust forming the base of this trough was susceptible to movements from below and from the west; and, after a considerable thickness of sediment had accumulated, with minor volcanic contributions, tectonism or folding started approximately 800–700 million years ago and lasted some 200–300 million years. As the folding started to abate, the large

Terroir

Terroir, which has been described as 'the whole ecology of a vineyard', starts with geology. The topography influences climate and defines aspect; both these, along with many other factors, such as the distance from the nearest coastline, the soil, its drainage, and the rock from which it comes bear upon the wine and its character. But all the other variables, both in the vineyard and in the cellar, make quantification of the effect of terroir on wine elusive, if not impossible.

Geologists have conducted surveys on the topic, trying to find some direct correlation between, say, the potassium content of the soil and the character of the wine it produces, but have always failed to quantify the relationship.

Others are in no doubt that the soil and rock types have a direct bearing on wines. We know that small grapes deepen the colour, and low yield intensifies the character of the cultivar; and that small grapes and low yield are a direct measure of how the vines have had to struggle, ranging from having to force their way up through broken shale with a thin soil cover to reaching easily from deep, well-drained alluvial soil. Dedicated cellar masters will continue to study the effects of terroir and strive to harness its benefits for the good of the industry.

When you're in this region, it's worth going to the tasting room at Fairview Estate and looking at the displays of the terroir of two different shiraz vineyards where their wine is sourced. With all other vineyard management and wine-making practices kept rigorously uniform, the difference in taste between wines produced from two different vineyards is dramatic. (See Bibliography on p. 247 for more on the role of terroir in wine-making.)

Different soils of the vineyards used for Fairview's Solitude Shiraz (left) and Beacon Shiraz (right), give tight consistent bunches from trellised vines on deep soil (Solitude) compared to looser bunches from bush vines in rocky 'soil' (Beacon).

The domed granite exposure on Paarl Mountain (seen here from the north) shines in the sun, which explains how the name (Dutch for 'pearl') was coined.

number of plutons in the Western Cape, including Paarl, were intruded, forming, for the most part, resistant masses, which were not themselves affected by the folding except in rare local instances. Both the tectonism and the granite emplacement happened in a series of pulses, which can be dated only approximately.

Although the folding would have built substantial mountain ranges, the fact that the folds were composed largely of quite soft rocks saw them being quickly eroded. By the time these ranges had been ground down to an almost level plain, the scene was being set for the next phase of sedimentation, again in an elongate arcuate basin around the southern and western margins of the craton. The first sediments of the Cape Basin were deposited some 480 million years ago, signalling the onset of a major phase of basin filling, which would last for the next 200 million years. Like the older Malmesbury sediments, those of the Cape Supergroup had no sooner been laid down than they were convulsed in a series of violent Earth movements. Thus were the Cape Fold mountains formed, a range that was probably as high as the more recently formed Himalayas before the inevitable erosion reduced them to the (still majestic) ranges we know.

In the case of Paarl Mountain and the other Cape plutons, erosion of inconceivable amounts of material has stripped the land to below the base of the Cape sediments, exposing the granite and Malmesbury rocks that were their floor.

But why are Paarl Mountain's granite slopes almost entirely devoid of soil cover? Rio de Janeiro's Sugar Loaf Mountain immediately comes to mind, and there are similar bare plugs in the escarpment forests of western Angola, all shaped from granite. Intrusive plutons like these comprise unusually 'massive' rock – a word used geologically to mean rock that's free of the joints and cracks that criss-cross most such bodies – and only with joints that are very widely spaced. (That's why it forms an ideal rock for dimension stone, with one of the most important quarries in the Western Cape mining the granite high above the southern residential suburbs of Paarl.)

The Cape's first stone-workers

From the almost-dark ages of granite intrusion and Cape Supergroup sedimentation and folding we emerge into the bright sunlight of the late Pleistocene, around 70 000 years ago. Imagine people – not that far removed in lifestyle and appearance from those encountered by the earliest 17th century settlers – sitting on the high slopes of Paarl Mountain. Perhaps they're shaping arrows and tools for digging, planning the next hunt on the flats spread out below them, gathering wood for the evening fire and generally attending to the domestic duties of the day.

The display of Stone Age implements on the outside wall of the winery at the Landskroon Estate tells us that people were working with stone long before the first slate was quarried in and around Cape Town for building the Castle in 1660. Even the strandlopers and pastoralists with whom the earliest settlers interacted in the late 17th century postdated the Cape's first stone-workers by thousands of years.

Landskroon farm owner Hugo de Villiers, a trained geologist, ensured that anything resembling an implement that his staff found while ploughing the lands or working the vineyards was brought to him. With time he noticed that his growing collection displayed a significant range of manufacturing skills and details, apart from which there were obvious differences in size and the uses to which the tools had been put. As with any craft, the degree of sophistication in tool-making had evolved over time, making it possible to estimate the era from which an implement came depending on the level of workmanship it showed.

The farm was especially well located for our early forbears. It lies on the slopes of Paarl Mountain, which gives on to wide plains, and which would at times have teemed with game. And the slopes are strewn with hard quartzite, which would have proved ideal for tool-making. Have a look at the tools on Landskroon, of a variety of applications and ranging in age from the Middle Stone Age (70 000–30 000 years ago) to Late Stone Age (30 000–10 000 years ago). There are hand-axes, hand-picks, scrapers, spear points and many other tools. The display makes a handy linkage from events we have reconstructed from many millions of years ago almost up to the present.

REFINED HAND PICKS
VERFYNDE HANDPIKKE

The many facets and cleavages of these tools are manifestly unnatural, leaving no doubt that they were shaped by practised human hands.

Imagine it: the fiery granite slowly ascending, pushing up a vast load of super-heated sediment above it, slowing down and finally coming to rest. Because the granite cools slowly under the cover of sediment, the crystals that make up the granite are tightly welded together and don't easily allow fracturing. Now, any number of millions of years later, the granite has been stripped of its cover. However, the rainwater that would start the weathering process in any crack or tiny cavity finds nothing of that sort: it simply runs off and down the slope. An hour after the end of a storm the rock is dry, unchanged from its pre-storm state – year after year, millennium after millennium.

Paarl to Franschhoek

Heading southeast towards Franschhoek now, you need to take the R301. This route passes, inter alia, Drakenstein Prison (formely Victor Verster), which for a few minutes on 11 February 1990 became a world stage when the first pictures of Nelson Mandela as a free citizen were broadcast.

To the south the country is broken, with hills big and small, and river valleys; to the north, on your left, is the sheer, towering range of Wemmershoek, imposing by any standards. Follow it with your eye and see it curve southwards behind the Franschhoek valley and then back again towards the west. Before it winds further southwards the range reaches its highest peak in the buttress of the Groot Drakenstein massif, every bit as precipitous and commanding as Wemmershoek, and all built of sandstone of the Table Mountain Group.

When originally deposited (horizontally) there were sandstones above and below the Cedarberg shale. Following the Cape folding, the sedimentary sandwich became steeply tilted, and in places the faulting that accompanied the folding cut across the entire package, displacing it along discrete fault planes so that the sedimentary contacts are not perfectly continuous, as shown.

Base of the
Cedarberg shale

The easily weathered Cedarberg shale forms gentle slopes that allow the preservation
of fallen snow long after it has melted on the more rugged rocky crags.

A staggering amount of quartz, or silica (simple silicon dioxide, SiO_2) now surrounds us, and it's interesting that nowhere in the world are there such extensive, high mountains of practically pure quartzitic sandstone as in the Cape. Not far to the east, the first dramatic folding of these seemingly rigid masses of sandstone can be seen, but around here the reaction to deep-seated forces hundreds of millions of years ago was different. In this part of the Syntaxis Zone, between the north-south and east-west belts of folding, the rocks underwent brittle fracturing. In this fragmented assemblage, bedding can be difficult to discern, but for that there is help at hand.

There is a conspicuous exception in this otherwise unbroken sequence of sandstone. Deep in its middle section is a shale band, which, compared to the sandstone above and below it, is extremely thin. In the mountains behind Paarl and quite conspicuously around Franschhoek, this band, with none of the blocky outcrop that characterizes the sandstone, is noticeably different. For the most part, in the mountains around you there are no smooth grassy slopes. However, after you have passed the Drakenstein Prison, have breasted a low rise and are dropping down to the flats, a narrow elongate belt sandwiched between the rugged, rocky slopes looms on the right: a pine-studded belt with no rocks **(geosite 3, map 1)** (GPS S 33° 51.237', E 19° 01.731'). Here it comes down to the road, but as you look ahead to the foothills of the Wemmershoek range, in a few places in the hills you'll see the same thin strip conspicuously distinct from the formations above and below it.

Once through Franschhoek, if you stand anywhere quite high on the southwest-facing slopes as you climb the Franschhoek Pass and look southwards, you will catch sight in the far distance of two high, rounded, soft-capped peaks. If you see them after a winter snowfall, you'll notice that they are islands of white long after the snow has melted on all the steeper, rockier slopes. These two peaks, Sneeukop and Victoria Peak, are capped by the same shale that has formed a band elsewhere, sandwiched between sandstone. It is their geology that keeps the snow on these peaks long after it has melted elsewhere.

This dark, soft shale bed, nowhere thicker than 150 m, is known as the Cedarberg shale. It is remarkable for its geographic persistence, from far in the northernmost Cedarberg, to where you are now, and on eastwards, where it is last seen just short of Jeffreys Bay.

As a rock type the Cedarberg shale is not particularly unusual. Much more interesting as a pointer to times past are the sediments directly below it, the Pakhuis sediments. This unit, even thinner than the Cedarberg shale, represents a glacial event that extended from North Africa to Antarctica.

The Cedarberg shale

In the northern and eastern parts of the winelands you will see many places where the Cedarberg shale presents itself in the scenery. Ironically, in a landscape of rolling lowlands towered over by craggy mountains, it draws attention to itself by its unobtrusiveness.

The Cedarberg shale is important because anything that contrasts with its environment as strongly as a narrow band of soft shale with thick layers of tough sandstone on either side is bound to be eye-catching. As far as geologists are concerned it is extremely useful, particularly when it comes to trying to make sense of the geological structure of a complex part of the Cape Fold Belt.

Without this shale band as a reference horizon it would be almost impossible, looking at an expanse of sandstone in a complex area of interrupted exposure, to know where one is in the Table Mountain succession. For example, the faults marked on the map northwest and southeast of Franschhoek would not have been possible to see, and to map, without the reference horizon that is the Cedarberg shale.

There's still more to this apparently insignificant geological unit: its basal part is globally celebrated for its extraordinarily rich content of fossils. These fossils are important because they mark a major stratigraphic boundary between two of the fundamental time units used by geologists around the world: the Ordovician and Silurian Periods. The basal Cedarberg shale is one of a few international palaeontological markers; doff your hat to those anomalous, smoothly landscaped strips that go on and on.

From kilometres away the Cedarberg shale, in some years supporting patches of dense Watsonia growth, is easily picked out once you have developed an eye for it.

The deformation of sedimentary bedding, to be seen across the valley as one descends the Franschhoek Pass, is not caused by tectonism but by the ice sheets that formed the Pakhuis tillite, rucking still-soft sandstones into the patterns you see.

The massive (i.e. unbedded) dark grey Pakhuis tillite, with conspicuous pebbles, mostly of quartz, forms a marked contrast with the much paler bedded sandstones elsewhere in the mountains.

A genetically similar rock unit that is better known and more widespread over southern Africa, and makes eye-catching outcrops, particularly in the Cape and KwaZulu-Natal, is the Dwyka tillite. Because there is still argument about the exact origin of the Pakhuis sediments, they are commonly known as diamictite, a descriptive term for unsorted sediments containing fragments ranging widely in size, rather than tillite, which is a genetic name applied exclusively to sediments of glacial origin.

Unlike the Dwyka tillite, which was the first depositional event after a long period of erosion of earlier formations, the movement of ice sheets during Pakhuis times happened in the middle of an otherwise normal cycle of sedimentation. In fact, it reflects an ice age in the middle of what the evidence tells us was a major period of greenhouse conditions.

What we see in the rocks today tells us that the recently deposited Table Mountain sands were not yet fully consolidated and hardened when the ice sheets crept over them. So, as the photograph opposite shows, the beds of sand could be deformed – in their soft plastic state – into bizarre shapes by the overriding ice. It is a complicated process, impossible to simulate in a laboratory today, and the above description is enormously simplified. Suffice it to say that this thin band of folding is dramatically displayed at a number of localities across the southwestern Cape.

The easiest place to see the diamictite and the folding it caused is on the road from Franschhoek to Villiersdorp. Over the top of the pass and just past the well-marked Jan Joubertsgat Bridge halfway down the eastern side of the pass **(geosite 4, map 1)** (GPS S 33° 56.364', E 19° 10.054'), there's a cutting through a rock type that's distinctly different from anything else you've seen – dark grey at first glance and not nearly as fractured as the other rocks in the area. Find a place to pull off and have a good look: here's hard evidence of a glaciation that covered the whole of Gondwana, from North Africa

The koffieklip (more correctly ferricrete) of local farmers denotes periods of prolonged stability and erosional stillstand of the surfaces where it is found.

to modern Antarctica; and that the Gondwana of 450 million years ago straddled the South Pole during a period of intense and widespread glaciation. Across the valley there are examples of the folding described above, but they're quite difficult to spot.

You could say that you have just looked at a memorial to the first of the five mass extinctions – this at the end of the Ordovician – that have punctuated 500 million years of the evolution of life. It is an event that saw 27 per cent of families that existed at the time and 57 per cent of all the genera disappear off the face of the Earth – or, more accurately, from the waters of the Earth, since life had not yet emerged onto land.

From those creatures that survived, diversification to fill all available niches proceeded apace and, in the cold waters that returned to lift sea level to earlier benchmarks and above – the Cedarberg sea, we might call it – an explosion of marine life took place. As old doors closed, new ones opened.

Find a place to turn and head back through Franschhoek.

Franschhoek through Stellenbosch to Cape Town

If you stop in Franschhoek, take a look up to the broad saddle behind the Huguenot Monument and you can't help noticing that it is dominated by a towering, almost vertical slope to the north of it. This rock face, known locally as Middagkrans, lies along a fault that separates the Table Mountain sandstone in the tall massif behind Middagkrans from the softer sediments below it. These belong

The Table Mountain Group sandstone buttress of Groot Drakenstein towers above the homestead of the Boschendal farm where Cecil John Rhodes pioneered the South African deciduous fruit industry.

to the older Franschhoek Formation, part of the Malmesbury Group, which, together with some granite that intruded them, were the floor rocks to the sediments of the Cape Supergroup. They also make up the base of the Franschhoek valley, their greater susceptibility to weathering and erosion explaining why the valley has formed where it has.

As you leave Franschhoek, stay on the R45 until you turn off to Stellenbosch (on the R310), keeping in the shadow of Groot Drakenstein. Soon after crossing the Berg River, in a cutting on the right as you approach the top of the first gentle rise **(geosite 5, map 1)** (GPS S 33° 52.559',

*This photograph shows the most dramatic of a series
of faults cutting the Franschhoek Formation, seen as
one descends Helshoogte into Stellenbosch.*

E 19° 00.617'), look for a layer just below the surface of dark brown nodular material that resembles gravel, rather than rock or soil. Farmers call it 'koffieklip' (coffee stone), geologists ferricrete (it's rich in iron) or laterite, and it's of interest because it forms on land surfaces that have been stable for prolonged periods of time. Around the world it is used in road surfacing.

Having left the R45, you pass Cecil Rhodes's old estate, Boschendal, with the high quartzite buttress of Groot Drakenstein towering over it to the east, and to your right the crags of Simonsberg.

You won't see rocks close to the road until you're over the saddle that locals know as Helshoogte, with wineries to both sides as you breast the rise. About a kilometre down the winding descent into Stellenbosch **(geosite 6, map 1)** (GPS S 33° 55.474', E 18° 54.489'), there is an interesting cutting to your left that shows good examples of faulting, where different lithologies (rock types) of Franschhoek Formation sediments are separated by a number of very clearly visible fault planes. The ochre smears conspicuous in the section nearest the top of the cutting result from oxidation (or rusting) of the iron sulphide, pyrite, which is quite common in sediments formed under anoxic conditions, and richly distributed here.

Once you reach Stellenbosch, a visit to the Geology Department in the Chamber of Mines building in Ryneveld Street is strongly recommended. Along the passages around a central atrium on the ground and first floors is a collection of minerals, rock specimens and geological memorabilia almost without equal in South Africa, added to which are some fascinating geological maps on the walls – and not just of South Africa.

Whichever way you choose to return to Cape Town, assuming that's where you're going, there's little new geology to look at. If, though, you find your eyes drawn to the mass of Table Mountain and the high peninsula beyond it, remember its former island status. Think, too, of other times when there were sandy flats between the krantzes of Cape Point and the hills beyond Gordon's Bay. And as you cast your mind back to the long history that preceded those comparatively recent days, mull over what we've seen in the winelands and marvel at the wonderful world we live in.

2 Paarl to Sutherland

GEOLOGICAL OVERVIEW

For those of you with a day or two to spare, there is a circular drive that showcases two of the most worthwhile geosites the country has to offer. In addition to these you will see magnificent scenery and a cameo of structural and sedimentary geology in the Cape and Karoo Supergroups, including a world-class oil industry 'laboratory'.

The 'Gansfontein palaeosurface' on this route is one of the true wonders of geology. Near Sutherland you'll see the impressive cone of South Africa's youngest and most complete volcano, and around Tulbagh the legacy of our most recent (1969) earthquake. Sutherland offers the opportunity to co-ordinate geology with astronomy, which resonates well with the purpose of these books: to add a dimension to travels you were planning anyway. Even if you do it for the geology alone, though, you are sure to be glad that you finished the circuit.

Be warned: the whole of the middle section of this trip is on gravel roads of varying quality, although mostly good. The Ouberg Pass from the Tankwa Karoo up the Roggeveld escarpment (to Sutherland) is steep and the last stretch of road to the foot of the pass may be corrugated, but not beyond the capabilities of an ordinary car. *Another important caution: some of the route is way off the beaten track and should not be attempted without GPS navigation.*

Mud cracks formed after a recent storm are superimposed on fossilized cracks incomprehensibly old. They differ just a little because of slight differences in the sediment, while the flora and fauna of those days would have borne little resemblance to that of today.

The highlight of the trip for many will be the Gansfontein palaeosurface,
the remains of a day frozen in time 260 million years ago.

Geology of the route

Paarl to Gouda

You start from the N1, which you leave in Paarl, and head out towards Wellington, through the edge of the town and on along the R44 across the gently undulating lowland plains, with the mountain rampart hard on your right. You're on the trail of the Voortrekkers of some 300 years ago, whose first route to the heartland of their new home left the coastal plains along a tight valley now known as the Nuwekloof Pass. Cut by the Little Berg River, the pass links the village and wine-growing area of Tulbagh with the outside world, as well as Cape Town with Johannesburg for those who prefer to travel by train.

The muted topography you cross after leaving Wellington is typical of ground underlain by the relatively ancient (600 Ma) Malmesbury Group. The low relief can be ascribed to three main factors: its composition of comparatively soft sediments; the fact that it was planed by erosion in very ancient times, before the Table Mountain sediments were deposited on it; and the much more recent mid-Miocene (15 Ma) erosional planation, when the sea level was nearly 100 m higher than it is today, and this was the low-lying coastal plain.

Before the fragmentation of Gondwana and the formation of a new coastline some 150 million years ago, southern Africa consisted of a vast inland plateau standing about 2 000 m above sea level.

The Cape Fold mountains were then a stretch of hills, rather than the high ranges we know today, from which rivers drained mainly northwards and eastwards onto the plateau. When the new coastline formed as the land that would become South America drifted away, rivers started cutting back into the high plateau. The Berg, Breede, Tankwa-Doring, Olifants, Sout and many other lesser rivers came into being. Low coastal plains were carved, and behind them was an escarpment and even higher Cape mountains. After the last of the Cape quartzite crust had been eroded, the underlying, much softer Malmesbury sediments would have been stripped off faster.

Soon after leaving Wellington, slightly to your left and ahead of you **(geosite 1, map 2)** (GPS S 33° 28.758', E 18° 57.656') you see the mountains of Riebeeck Kasteel and Riebeeck West – isolated massifs that seem inconsistent with the processes just described. Most of the isolated uplands on the coastal plains are durable granite, intrusive into the softer Malmesbury sediments. But these massifs are different: they are formed by a fault that dropped the basal units of the younger Cape Supergroup, including the highly resistant Peninsula Formation to the east of the fault, to abut against the more yielding Malmesbury formations to its west. As erosion lowered the land surface, made – at this level – predominantly of the older soft sediments, it encountered a block of anomalous resistance. While levels were lowered all around them, the hard Peninsula quartzites gradually gained ascendancy, ultimately standing up as the high 'castle' of Riebeeck Kasteel.

LEFT: *In the Tulbagh valley the rolling lowlands are carved from Malmesbury shales while the range in the distance is made of Table Mountain sandstone.*
BELOW: *The prominence of Riebeeck Kasteel is the result of faulting.*

MAP 2

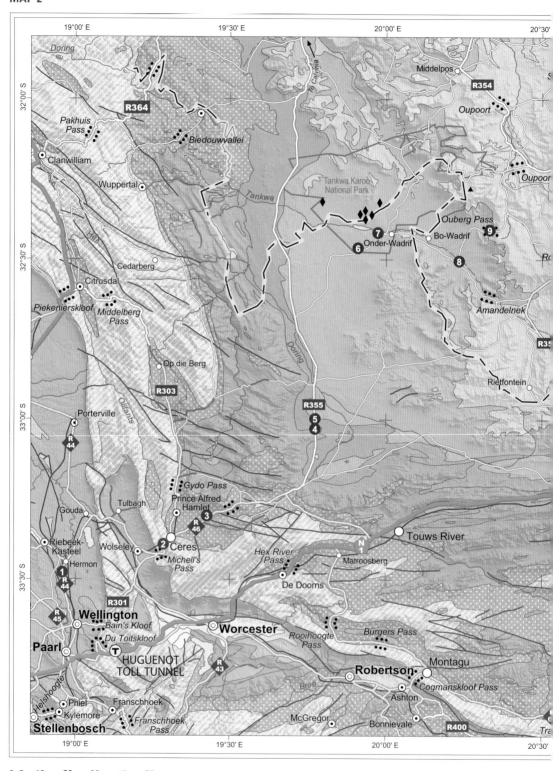

0 5 10   20   30   40   50
Kilometres

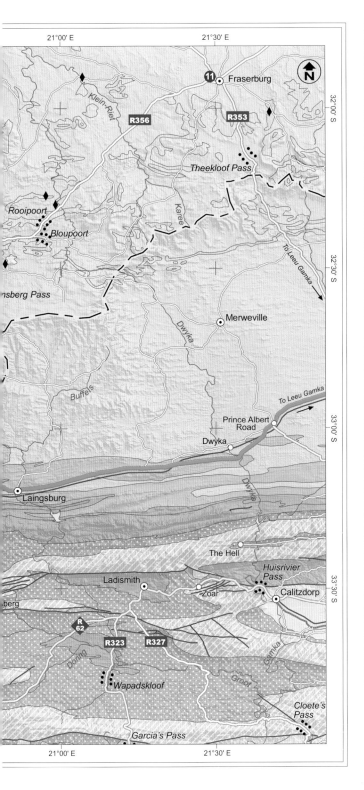

21°00' E   21°30' E

11 Fraserburg

R356   R353

32°00' S

Klein-Riet

Theekloof Pass

Karee

Rooipoort

Bloupoort

...sberg Pass

32°30' S

To Leeu Gamka

Dwyka

Merweville

Buffels

To Leeu Gamka

Prince Albert
Road

33°00' S

Dwyka

Dwyka

Laingsburg

The Hell

Huisrivier
Pass

33°30' S

Ladismith

Zoar

Calitzdorp

...berg

R
62

Gamka

R323   R327

Doring

Groot

Wapadskloof

Cloete's
Pass

Garcia's Pass

21°00' E   21°30' E

ABOVE: *This major rockfall in the
Skurweberge behind Tulbagh very
probably dates from the 1969
earthquake, when a fault running
through the mountains became
briefly active.*

Faulting

Faults abound in this part of the world. Mostly they are seismically inactive in crust that has been stable since South America broke away from Africa in the deep geological past. Long before that, tectonic activity had given rise to the Cape Fold mountains in phase after phase of intense crustal shortening – a response to contraction taking place deep below the fold belts, as happens when crustal plates collide far below the surface. The fluid mantle is, in a geological time scale, dynamic, with convection currents slowly churning its material over (see fig. 1, p. 12), much like molten toffee being cooked. This slow churning causes the regime above to change. Where the crust along the Cape Fold Belt had been in a state of contraction and thickening through multiple stages of folding, it gradually stabilized, then started to stretch, thinning in the process. Gondwana was about to fragment. The main northwesterly-trending faults you see on map 2 were formed as part of the last major tectonic event to affect southern Africa. It was a time of huge earthquakes.

Activity of these fault systems has not been permanently consigned to the history books, as was shown with damaging and fatal consequences during the night of 29 September 1969. Apart from destruction of property estimated at many tens of millions of rands, nine lives were lost and dozens badly hurt in the Ceres-Tulbagh earthquake that night. At magnitude 6.3 on the Richter Scale, it was the biggest in local recorded history. The worst devastation was at the Rhenish Missionary School at Steinthal, in a tight valley in the foothills east of Tulbagh. It seems that the fault responsible for the quake, part of the system of faulting that characterizes the fold belt, passes through the head of the valley.

During the quake itself and aftershocks that continued until the middle of April the next year, rockfalls were frequent on the slopes above the valleys of Ceres and Tulbagh. Anyone who has driven through these parts will have been struck by how rocky those slopes are. Given that September to April spans the hottest, driest months of the year, it is no surprise that it was a summer of recurrent veld fires as sparks caused by quartzite striking quartzite ignited the tinder-dry fynbos.

The 1969 earthquake that shook Tulbagh and Ceres most severely left many of the older houses in ruins.

Gouda to Wolseley

As you pass Gouda and head for Tulbagh along the R46, you turn from a northerly direction of travel towards the east, leaving the lowlands and entering hilly country via the Nuwekloof Pass. It's not hard to imagine the excited anticipation the trekkers of hundreds of years ago must have felt on entering the pass and leaving behind the familiar coastal plains, and to share their sense of curious expectancy. Not only are you entering a majestic mountain realm, but geologically you are about to explore a challenging tectonic environment – the heart of the so-called Syntaxis Zone of the Cape Fold Belt.

A glance at the geological map of South Africa shows two elongated belts of formations parallel to the south and west coasts converging inland of where the coastline makes a right angle at Cape Town. (Topographic maps show the same belts as high mountain ranges.) These strips are the southern and western parts of the Cape Fold Belt – let's call them the Swartberg Branch and the Cedarberg Branch, respectively – and the zone where they meet is called the syntaxis. Such areas where two fold systems meet at a high angle (in this case practically a right angle) are not common: they are inevitably geologically complicated. Council for Geoscience geologist, Coenie de Beer, has done a masterly job of unscrambling the complexity, his task made more challenging by the fact that many of the answers lie high up steep mountain slopes liberally strewn with loose rocks up to several metres in diameter. Spare him a thought as you wind along in your comfortably upholstered air-conditioned vehicle.

FIGURE 3 **THE SYNTAXIS ZONE OF THE CAPE FOLD BELT**

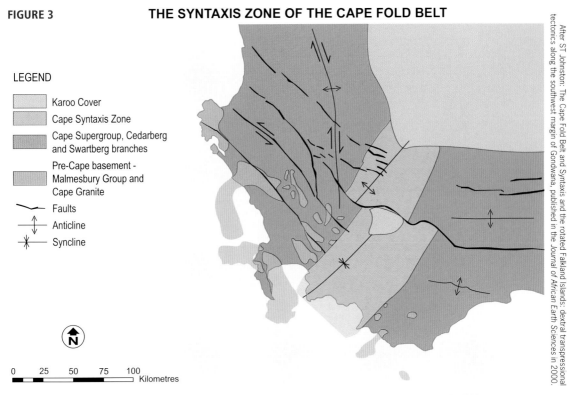

LEGEND

- Karoo Cover
- Cape Syntaxis Zone
- Cape Supergroup, Cedarberg and Swartberg branches
- Pre-Cape basement - Malmesbury Group and Cape Granite
- Faults
- Anticline
- Syncline

0 25 50 75 100 Kilometres

After ST Johnston: The Cape Fold Belt and Syntaxis and the rotated Falkland Islands: dextral transpressional tectonics along the southwest margin of Gondwana, published in the Journal of African Earth Sciences in 2000.

A sketch showing the Syntaxis Zone in relation to the two 'branches' of the Cape Fold Belt. The fold structures in the Syntaxis Zone, shown in pale grey, have been substantially displaced by the regional Worcester Fault.

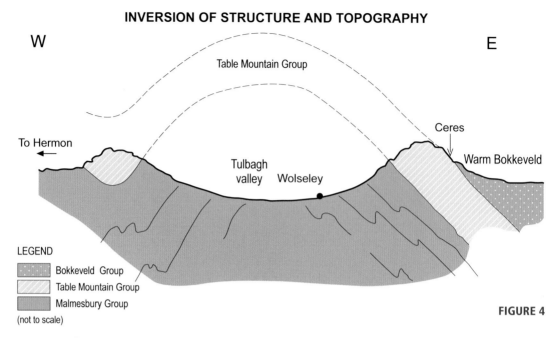

INVERSION OF STRUCTURE AND TOPOGRAPHY

*This illustrates the inversion that caused the Tulbagh valley, in the 'core' of an anticlinal structure, to be
more deeply eroded than the surrounding ranges of hard Table Mountain sandstone making the limbs.*

In the Syntaxis Zone, the north-south zone shows less intense folding and thrusting than the more extreme east-west branch: both happened in multiple phases that 'overlapped' where the branches meet. The directions of the folding in the Syntaxis Zone lie between the directions of the elongate zones on either side, in other words northeast-southwest (see fig. 3, p. 49).

Let's look at the grand structure of where you are before proceeding. You've crossed from Malmesbury sediments on the coastal flats through a thin slice of Cape Supergroup sediments in the Nuwekloof Pass and back onto the Malmesbury Group in the Tulbagh valley. You may remember that if you go from older sediments to younger and back to older, with no appreciable change in elevation, you've gone through a 'syncline', a boat-shaped fold. However, the big fold between the pass and the mountains behind Tulbagh and Steinthal is an anticline, shaped like an upturned boat. You now travel along the axis of that anticline, heading slightly east of south, and passing close to Wolseley. Along this part of the trip there's an inversion of topography *vis-à-vis* geology: the younger (harder) sediments stand much higher than the older (softer) ones (see fig. 4, above). It's not particularly unusual – even if it is quite exaggerated here – and you should keep a lookout for it in other parts of your travels.

Wolseley to the Tankwa Karoo

Just as you entered the Tulbagh-Wolseley valley through a pass, so you leave it – and Wolseley – through Michell's Pass, on the R46, which takes you into the Ceres valley and the Warm Bokkeveld beyond it. You are now entering a wide 'synclinorium', where the overall structure is synclinal, but which contains subsidiary synclines and anticlines within it. The syncline opens to the northeast (in other words, the synclinal axis dips in this direction), so travelling quite close to the fold's axis, you cross from older sediments to younger.

At the start of Michell's Pass, you're dwarfed by the precipitous, towering mountains to either side – the awe-inspiring scenery attributable here, as is usual in the Cape, to the lowest member of the Cape Supergroup – the Peninsula Formation (of the Table Mountain Group, or TMG). The far gentler topography of the wide, rolling Ceres valley around the corner ahead of you is made by shale and mudstone of the Bokkeveld Group, with only minor outcrops of interbedded sandstone.

But before reaching the soft sediments of the Bokkeveld, you must traverse the sandstones of the upper part of the TMG. To begin with, all you see are the steeply dipping beds of the Peninsula Formation. If you keep an eye on the rock in the pass cuttings, you should be able to see when you come to the Pakhuis tillite **(geosite 2, map 2)** (GPS S 33° 23.611', E 19° 17.246'). In contrast to the well-bedded, almost white Peninsula sandstone, the massive (i.e. unbedded) dark grey tillite, studded with small quartz pebbles, is conspicuously different. This is the unit that signals the top of the Peninsula Formation; the next quartzites you see will be those of the upper part of the TMG. These make up the slopes overlooking Ceres from the west and south. The most prominent unit of the upper TMG is called the Skurweberg Formation, named after the Skurweberge overlooking Ceres from the west – 'rough mountains' being an apposite description of the unit.

Proceed along the attractively tree-lined main street of Ceres and out into the orchards of the Warm Bokkeveld. Having zig-zagged so far on this route, you now strike out in a northeasterly direction, which you will follow for most of the rest of this trip, across the Tankwa Karoo, up the Roggeveld Escarpment, through Sutherland and to the turning point near Fraserburg, where you head south to the N2. As you leave Ceres behind and head towards Theron's Pass, there are high mountains to both the north and south. To the right, further from the road, are the Hex River Mountains,

built of an anticlinal core comprising mainly Peninsula Formation quartzite, and including the Matroosberg, which is some 2 250 m high and often snow-capped for weeks at a time in the winter. But turn your attention now to the precipitous slopes closer to hand and to your left **(geosite 3, map 2)** (GPS S 33° 18.294', E 19° 25.956').

Before proceeding, a reminder about the Cape Supergroup stratigraphy. At the base of the succession of sedimentary units is the Table Mountain Group (almost exclusively hard quartzitic sandstone), above it the Bokkeveld Group (predominantly soft siltstone and shale, with minor sandstone) and above that the Witteberg Group (mainly sandstone with some siltstone and shale). In the Western Cape you generally see much less of the Witteberg Group above the Bokkeveld than the TMG below it. To the north of you now is the first exposure of the Witteberg Group you've seen on this route. It is a very different package of rocks from the Table Mountain sandstone

Dark grey massive (i.e. unbedded) Pakhuis tillite in Michell's Pass, of glacial origin, is conspicuously different from the pale, bedded sandstone elsewhere in the pass, not least because of the quite large pebbles it carries.

How clastic sedimentary rocks form

So much of South Africa is covered by the predominantly sedimentary units of the Cape and Karoo Supergroups that it is as well, at this point, to try and develop a feel for how such rocks form.

It is helpful in such an exercise to make the connection between process and product. While the products are visible just about anywhere in South Africa, and more particularly in the Karoo or the Cape, you don't see much of the processes at work. If you lived in Cairo or Calcutta you'd see very active sedimentation under way as the Nile or Ganges brought thousands of tonnes of detritus into their deltas, day after day. If you'd been in New Orleans in August 2005 when Hurricane Katrina struck, you would have seen what happens when a river like the Mississippi breaks through the levees constructed to keep it out. You would have witnessed the deposition of tonnes of sand, silt, mud and clay in downtown suburbia, and the resulting devastation.

Rivers have steeper degradational parts in their headwaters where they accumulate sediment. Then they have flatter aggradational parts where the sediment, whether from floods or normal flow, settles, both in the river channel and, in times of flood where natural levees are breached, on the floodplains. The coarseness of the sediment picked up and deposited depends on the energy of the current, or the rate of flow. River channels and deltas, because of their high energy, are commonly where coarse clasts, from big boulders to pebbles and sand, are deposited. On floodplains, on the other hand, where the water is shallower, the finer detritus, carried higher in the stream profile, settles out from sheets of shallow, slow-moving water. The oxygen-rich environment of such sediments often shows itself as red or mauve coloration, derived from the oxidation ('rusting') of iron, a common component of the sedimentary package.

As rivers reach a shoreline, their energy level drops and they soon dump their 'bottom load', of bigger clasts and sand. The mud and clay keep going, though, sometimes far out into the body of water beyond the shore, and settle slowly. The floor where they finally come to rest is usually deep below the surface, beyond any surface aeration. Sediments formed at these depths are called subaqueous, and because they usually have variable – often significant – amounts of organic material added, they are dark grey, almost black.

In the case of rivers reaching the coast where strong longshore currents or wind regimes prevail, such as at the mouth of the Orange River, the coarser material may be moved down-current for long distances, keeping the mouth clear. Otherwise, load-bearing rivers may build deltas. As long as sea level does not rise these will continue to build out from the river mouth, a spectacular example being the delta of the Ganges and Brahmaputra rivers in the Bay of Bengal.

Where there is a plentiful supply of sand, the coastal plain is low and wide; and wind with an onshore component is a factor, such as around Wilderness or St Lucia, where river mouths may be temporarily sand-blocked and estuaries form. Energy levels are low here, except in times of occasional flooding, and the sediment is mostly fine-grained.

As you journey across South Africa, you will continue to see modern examples of the end products of all the above processes: sedimentation in river channels, across wide floodplains, in different stages of building deltas and in unoxygenated depths of oceanic abysses. If you don't see much of the processes in action right now, perhaps it's a reminder of the millions of years that they've been at work.

The central bed in this photograph shows the red shale that typifies onshore deposition of fine detritus, where any iron present is quickly oxidized, imparting its colour to the entire bed.

The kink-folding in the range north of the road out of Ceres characterizes the Witteberg Group, and is absent from the older Table Mountain Group, with its higher content of quartzitic sandstone.

The Dwyka tillite in the Ceres Karoo shows a much wider variety of clasts than the more locally derived Pakhuis tillite seen on the other side of Ceres.

It's not on top ...

... it's inside. It would be no surprise if, in tracing our ancestry deep into prehistory, there were missing links. The extraordinary luck required to find fossils is touched on elsewhere in this book, and this entombed young Mesosaurus illustrates the point. On the outside this is an ordinary chunk of rock, one of a huge number strewn across the veld: inside is a treasure.

Mesosaurus tenuidens was an aquatic reptile that has been found in quite large numbers in the Whitehill Formation of the Ecca Group that covers a lot of the western Tankwa Karoo, as well as in southern Namibia. These fossils represent the oldest reptiles known in South Africa, with adults reaching about a metre in length. The closely related M. brasiliensis from southern Brazil and Uruguay supports a Gondwana origin for both some 280 million years ago.

you've just left behind – and the most intensively folded part of the fold belt. The Witteberg, with minor interbedded shales and siltstones, comprises a less rigid block than the TMG when it comes to folding. It behaves conspicuously differently from the pure sandstone sequences of the TMG, and if you look at the slopes to your left you'll see excellent examples of 'kink folds', which you won't find in TMG folding.

Soon after reaching the bottom of Theron's Pass, you'll find the tar road turning off to Touws River, but rather take the road straight ahead, which links Ceres and Calvinia. A good road, it takes you through Karoopoort, with its folded Witteberg sediments now on both sides of the road, and then onto the R355, northwards across the wide plains of the Ceres Karoo and beyond them through the Tankwa Karoo. As you leave the pass, the mountains of Witteberg sandstone can still be seen to your left and quite soon you are travelling over Dwyka tillite, though outcrop is sparse.

Keep a lookout for the distance indicators to the left (west) of the road: soon after the 25 km marker plate you breast a low rise with some fresh outcrop and lots of loose material from the road cutting **(geosite 4, map 2)** (GPS S 33° 01.979', E 19° 46.321'). This is the glacially derived Dwyka tillite, full of clasts of varying size and of a huge variety, including quartzite from Archaean basement rocks near the gold fields far to the northeast, and also stromatolite fragments from those parts. Were you anywhere else in the country you would see waving grass, or scrub, or forest; but because you're in the Karoo – the driest part of it, what's more – you will see the tillite-borne clasts strewn over the surface. If you look hard, you may even find a clast with striations or scratches on it from grinding along in the ice sheet of 300 million years ago. A few kilometres from here, you start to see flaky shale at the side of the road, and it is here that the black surface coating, or desert

You might feel this rock surface has a 'burned' look: in fact, it is 'desert varnish', caused by aridity rather than heat, the colour mostly due to black manganese oxide which is concentrated from traces in the shale.

On the image: Fan 5 ± 75 m, Fan 4 ± 60 m, Fan 3 ± 15 m

De Ville Wickens: Statoil field excursion guide book, December 2011

From any angle the 'chimney' topping this sedimentary massif, known as Skoorsteenberg, is a distinguishing feature, visible from tens of kilometres away. Three of the fans of interest to petroleum geologists are shown.

varnish, first makes its appearance **(geosite 5, map 2)** (GPS S 33° 00.109', E 19° 46.272'), on rock outcrops and loose material. You'll see plenty of this for a while. The shale is of the overlying Ecca Group, onto which you've progressed from the Dwyka – an important change.

Note, too, that you're in one of the driest parts of the country, with much of it recording less than 100 mm of rainfall per annum and average daily maximum temperatures in January and February approaching 40°C. The width of this valley floor, with the Roggeveld Mountains far to the east and the Cedarberg closer by to the west, suggests that you're travelling over a very ancient erosional surface, which was formed by the Tankwa-Doring river system in the time since the break-up of Gondwana. Then you will notice wide areas where all that covers the sun-baked surface is scree of black, pebble-sized chips of rock: this is called a deflation surface, meaning that only the most resistant silica- and iron-rich fragments from the original soil profile have remained. Over the aeons, every other last grain has been blasted by wind into the distance, with here and there a gnarled plant bravely standing its ground. It is an extreme, bizarre landscape. It wasn't always quite as bleak as you see it now: overgrazing over decades has exacerbated the barrenness.

Keep an eye open for Skoorsteenberg (Chimney Mountain) in the distance to your right; it's easily identifiable because of the short 'chimney' that forms the top part of the mountain. This distinctive landmark can be seen from all sides and for many tens of kilometres. Consider it a pivot about which you'll turn eastwards up ahead.

Let's step back briefly, though. You are now traversing the lower part of the Ecca Group. In the northeast of the country the Ecca hosts our coal deposits, so for 100 years the economic significance of the Ecca Group has been well established. More recently the Ecca has come into prominence for another reason, also related to fossil fuel – this time oil and gas, and at the diametrically opposite side of the country from the original discoveries, right where you are now.

If the coal beds gave the Ecca its early fame, the rocks for which it is now celebrated are turbidites (see text box opposite), which built huge submarine fans on the floor of the ancient Karoo Basin. These potential petroleum reservoir rocks are sandwiched between the deep-water sediments where oil is formed in the first place. The shales, usually black, arise from extremely

The oil industry in South Africa

It's common knowledge that there is no 'South African oil industry'. But during South Africa's years of political isolation, when there was the possibility of being cut off from external supplies of this vital lifeblood, there was good reason for oil exploration in South Africa to be pursued with zeal and intent.

Three basic criteria must be met for economic reserves of oil to accumulate: (i) there must be a source rock containing enough organic carbon to generate oil, drop by precious drop; (ii) this oil must be pressed out of the source rock; and (iii) it must concentrate in a porous reservoir rock, usually sandstone, from where it can be tapped. The first and last requirements were thought – and found – to be well accommodated in the enormous Karoo Basin, particularly the southwestern part of it. However, long and exhaustive research spanning many years from the early 1970s by Soekor (Pty) Ltd showed that temperatures in the source rock at the critical time of oil formation had been too high, and the droplets formed had been turned to gas and driven off, never to concentrate in any of the reservoirs that were present in abundance. There remains, of course, the possibility of stimulating the more organic-rich source-rocks of the Ecca for unconventional shale gas, i.e. dry methane gas. At the time of going to print, the whole question of 'fracking' in the Karoo is an open – and very emotive – question (see text box on fracking pp. 108–109).

At about the same time that South Africans were coming to terms with the apparent lack of commercially exploitable petroleum in the Karoo, a new discovery was sweeping through the oil exploration business: 'turbidite', until then almost unknown outside classrooms and textbooks, was now recognized as reservoir rock par excellence. Soon turbidites in offshore sediments much younger than the Ecca Group were producing petroleum south of Mossel Bay. While, for the most part, the turbidites being identified in producing and pre-production oilfields were in places like the storm-churned North Sea or under the sands of Arabia, the South African examples were extravagantly shown off in wide expanses of easily accessible land in the southern and western areas of what was then the Cape province. These turbidites offered petroleum geologists a unique opportunity to study their architecture side by side with seismic profiles and drill cores.

News and research results on the turbidites in the Ecca of the Tankwa Karoo and the Laingsburg Karoo soon reached the ears of the petroleum industry and its geoscientists came to see for themselves. The global oil industry is now familiar with these Ecca turbidites, and has spent much time and effort mapping outcrops in minute detail, carrying out seismic surveys, drilling boreholes and logging them geologically and geophysically – all for a better understanding of submarine-fan architecture. On this route you are travelling through a world-famous, world-class oil industry open-air 'laboratory', which companies visit on a regular basis to see for themselves, and to understand nature's processes of building submarine fans.

Turbidites and submarine fans

The term 'turbidite' alludes to the process by which the sediment is transported and laid down – muddiness created by stirring up sediment or where foreign particles are suspended – rather than describing the rock itself. Turbidites are the depositional products of silt- to sand-rich turbidity currents, commonly interbedded with shales. Turbidity or 'density' currents usually originate at the head of submarine canyons cutting the steep continental slope, where they form accumulations of relatively coarse-grained sand at the shelf edge, not far from the wave-washed shoreline. More and more sand accumulates until it reaches a critical mass, when the break of slope becomes unstable and the whole body of sand slides off the shelf edge and down the canyon in a mighty turbidity current. This is no trivial event: millions of tons of wet sediment careering down the slope come to rest hours later as a great splayed fan at its foot.

Once the sand has finished churning and swirling following its descent, the water slowly clears and things return to normal. As usual, the fine clay particles washed out after storms in the source area continue to settle on the sea floor, gradually covering the turbidite sand.

Turbidites are single events comprising the building blocks of fans. The formation of submarine fans results from a continuous process of slumping – or turbidity – events that are predictable in distribution, but also complex and infinitely variable. That's what petroleum geoscientists seek to explore: the regional development, continuity and connectivity of sand bodies in deepwater fan complexes.

FIGURE 5

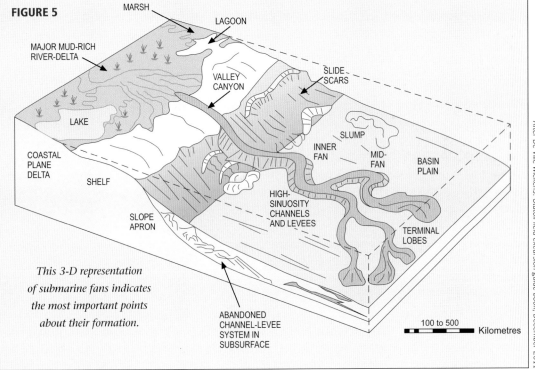

This 3-D representation of submarine fans indicates the most important points about their formation.

After De Ville Wickens: Statoil field excursion guide book, December 2011

fine-grained clay that reaches the seashore in rivers. Wafted far out into the deep, still water, the clay particles very slowly settle out of suspension, layer after thin layer, to become shale. The sediment often contains a high percentage of organic material, which, in the right circumstances, for example high temperatures during deep burial, will form droplets of oil or bubbles of gas.

River-borne cobbles deposited by streams in the recent geological past overlie black (deep-water) Ecca shale, deposited nearly 300 million years ago.

R355 to Sutherland

You will pass the turn-off to Sutherland and Rietfontein just after the 43 km marker plate on the Ceres-Calvinia road that you're on (the R355); at the 66 km marker plate (GPS S 32° 40.887', E 19° 42.480') take the turn-off to the east marked 'Sutherland and Middelpost'. Skoorsteenberg is now over your right shoulder.

You're heading for the escarpment far to the east, though at times you might wonder about the direction, as the road winds this way and that. Skoorsteenberg stays on your right and, after a while, you'll see a lower, flat-topped bluff behind it, protruding into the valley. This is Katjiesberg, northernmost point of the Koedoesberg mountain range, which you will approach quite closely in due course. You will notice on both Skoorsteenberg and Katjiesberg the soft shale slopes with contrasting thinner resistant bands that stand out clearly. These are turbidite sandstones of fans in the Ecca in these parts – the Holy Grail of petroleum geologists.

As you pass the 30 km marker plate (attached to the fence at the roadside), you'll notice a low ridge of dark rock about a kilometre from the road to your left **(geosite 6, map 2)** (GPS S 32° 28.960', E 19° 53.869'). This is your first sighting of dolerite – here a 'dyke' – on this trip, and you'll see lots more of it. Its presence signals that you're getting far enough away from the Cape Fold Belt to be within the Karoo Igneous Province, where tensional cracks heralding the break-up of Gondwana permitted the ascent of pressurized basaltic magma from great depths. Up through the thick cake of Karoo sediments it came – long after the Ecca shale through which it cuts had been deposited – to flow over the surface as sheet after sheet of lava; where it didn't make it to the surface, it squeezed between layers of sediment to form 'sills'. Ten kilometres ahead you drive through a cutting in a dyke and soon after this you see low mesas off to the left, which are remnants of a sill.

About 300 m after the 44 km marker plate, take the turn-off to the right marked 'Sutherland and Skurweberg via Oubergpas'. Soon after turning, you cross a dry river course **(geosite 7, map 2)** (GPS S 32° 25.274', E 19° 59.617'), with conspicuous alluvial gravels over the Ecca shales, and as soon as you come out of this slight valley, looking to your left, you'll see the wooded valley of the Tankwa River with a very conspicuous terrace some tens of metres above the river, marking an old base level of the river before it cut down to its current course.

With the majestic Katjiesberg rising on your right-hand side, you see Fans 4 and 5 wrapping around its foot and capped by 200 m of deltaic deposits. Some time after this you cross a main tributary of the Tankwa River, where you will see some wonderful exposures of what is called Fan 5 (the fifth from the base) of the Tankwa Karoo Ecca Basin **(geosite 8, map 2)** (GPS S 32° 30.163', E 20° 14.047'). Stop your car, get out, walk around on the top of the fan, scramble down the face (which becomes a waterfall when the river flows) and get a feel for what a turbidite deposit is like. Note that the sandstone is quite fine-grained and that it's massive, i.e. unbedded or devoid of any layering – it came rumbling down the slope in a single dramatic event, to splay out on what was then the sea floor.

A hundred metres after the drift you reach a T-junction (GPS S 32° 30.187', E 20° 14.181') where you turn left, following the arrow to Sutherland. Soon you will cross the Tankwa River. After you have wound out of the valley and travelled a few hundred metres along the terrace, there is another T-junction, where you should turn right. A big board points in this direction, which once must have said 'Sutherland', but which is now plain green. You are heading for the foot of Ouberg Pass, better suited, perhaps, to 4x4 vehicles, but which my 'on-road' station-wagon managed quite easily.

A buttress of turbidite sandstone of Fan 5, in the low cliff just below the road as one crosses the Tankwa tributary stream, is conspicuously devoid of bedding, indicating its very rapid deposition.

On the pass, having climbed and climbed, you reach a hairpin bend to the left where you might think you're just about on the plateau, but which turns out to be only about halfway up **(geosite 9, map 2)** (GPS S 32° 24.280', E 20° 20.005'). Here you will see a change from grey sediments to beds with a variety of colours: pink, maroon, beige and some green. This colour change marks the contact between the subaqueous Ecca Group (formed offshore) and the subaerial (river channel and flood-plain) Beaufort Group. You have climbed up through over 1 300 metres of Ecca sediments, from deep-water shales, which you first saw not far out of Karoopoort, up through the fan succession to the deltaic sandstones and siltstones, and now you've crossed the palaeoshoreline onto the land.

As you have climbed from the low plains and up the escarpment, you have also been travelling upwards in geological time, from old to steadily younger beds. When the oldest sediments (the lowermost Ecca) were deposited it was into the deep waters of the great inland Karoo Sea. Gradually the basin was filled, until finally it was a vast swamp. Imagine an enormously scaled-up version of the Okavango Delta, with river channels flowing across sandy plains. The red- to green-coloured siltstone and shale you start to see near the top of the Ouberg Pass – and from here onwards – are testimony to the shallow water in which the sediments of the Beaufort Group were deposited (see text box on 'How clastic sedimentary rocks form', p. 52).

The main geological attraction in the Sutherland district is the striking Salpeterkop volcano. Unfortunately, you will not see steam rising from fumaroles in its crater, but it is the youngest, most complete volcano in the country, and is a prominent topographic feature. You can easily see it from the road leaving Sutherland towards Matjiesfontein, via the R354, if you have chosen to drive out along this road **(geosite 10, map 2)** (GPS S 32° 30.594', E 20° 38.242'). Or, on your way to Fraserburg following the route we've proposed, as you leave the bowl in which Sutherland is situated and breast the rise where you turn left to the observatory, the volcano is clearly visible not far to your right.

The grey mudrock below the road is of the deep-water Ecca Group; the maroon above it is of the Beaufort Group, laid down inland of the shoreline, where the iron in the rock was oxidized to give it its colour.

Sutherland to Fraserburg

You're heading for Fraserburg and one of the 'high' points of this journey, the 'Gansfontein palaeosurface', just outside that town. At the municipal offices in Fraserburg you can pick up a guide – or directions – to the locality, well-known to locals and situated on the farm Gansfontein **(geosite 11, map 2)** (GPS S 31° 54.136', E 21° 28.898'), 4.5 km out of town on the Williston road, the R353.

Imagine the scene. On a quiet day in the age of deposition of the Beaufort sediments, the pre-dinosaurian creatures, large and small, went about their business. They picked their way over the mud left by recent flooding, leaving tell-tale prints as they did so. The sun blazed down. The remaining pools of water evaporated and shrank, and ultimately the delicate ripples that had been formed by the slow flow of the receding water were exposed. The mud baked, cracked and dried under the Gondwanan sun, immortalizing the scene in time. Then, as the rains returned, *Bradysaurus* and other denizens of the swamps moved to higher ground. Rising waters brought new mud and silt in, covering the traces of everyday life in Gondwana. Years went by, then hundreds, millions, sometimes leaving no sediment,

Coenie de Beer (CGS)

Tetrapod tracks across this mudflat, made some 260 million years ago, show that the animal was walking along a gentle slope, with the prints more deeply impressed towards the left of the photograph. The slope at that time was the same as it is today.

other times layers of mud and sand, until the scene was buried by thousands of metres of sediment.

Then Gondwana began to dismember; African coastlines were formed for the first time, new rivers cut down into the sediments, down, down, down. Finally that everyday scene from 250 million years ago was once again exposed as the last layer of mudstone that had entombed it went the same way as the thousands above it. And there the palaeosurface is for all to see: a memorial more vivid than any created by human hand. What a privilege to see it!

The memory will surely stay with you as you head south from Fraserburg towards the N1. You'll join the highway at Leeu Gamka, but on the way you'll see dramatic exposures of the Beaufort sediments as you drop down off the 'High Karoo' to the area below the escarpment. You saw just about the whole of the Ecca Group as you came up the Ouberg Pass: now, to complete the 'Karoo Supergroup experience' you are treated to most of the Beaufort Group as you descend the Theekloof Pass. You saw the Dwyka, at the base of the entire sequence, as you entered the Ceres Karoo, although you are tens of millions of years too late to see the top units of the Supergroup, long since removed in the shaping of the subcontinent we know. You've seen just about all that there is to see in the southwestern Cape. As you approach the N1, the Cape Fold mountains to the south of it loom large, recalling the towering krantzes near Ceres, the folding and the almost indestructible Cape Supergroup quartzites.

Casting your mind back even further, you'll remember the rockfalls around Tulbagh, a testament to the 1969 earthquake there, the most destructive in living memory. Surely it has been a few days of unforgettable geology.

The Salpeterkop volcano

Look at the aerial photograph below of Salpeterkop and marvel at the concentric, bull's-eye arrangement of the topography around the volcanic crater, remembering that the outward-sloping beds were horizontal before the volcano punched its way to the surface. Now those beds dip away from the neck on all sides – with pleasing symmetry – at angles of up to 30° and 2 km away from the neck.

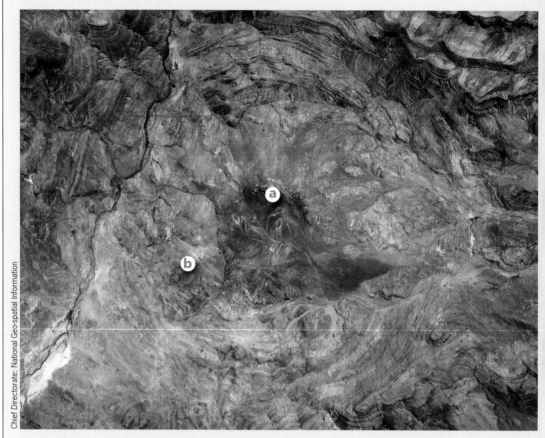

This aerial view of the Salpeterkop volcano, in the centre, shows the concentric, outward-dipping beds, domed upwards by the intrusive body below the volcano. Elsewhere these Beaufort sediments are horizontal. The view of the remnant of the main crater, pictured opposite – (a) in this photograph – was taken from a subsidiary eruptive vent to the southwest (b).

If you were to look at the geological map of the volcano you could imagine the excitement the geologists must have felt as they pieced the picture together. The fragmentary outcrop, mainly breccia-country rock, would have been shattered by the force of the explosion as it burst to the surface – these fragments now giving a clear indication of what happened. Most exciting would have been the unusual rock types they found: rocks with names like K(potassium)-trachyte, carbonatite, and float (loose blocks on the surface) of olivine melilitite. Most telling, though, is the tuff (sedimentary volcanic ash washed in from the crater rim) in the centre. From this, the only interpretation can be that one is looking at an almost completely preserved volcano whose rim has mostly been eroded away over the 66 million years since it last erupted. Salpeterkop is, therefore, not – as was earlier thought – just the 'neck' of a volcano whose top has been stripped off by erosion, but rather a well-preserved volcanic dome itself. That it never formed a Kilimanjaro-like peak was because it was formed by an explosion of short duration, as opposed to the Rift Valley volcanoes from which molten lava flowed, layer after layer over a prolonged period, to build up the imposing structures we see there and in other volcanic belts.

You may wonder whether the volcano was forceful enough to dome well-consolidated sandstones and mudstones into the attitudes shown in the photograph below. The answer is, probably not. Geophysical and other data suggest that not far below the surface is an igneous intrusion, a very large, irregular-shaped mass of rock, which geologists call an 'intrusive ring complex', through the centre of which the volcano burst.

There was not just a single vent of eruption. This photograph shows the main volcanic neck and crater rim – (a) in the aerial view opposite – but there were also multiple smaller volcanic vents and intrusions, one of them easily accessible from the farm road, and from which this photograph was taken – (b) in the image opposite.

3 N15/R62: Worcester to Zoar

GEOLOGICAL OVERVIEW

The R62 is one of the most popular diversional routes in the Western Cape. To get from Cape Town and its surrounds to Oudtshoorn (the setting for the festive annual Kunstefees) and the Little Karoo, the obvious route takes you via Montagu, Barrydale, Ladismith and Calitzdorp. And from the north, Seweweekspoort offers a spectacular approach to the Little Karoo, so that the popularity of the R62 is no surprise.

Of all the routes in this book, this one – the N15 from Worcester to Ashton, and the R62 eastwards from there – ranks as one of the most interesting. Apart from its spectacular scenery, the route takes you through a comprehensive spectrum of well-exposed geology from ancient to modern; and the folding – around Montagu, in particular – is a delight to behold.

Not only do you cut across the Syntaxis Zone (see more about Syntaxis Zones in ch. 2 – Paarl to Sutherland), but you travel close to one of the most important geological faults in the country, known as the Worcester Fault, which has moved the blocks on either side of it a substantial distance vertically. This varies from place to place along the fault, but geologists who have analyzed the system believe the maximum displacement to have been well in excess of 5 km. This faulting, *inter alia*, means that as you travel you will see rocks of the Precambrian Malmesbury Group, representatives of every part of the Cape Supergroup from bottom to top, the lower parts of the Karoo Supergroup (not seen elsewhere within the Cape Fold mountains) and the Jurassic Enon conglomerate. It's as though all the various strata we know of in the south of the country have been lined up for roll call: all present and correct along this one short route.

This spectacular example of text-book Cape folding to the right of the road as you approach Montagu is within easy reach of Cape Town.

Geology of the Route

Worcester to Ashton

To access this cornucopia, turn off the N1 where it by-passes Worcester, pick your way through the town and head east onto the N15, which you will leave just beyond Ashton where you join the R62.

The town of Worcester lies just off the northern edge of the Breede River floodplain, with the underlying geology unobtrusive. The valley-floor sediments you cross as you leave Worcester are geologically young – formed by the Breede River a few million years ago, at most; heading eastwards takes you progressively further back in time. Look to the right as you approach the first river east of

The abundant green pebbles in the overwhelmingly red sediments, by no means typical of Enon conglomerate, make it worth taking the short drive down the road to Nuy.

Worcester, the Nuy River: you will see a collection, too dispersed to be called a 'bed', of rounded white cobbles of the sandstone that flanks the valley – the general impression is of paleness. A short way on is a low hillock on the left, just before the turn-off to the winery and farms of Nuy. If you take the gravel turn-off **(geosite 1, map 3)** (GPS S 33° 41.160', E 19° 35.380'), you will see cuttings where there are layers of conglomerate not very different from the white cobbles of the Nuy River gravel you've just passed, except for their conspicuous red coloration, which is distinctive of the Enon conglomerate. There is, however, a conspicuous difference between this and most of the Enon elsewhere. Firstly, it

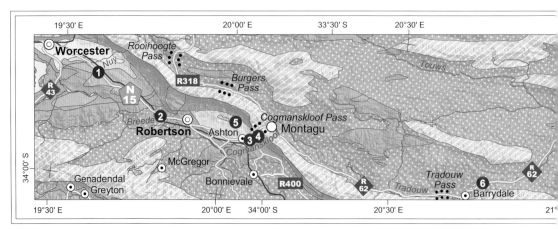

MAP 3

The folded Ecca shale to be seen before Robertson is noteworthy because this is the only case where Karoo Supergroup sediments are seen well within the Cape Fold Belt.

is finer-grained, with lots of interbedded sandstone; and, secondly, its smaller pebbles include a high proportion of shale and fine-grained sandstone, which are conspicuously green. Examined closely, the combination of red with bright green pebbles makes it a very striking rock.

The presence of green clasts in Enon conglomerate is extraordinary: usually they are shades of cream, brown or red. However, a little further on are steeply dipping, thinly bedded sediments in a cutting to the south of the road that are distinctly green: they are 250 million-year-old Ecca shales, and it's worth stopping and having a closer look. It is only around these parts that you will see the Ecca Group within the Cape Fold mountains and anywhere near Enon conglomerate. The connection between these outcrops and the fineness of the Enon sediments a little further west with their green pebbles is that this is the only Enon Basin where the rivers of those times traversed the Ecca Group.

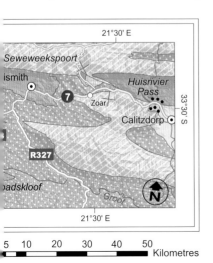

Elsewhere in the mountains in Enon times, flash floods resulted in 'debris flows', which created 'fans' of scree or talus of Cape Supergroup sandstone, along steep, fault-induced slopes. That sandstone is white or pale grey and, being hard, would survive the erosion and transport in the form of boulders or large cobbles. Minor amounts of iron in the Cape sandstone were released and oxidized, which coated the boulders to give the conglomerate the reddish colours so typical of the Enon. In this basin, by contrast, the floods and streams traversed much younger, softer, partly greenish-hued Ecca sediment, giving quite different Enon conglomerate with smaller clasts, many of them green.

The cosmopolitan family of formational names

Though intimidating at first, formational names tell their own story.

The first major split of formations is into two groupings: the eon called the Precambrian (including all the really ancient rock units) and the younger eon called the Phanerozoic.

1   **The Precambrian,** *meaning 'before the Cambrian', comprises ancient rocks almost devoid of fossils except for the most simple marine creatures such as stromatolites and algae. Cambria is the Latin name for Wales, where a group of mainly sedimentary rocks, quite distinct from those above and below, is best exposed. These rocks consequently became grouped together by early mappers as the 'Cambrian'.*

2   **The Phanerozoic** *includes all rock units younger than the Precambrian. It derives its name from the Greek for 'apparent or visible life', because it was only after the beginning of the Cambrian that complex, multicellular life forms evolved, and they are found in sedimentary rocks around the world.*

*The Phanerozoic is split into three eras: the **Palaeozoic Era** (from the Greek for 'ancient life'), **the Mesozoic Era** ('middle life') and **the Cenozoic Era** (originally Cainozoic from the Greek for 'new life').*

*The **Palaeozoic Era** is itself divided into a number of Periods, which in the United Kingdom give their name to the Systems of rocks falling in those time spans. They are named mainly after geographic regions where the rocks are best represented or were first mapped. From youngest (top layer) to oldest (bottom layer) they are:*

- *Permian, from a part of Russia, the district of Perm; at the end of this Period (end-Palaeozoic), some 250 million years ago, occurred the greatest mass extinction of all time of living forms.*
- *Carboniferous, from the Latin for 'coal-bearing', because it is the period during which most coal around the world formed, although in South Africa the Permian and Triassic also saw the deposition of coal seams.*
- *Devonian, after the English county where this particular package of rocks was first studied.*
- *Silurian, a distinct succession of rocks named during the earliest days of British geological mapping, after a Celtic tribe, the Silures.*
- *Ordovician, similarly named, after a tribe called the Ordovices.*
- *Cambrian, near the start of which occurred a phenomenon named the Cambrian Explosion, when a unique and dramatic proliferation of complex and drastically different life forms took place.*

The South African names of rock units derive, more simply, from the areas where they were first recognized as distinct sequences, clearly different from those above and below them.

To the north of the road, about 14 km from the Nuy turn-off there's a white scar on the hill slope some 4 km from the road, where Malmesbury Group dolomitic lime is being quarried. A little further on, right next to the road, is the Langvlei Cape Lime factory, where lime is processed for a variety of uses. Most of the lime in the Cape is quarried from the Neoproterozoic Malmesbury Group and its equivalents.

After passing the Rooiberg Winery on your left, and approaching the Graham Beck vineyards, you will notice ahead of you, as the road curves away to the left **(geosite 2, map 3)** (GPS S 33° 47.575', E 19° 47.281') , a patch of pale sand high up on the slope overlooking the vines. This is river sand thought to have been blown out of a tributary of the Breede River on the other side of the ridge, and over the top. It's a good example of a geological process at work.

If we think of accumulations of wind-blown sand as dunes, then what you see near the crest of the hill behind the Graham Beck vineyards are indeed sand dunes, thought to have been blown over the ridge from a tributary of the Breede River on the far side of the ridge. Note the fold to the left of the 'dunes'.

The strata below the Witteberg are shales (and subordinate sandstones) of the Bokkeveld Group, of which there are good examples as you cross the last ridge before the next town, Ashton. The high hills at a distance from the road and to the north are granite – the same granite as elsewhere in the Cape, here of the Robertson Pluton. Notice the scattered bare patches of granite in the fynbos and the lack of layering (bedding) which is a prominent feature of sandstone outcrops and crags elsewhere. As promised at the start of this chapter, the geology of the route has taken you steadily back in time, from a few million years to about 480 million years ago, the estimated minimum age of this pluton. And there are still older rocks ahead.

It seems you have only just left Robertson when you find you're approaching Ashton. As you drive through this village you drop noticeably to cross a small stream running through it. Looking back after you have crossed the bridge, and in the direction of the mountains to the north, you will see a high vertical river bank facing you in the distance. Were you to stop for a careful look, or drive through the town towards it, you would see in the bank one of the best exposures of Enon conglomerate in these parts. Remember that these conglomerates were formed on the downthrow side of faults formed as Gondwana was splitting up, faults analogous to the rifts in the Rift Valley of Central and East Africa.

The fault responsible for the conglomerate in Ashton is one of the major such features in southern Africa, the Worcester Fault, running to the north of the R62. It is part of a system of broadly east-west faults that run from Worcester in the west to beyond the Baviaanskloof in the east. At points along their length they are invariably associated with Enon conglomerate.

The lower, better-sorted and faintly layered sediments in the river bank in Ashton are Jurassic Enon conglomerate and unrelated to the river they overlook; the overlying, coarser and poorly sorted gravel relates to a comparatively recent time before the river had cut its present channel.

If you drive close to the vertical river bank in question **(geosite 3, map 3)** (GPS S 33° 49.733', E 20° 03.912') you will see that overlying the conspicuously layered and compacted Enon conglomerate (approximately 150 million years old), which makes the basal part of the bank, is a layer of unbedded and less compacted material with some large, pale-coloured boulders. This is a much younger river gravel, unrelated to any faulting, which is all but dormant. It formed during floods in the rivers before they cut down to their present level.

Ashton to Montagu

Leaving Ashton, you drive past the turn-off to Swellendam and turn northwards along the Cogman's River, which has cut the poort through the rampart formed by the Table Mountain sandstones. Before entering the poort proper, though, you can see rocks exposed in the high cutting to your right that are quite different from anything you have seen since leaving Worcester. They are finely banded and cleaved phyllitic shales, conspicuously veined with quartz and stained with red-brown iron oxide. Although widespread almost wherever the rift- and drift-related mega-faults cut through the southern Cape, these Malmesbury sediments are the first and only Precambrian rocks you will see on this drive. They are about 560–580 million years old, formed a little before the granite north of Robertson.

Up until now on this route, you have travelled back in time, stratigraphically. Now, after 100 m of ancient Malmesbury phyllite, you cross back from old to younger formations **(geosite 4, map 3)** (GPS S 33° 49.440', E 20° 05.422'). The next rocks you see are significantly younger: they are the high-standing quartzitic sandstones of the Table Mountain Group (TMG). They were deposited on the Malmesbury sediments after these had been folded and planed off to form the floor of the TMG basin. In Cogmanskloof the once horizontal TMG quartzite beds now stand vertically, tilted into this attitude during the formation of the Cape Fold Belt.

The basal conglomerate of the Peninsula Formation of the Table Mountain Group (TMG), seen here (inset), marks the unconformable contact between this group and strongly cleaved and substantially older Malmesbury phyllite, already folded and planed off when the TMG was deposited.

The geological setting as you approach Montagu is magnificent: bed after bed of seemingly indestructible quartzitic sandstone towers vertically above you with geometric precision. The effect calls to mind a pack of giant playing cards stood on end, except where the linear pattern is disturbed by folding, and even this is so elegantly sculptured as to make a mockery of the hardness of the ancient rocks. It's a very different setting from the flats you've just traversed.

Lying stratigraphically above the thick sequence of rigid quartzitic sandstone of the TMG, the thin (less than 100 m thick) Cedarberg shale, being soft and easily deformed, acts as a lubricating layer, allowing detachment of the overlying strata. These, the much less rigid sequences of less quartzitic sandstone of the Nardouw Subgroup, have been folded into swirling patterns that you see to your right as you approach Montagu. These spectacular folds are the hallmark of the grandiose scenery further east, most famously in Meiringspoort and the Swartberg Pass. For more detail of the folding and geological events before and after the folding, view the plaque erected by the Geological Society of South Africa, which can be found after driving through the little tunnel above which the fort from the Anglo-Boer War stands. It is fixed to the rock slope above a shady parking area to the right of the road. To see folding of the post-Cedarberg sandstones head-on, you need go no further than the west bank of the Keisie River as it runs through Montagu **(geosite 5, map 3)** (GPS S 33° 46.906', E 20° 0.696'). Turn left into Barry Street, and left again, and over the river into Meul Street. The river has cut a vertical cliff below Kanonkop, which you can reach via Kohler Street. From this vantage point there are magnificent views over the town and eastwards along the mountain face for tens of kilometres.

What you see as you pass through Montagu is the result of deformation of sedimentary rocks that took place many kilometres below the surface. In order to see the results of processes that took place so deep in the crust, huge thicknesses of overlying rocks have had to be stripped off. Here, the very core of the fold belt has been exposed.

If you have time you should stop at the museum in Montagu's old Dutch Reformed Church in Long Street, and ask to be shown the fossils. They are from a farm in the Warmwaterberg north of Barrydale, and are of perfect little shells and crinoid 'stems' from the Bokkeveld Group to the east of Barrydale. Crinoids (from the Greek meaning 'lily-like'), though resembling water lilies, are in fact animals. Although there are many species still living, they were much more abundant and diverse deep in the geological past.

Casts of fossilized bivalves (left) of the sort we might see on beaches today, and impressions left by crinoids (above) from the Bokkeveld sediments east of Montagu.

Among other attractions, Montagu is known for its hot springs. The calorific input can be ascribed to extremely deep circulation of surface water, down to warmer levels in the Earth's crust – and back – via joint planes close to the contact between the Table Mountain and Bokkeveld Groups, which were opened more widely than usual during folding. As with all South African hot springs, there is no volcanic input into any of them – just unusually good 'plumbing'. Water filters down to depths that are naturally hotter, and circulates up again fast enough not to lose the acquired heat. The better the plumbing, the warmer the water.

Montagu to Zoar

After the rich geological experience that Montagu boasts, the road onward from here offers a breather. To begin with, while the road still runs quite close to the steep northern slope of the sandstone Langeberg range, you catch glimpses of the folding of the Upper Table Mountain Group sandstones; and in the road cuttings, highly cleaved Bokkeveld shales, with occasional uncleaved dark grey sandstone and greywacke.

Soon after leaving Montagu you'll notice boards advertising the Guano Cave. Over the centuries, bats living in this small cave near the foot of the steep face of Table Mountain sandstone have left a legacy of nitrate-rich droppings, which used to be extracted by local farmers and spread over their lands. There are Khoi-San paintings in the cave, too.

The best exposure of the Bokkeveld shales is in the cuttings near the top of the Tradouw Pass, which drops you down into the valley in which Barrydale nestles. Whereas the cleavage in the Malmesbury shales as you came into Cogmanskloof was along the bedding, this is not the case here, as you will see if you stop at the top of the pass: the cleavage, or fine splitting of the rock during folding and often not aligned along the bedding, is steep to the south, parallel to the axial plane of the folding (see *Geological Journeys*, p. 121), while the much flatter bedding cuts across it at a high angle. A close look shows you bedding on a variety of scales, from many centimetres, down to beds of only a millimetre or two thick.

The Tradouw Pass shows typical Bokkeveld shales, with strong almost vertical cleavage (parallel to the pen) and quite subtle bedding perpendicular to it.

The Tradouw Pass that you drive through on the R62 is, in fact, only the first part of the pass; the second, much more dramatic section leaves the R62 heading towards the coast, through the Langeberg range, where you enter Barrydale. The Tradouw River, today a fairly insignificant stream, is a mere shadow of its former self, when it cut a couple of important valleys, the second a spectacular gorge.

To the east, the next defile through the range would take you through Garcia's Pass to Riversdale, mentioned here only because it illustrates the curious phenomenon of river capture, or, more evocatively, 'river piracy'. It is generally accepted by geologists that the Groot River, which has its source north of Laingsburg and flows past that town as the Buffels River, formerly cut through Garcia's Pass. That was until a deeper-cutting tributary of the Gouritz River, gnawing its way upstream, as rivers do, cut through the minor watershed between it and the Groot. In so doing, it captured the substantial system of headwaters that had formerly flowed through Garcia's Pass, leaving a very truncated Vetrivier to make its way to the coast through the poort that's followed by the pass. The R62 travels through that part of South Africa where river piracy has been at its most pervasive (see a more comprehensive treatment of this intriguing subject in ch. 4, p. 94).

The mesas east of Barrydale, as well as the conical koppie, are remnants of the valley floor during a prolonged period of stability millions of years ago, before the surface was cut down to its present level.

The soft white kaolin in the koppie is the result of prolonged leaching of Bokkeveld shales, the hard iron- and silica-rich layer above it telling of later upward movement of those elements to form the resistant capping.

Landscapes of yesteryear

There are not that many obvious reminders of the transience of landscape – in a human lifetime the topography changes so little that there's scant evidence it was ever any different. We know that it changes, if for no other reason than that seashell fossils are found on hillsides far from the nearest beach, and in the semi-desert Karoo, which was clearly once a vast inland sea.

Something that we can relate to are times when the rivers we know had not yet quite cut down to their current level, and when the mountain ranges so familiar to us were exactly where they are now, only a little higher. The valley floors were higher, too; and the flat-topped koppie south of the road just outside Barrydale, and other koppies ahead, help us reconstruct the landscape of long ago. This ancient land surface existed during what was – quite recently, in geological terms – a very prolonged period of stability on the Earth's surface. The inevitable processes of cutting down through erosion had slowed down considerably under the stable conditions. Away from the mountains were wide plains stretching to the horizon, crossed by languid rivers that meandered seemingly aimlessly. In the Cretaceous climate, which was wetter than today's, rain fell and gradually the rocks near the surface were leached, all the silica and iron being washed out of them and draining downwards. When the climate turned drier again in Tertiary times and the land surface became periodically desiccated, the silica and iron were drawn back to the surface by capillary action and reprecipitated. A hard capping of surface material cemented by this 'silcrete' and 'ferricrete' formed above an uppermost layer of rock that was leached, in extreme cases, to pure kaolin.

At this point in time, Earth's axis tilted and an ice-age froze increasingly bigger polar ice caps, causing sea levels to fall. The stability that had ruled for so long came to an end as the next cycle of lowering of Earth's surface began. Gradually the iron- and silica-capped surface fell prey to down-cutting by re-energized streams and rivers. Today, that age-old surface has all but disappeared, the only remnants being the scattered, flat-topped koppies (locally known as 'oervlakte') you see in this region. The silcrete and ferricrete remnants are grouped as the Grahamstown Formation, with an estimated age of some 70 million years.

FIGURE 6   CROSS-BEDDING – CLUES TO ORIENTATION

RIGHT: *In situations such as the Cape Fold Belt, where horizontally deposited beds stand vertically, cross-beds form a useful clue as to the correct 'way up'. Their elegantly arcuate form is very commonly asymmetric and it is this asymmetry that tells beyond any doubt which was the top of the bed and which the bottom, as these three diagrams show. The 'missing' (truncated) section of a complete cross-bed form will always lie at the top of the curved surface.*

OPPOSITE: *Siltstone of the Witteberg Group west of Ladismith offers a good example of this cross-bedding, showing truncated topset beds (and top of the sequence) to the left in the photograph.*

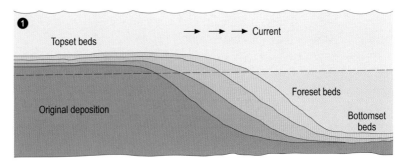

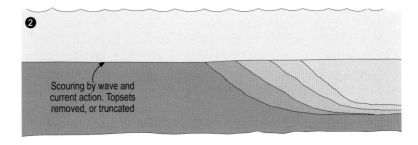

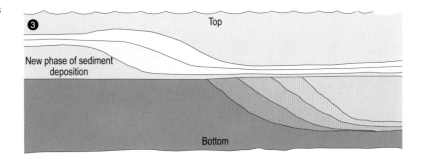

Not far beyond Barrydale you cannot miss, on your right-hand side, a flat-topped koppie that, in this landscape of rolling hill and dale, is conspicuously different **(geosite 6, map 3)** (GPS S 33° 51.721', E 20° 46.352'). It's too small to show on the map but take note of it because it's part of an interesting story, enough so to warrant its own text box.

From Barrydale, you drive through a broad valley system carved mainly from Bokkeveld shales and lesser amounts of Witteberg sediments, beds of sandstone alternating with siltstone and shale. To both north and south, even if these are not always visible from the road, high ridges and ranges of Table Mountain sandstone contain the rolling lowlands – a reminder that you're moving into the Little Karoo, where this is the norm. Far to the north lie the great plains of the Karoo proper, to the south, the thin strip of coastal plain. Between Barrydale and Ladismith the country is still as hilly as further west, but the valleys are broader. This is because you are entering the heartland of some of the most important landscape-forming rivers in the southern Cape, the Touws and the Groot, together with their tributaries. They are themselves tributaries of the Gouritz, and make up a system with a catchment of tens of thousands of square kilometres. Earlier progenitors of these rivers – in wetter times – formed the wide plains of which the flat-topped koppies referred to in the text box (p. 77) are remnants.

While this route generally runs from west to east, in the stretch from Barrydale to Ladismith you are heading more north than east, which means you are cutting across the east-west axis of the Cape folding. Not far out of Barrydale you cannot miss the famous landmark of Ronnie's Sex Shop, soon after which you'll see a turn-off to the left to Warmwaterberg and Brakrivier. The broad whaleback, known as Warmwaterberg because of the presence of a hot water spring similar to that in Montagu, towards which this road leads, is made by a gentle anticline of upper Table Mountain sandstone in a sea of softer Bokkeveld sediments. It was in the Bokkeveld shales and mudrocks draped over this anticline that farmer De Vries collected the fossils now in the Montagu Museum. If you look in the road cuttings, and at the dips in the hills, you will see the broad anticline you are travelling through.

As you move off the Bokkeveld and towards Ladismith you will start to see more of the Witteberg Group in the hills and next to you in road cuttings. Even without the krantzes that you would see, for example, around Ceres, there is conspicuously more ridge-forming sandstone here than on the Bokkeveld Group further back, whose predominant shale and mudrock tends to make rounder, soil-covered hills.

At Ladismith, you are close to the northern edge of the Little Karoo. The imposing landmark of Towerkop (2 295 m) is clearly visible, the wide, river-carved lowlands now behind you. Crowning the Klein Swartberg range, and like the Groot Swartberg to the east of it, Towerkop is formed by

FIGURE 7

FAULTING NEAR LADISMITH

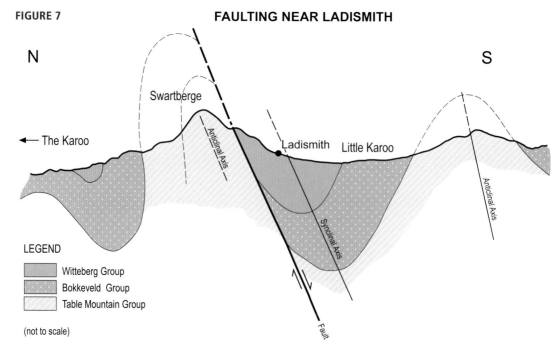

Sketch showing how at Ladismith the top member of the Cape Supergroup lies adjacent to the lowermost Table Mountain Group, with the middle of the 'sandwich', the Bokkeveld Group, missing as a result of faulting.

As you approach Zoar, the extensive mesa to your left is another remnant of the ancient valley floor, subsequently dissected by erosion of the present valley. The Swartberg range appears just behind the cloud.

the ultra-resistant Table Mountain sandstone. Note that the high Swartberg crests making the northern skyline are separated by a major fault from the Witteberg-built hills in which Ladismith nestles, the whole Bokkeveld Group having been removed by faulting.

The Swartberg range, at its highest in these parts, marks the northernmost TMG-cored anticline of the fold belt. Beyond it lies the Karoo where folding of reducing intensity rucks softer overlying formations of the Bokkeveld and Witteberg Groups into gentle ridges and valleys. Gradually the folds die out until one is finally in the vast expanse of horizontal Karoo formations.

Heading eastwards from Ladismith towards Calitzdorp, the mountain range remains hard on your left. In this stretch, before going through the passes and down to Calitzdorp, the road passes Zoar and Amalienstein, where it links up with the route out of the Little Karoo via the Seweweekspoort (covered in *Geological Journeys*).

There is still one treat in store, though. About 12 km out of Ladismith, after quite a marked turn to the left and as you enter a long, straight section, you will see pronounced and extensive flat hilltops across the valley **(geosite 7, map 3)** (GPS S 33° 30.649', E 21° 21.935'). These result from the same processes as the flat hills outside Barrydale, the important difference being that this remnant of the ancient surface lies at the northern edge of the valley. All the others were against the southern boundary slopes. North or south, they are the last surviving vestiges of what were once broad valley floors where rivers meandered, shaping the new continent.

4 R322: Baviaanskloof

GEOLOGICAL OVERVIEW

The single, tight valley of the true Baviaanskloof is sandwiched almost secretly between the wide plains of the Karoo and one of South Africa's most popular tourist coasts. It offers not only truly spectacular scenery but, together with the sections linking it to the N9 in the west and the N2 at the other end, some remarkable and educational geology. The chronological continuum it offers from the folding of Cape Supergroup sediments, through the break-up of Gondwana to the present day gives vivid accessibility to geological processes at work, step by giant step.

Dave Rogers

The Baviaanskloof River has, for the most part, carved itself a valley just wide enough to accommodate a road. The latter cannot meander like the former, though, so crosses it in a succession of drifts, some deep enough for the water to reach well up the sides of cars. Elsewhere the river squeezes into slit-like defiles and the road has to climb onto the upland interfluve up steep and winding passes, mostly too narrow for two vehicles to pass. Four-wheel-drive is not essential but a bakkie with big tyres would be fine – this is definitely not a route for your highway sedan.

Some of the outcrops of Enon conglomerate referred to in the text cannot be shown on the map because they are small and the area covered by the map large by comparison.

LEFT AND INSET: *From high points in the Baviaanskloof, the planar African Land Surface can be clearly seen, deeply dissected by comparatively recent valleys.*

Geology of the route

Willowmore to Studtis

There are two ways of getting into the Baviaanskloof from the west: the route described here follows the R332, branching off the N9 towards the southeast, some 3 km south of Willowmore, rather than the lower-ranked road closer to Uniondale. From where you leave the N9 until a little before Patensie in the east, the road is gravel, but the surface, though corrugated when we drove it, is mostly not bad.

To begin with you pass close to the axis of a synclinorium filled mostly with soft shale and mudrock of the Bokkeveld Group. Then, after about 10 km, you go through a low sandstone ridge of the uppermost part of the Table Mountain Group (Baviaanskloof Formation), and from here on, what has so far been gently rolling upland becomes more rugged. You're approaching the Baviaanskloof Mountains to the east, with peaks higher than 1 500 m, and west of the road lies the more restricted range, capped by the 1 720 m-high Antoniesberg peak – all cut from the ever-dominant Table Mountain Group.

As you start to descend the Nuwekloof Pass you see well-bedded sandstone and mudrock of the Baviaanskloof Formation in a road cutting. After this, you drop down in the stratigraphy until you're in the kloof from which the pass gets its name, where the vertically standing quartzite beds that tower over you on both sides are of the Peninsula Formation, which lies at the base of the Cape Supergroup.

As you see the poort opening up into the broad Baviaanskloof valley beyond, look to the right (west) of the road and you will see a beautiful example of the breccia formed in the fault zone that has defined the location of the valley **(geosite 1, map 4)** (GPS S 33° 31.372′, E 23° 39.445′). This is a key element of the geology of this route – essentially it is the reason the Baviaanskloof exists. The fault runs for tens of kilometres along the north side of the length of the valley, by no means always forming its northern edge, but never very far from it and clearly its *raison d'être*.

These iron-rich and iron-poor sediments of the Baviaanskloof Formation, originally laid down horizontally and now (after Cape folding) steeply dipping, are stratigraphically near the top of the Table Mountain Group.

With stress fields in the crust during the unimaginably complex tectonic disturbance, faults seldom run as straight as one might think they should. The Baviaanskloof Fault is an example of such a 'bent' fault, making a pronounced – almost right-angled – curvature at the portal of Nuwekloof, following the eastern wall of the kloof into the northern face of the main valley you're entering. The breccia occupies a thick zone, thereby exploding the notion you may have had that a fault always happens along a single plane of movement. Have a good look at the fault breccia where the road turns to the left out of Nuwekloof: it's fundamental to an understanding of the genesis of the Enon conglomerate, and key to the geological history of these parts.

The story of the Cape Fold Belt has been told quite fully in earlier chapters and will only be summarized here. Subduction of a proto-Pacific

The fragmented nature of the Baviaanskloof Fault shows dramatically what happens when one block of Earth's crust moves against another as forces deep in the mantle are accommodated at the surface.

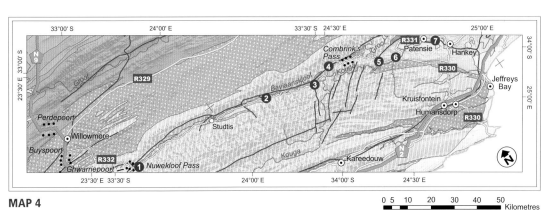

MAP 4

0 5 10 20 30 40 50
Kilometres

plate under Gondwana, between about 200 and 100 million years ago, caused folding and thrusting of a package of sediments deposited in the elongate Cape Basin, broadly parallel to, and some distance from the edge of the Gondwana plate. It happened in a number of pulses and brought about substantial crustal shortening.

Not long after the conclusion of Cape sedimentation and the onset of folding, a massive glaciation event occurred, giving rise to the Dwyka tillite, not found in the Baviaanskloof but widespread elsewhere in the Cape. After this, and with Gondwana moving away from the polar region, sedimentation continued to the north of the Cape trough in a vast subsiding repository that we know as the Karoo Basin. The continued tectonism in the Cape Fold Belt now involved the southernmost part of the Karoo Basin until its sedimentary history was well under way. Folding died and, some time later, Karoo sedimentation came to an end too. Deep-seated events caused the crust to start stretching, the cracks thus formed giving access to huge amounts of basaltic magma, which rose to the surface to cover large parts of Gondwana. What didn't reach the surface squeezed into partings in the crustal rocks, mostly the Karoo sediments, as dolerite dykes, sills and sheets.

Crustal tension continued and major zones of weakness, dormant since the end of Cape tectonism, were reactivated, this time as normal faults. Grabens, or rift valleys, and half-grabens were formed. Half-grabens have faults on one side and hinges on the other, where no rupture takes place, just downwarping. In the Cape Fold Belt the pre-existing tectonic 'grain', in these parts aligned east-west, set the scene for normal faulting, which also runs east-west. As crustal stretching continued, Gondwana ruptured piecemeal into the fragments we know today – continents such as Africa and Australia, and islands like Madagascar.

FIGURE 8a

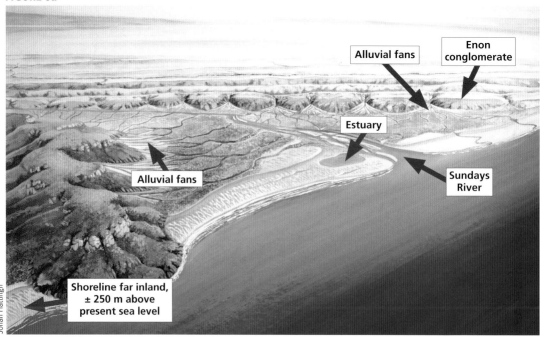

An artist's portrayal of the changes along the Algoa Bay coastline over geological time vividly illustrates the dynamic nature of river and coastal evolution. The above is a reconstruction from the Late Miocene, some 8 million years ago.

FIGURE 8b

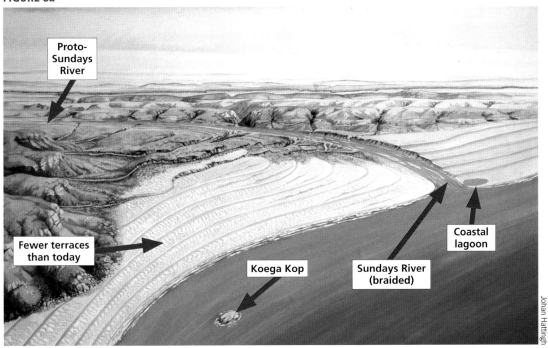

*A slightly closer view, from the Middle Pliocene, some 4 million years ago,
sea level having fallen substantially and the coast receded.*

FIGURE 8c

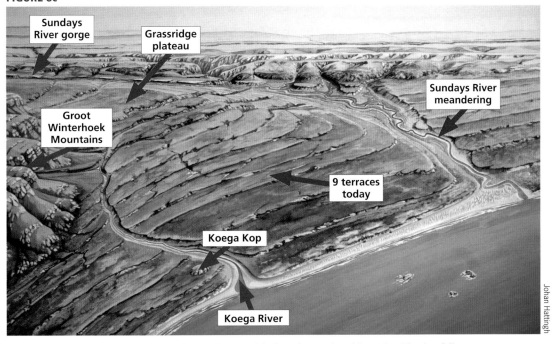

*Algoa Bay as the early strandlopers might have known it, with sea level having fallen
still further and the formerly extensive sandy beaches now mostly vegetated.*

Building blocks

In a nutshell, and working from oldest to youngest, we can summarize the sequence of events described on the previous pages as follows:

- Formation of the E-W and N-S Cape sedimentary troughs
- Glaciation (Dwyka Group)
- Commencement of folding
- Start of Karoo sedimentation
- Termination of folding, with compressional faulting
- Completion of Karoo sedimentation
- Start of tensional regime in the crust
- Outpouring of basalt
- Reactivation of faults, now tensional
- Formation of E-W grabens and half-grabens (rift valleys)
- Deposition of Enon conglomerate in the 'rift valleys'
- Commencement of Continental Drift, starting with a new Indian Ocean, and, slightly later, the Atlantic
- The subcontinent, much as we know it today, was being shaped
- Development of river systems in the same 'rift valleys', with silcrete terraces and the 'African Land Surface' of erosion
- Formation of present valleys, with terrace remnants.

Baviaanskloof Formation mudrock and sandstone, showing the near-vertical bedding.

As you look around you, travelling through the Baviaanskloof, almost all the building blocks are present. While you won't see Karoo sediments and basalt on this route, you've probably seen them elsewhere and will understand their inclusion in this potted history as an integral part of it.

New river systems cutting back from a virgin coastline were, to a large extent, guided by the architecture resulting from the earlier Cape folding. Hard sandstone formations made ridges, and soft shales and mudrocks were shaped into valleys. Rift valleys (strictly half-graben) that subsequently opened by faulting during the Gondwana break-up became filled with conglomerate of the Enon Formation. This was derived mainly from the southern, downwarped (i.e. not faulted) edge of the valleys and generally transported from west to east.

With the whole Baviaanskloof ahead of you, you can now appreciate how faulting formed the valley. From the time you emerge from the tight Nuwekloof gorge until the fordable valley stream has fed into the mighty Gamtoos River, far to the east, you will see regular patches of Enon conglomerate, and will know how it got there. Remember that the impressive alluvial fans, formed by water washing rock debris down the slopes, would have fanned out at the base of the slopes – testimony to the breaking down since those times (140 million years ago) of towering mountain ranges. What we gaze up at today are the mere stumps of mountains, truncated by millions of years of erosion.

As the faulting slowed and finally stopped, with drift now well under way, the drainage patterns we know today started to form. Sea level fluctuated globally and forces in the mantle lifted the land, resulting in a coastline that is forever shifting. Regardless of any considerations of global warming that may concern us today, what yesterday was deep out to sea, tomorrow could be far inland.

When sea level was relatively higher than today's, river base levels were higher, too, although – and this is important to remember – the river systems were essentially where we find them now. Over much of the Eastern Cape, wide valleys were carved out by rivers like the Baviaanskloof. This was particularly pronounced during the long period of stability when the so-called African Land Surface (of erosion) developed. African Surface terraces were generally capped by a duricrust of silcrete or ferricrete; this gave them a greater capacity to survive erosion as rivers cut down in response to the falling sea level, particularly where the underlying rock was soft. Remnants of this silcretized surface, called the Grahamstown Formation, are common in the Baviaanskloof and other valleys in the Eastern Cape.

The Enon conglomerate across the valley as you enter it is more iron rich than the grey conglomerate near the road where the Nuwekloof gorge joins the Baviaanskloof valley.

Having seen the fault as you leave Nuwekloof, right ahead of you as you enter the main valley, is a lot of Enon conglomerate, across the valley as well as much nearer. Although Enon is usually stained red by small amounts of oxidized iron minerals coating the clasts, sometimes conspicuously so, the closer outcrops are practically devoid of colour and the more distant, southerly outcrops are only partly red, probably because there was less iron present.

As you pass the farm Verlorenrivier, the scarp edges of the old valley floor appear pronounced.

For 5 km the valley is quite broad, with Enon conglomerate conspicuous, particularly to the south (on your right), after which you climb away from the river slightly. As you come into the next wide valley eastwards, after the farm Verlorenrivier, you will see the strikingly flat-topped slopes at the far end of the valley, on both sides tilting very slightly towards the centre of the valley. This is the old valley floor surface at its most obvious. Perhaps most diagnostic are its sharp, stepped edges.

You drive on with farms on either side of the road, where the scenery is pleasing but not yet spectacular. After the Verlorenrivier flats the valley narrows and you pass through the Sewefontein communal farming area and the tiny settlement of Studtis, where the valley now widens conspicuously. On the farms you will see small groups of domestic stock: further on, in the Baviaanskloof Nature Reserve, you will see kudu, bushbuck and, if you're lucky, buffalo.

Studtis is well known to local geologists and hydrogeologists because of the strong artesian water supply near the town: water that is retained in the Baviaanskloof Mountains to the north bubbles to the surface along a fault running very close to the road, and is supplemented by a free-flowing supply from boreholes drilled next to the fault so that quite intensive farming is possible here.

Studtis to Jeffreys Bay

After a short constriction the valley opens again as you pass the farmstead and store at Kleinpoort (the last place where diesel can be bought until Patensie, 133 km down the track). By the time you get here you may have noticed a difference in the setting. As the road hugs this northern side of the valley, the slope just to your left is far smoother than the chaotically irregular slopes that have

The smooth continuous slope north of the valley at Kleinpoort is a good example of a dip slope, where softer layers of a tilted package of Table Mountain sediments have been weathered away until a layer of exceptionally hard sandstone formed a more durable surface.

As you enter the Baviaanskloof Nature Reserve you are confronted by this magnificent face of Enon conglomerate.

flanked the route up until now. From time to time there are narrow gorges cutting through the ridge: have a look at the exposure in these kloofs and you will see the reason for the difference. In a general sense the bedding, like the hillside itself, is dipping down towards you. The slope is a dip slope, meaning that it has been controlled by the dip of the sedimentary bedding of the Peninsula Formation that makes the ridge. For quite a few kilometres the Baviaanskloof Fault runs along the foot of the slope, under – or at least very close to – the road.

There is lots of Enon conglomerate now on both sides of the road, near and far, but undoubtedly the most impressive exposure is in the almost vertical face that you see as you approach the western gate of the Baviaanskloof Nature Reserve **(geosite 2, map 4)** (GPS S 33° 36.214', E 24° 11.992'). Most of it is conspicuously red, and even in places where conglomerate has been stripped off, the ancient underlying Cape sediments themselves may be strikingly iron-stained. There's more conglomerate ahead, but the valley narrows from here, in places to a tight cleft between jagged rock faces, and there's not always space to pull off the road for sight-seeing, especially on the two passes where the road leaves the river. Close up you'll see that most of the sandstone is conspicuously fractured, testimony to repeated phases of both folding and faulting, first compressional and then tensional; and you get regular glimpses of panoramic vistas showing good folding, mainly in the Goudini Formation, the middle main unit of the Table Mountain Group. Soon after the birth of the African continent, the scenery levelled off – a phenomenon that is borne out by the longer views here, where the flat African Land Surface sharply bevels steeply dipping beds.

You can see the full development of the African Land Surface in these parts from the tops of the passes. The first, more westerly one is the Grasnek Pass, which offers views of the Cedarberg shale – beige-weathering and finely cleaved – in roadside cuttings as you ascend the pass. This is the first rock other than sandstone or Enon conglomerate that you've seen in the Baviaanskloof. Remember that it separates the basal Peninsula Formation, here lying to the north of you, from the overlying Goudini Formation to the south. You do not stay long at the top before starting the descent to the east. In the middle distance ahead of you as you pass the 116.0 km marker plate is a prominent hill of Table Mountain sandstone, striking because of its unvegetated western slopes, reminiscent of the smooth granite domes of Paarl Rock.

Back in the valley, it's not long before you're aware of the red conglomerate again. You will see it ahead of you to the left (north) of the road, a few hundred metres after passing the 121.0 km board, in a beautiful exposure of a fault contact. The contact is just about vertical, the Enon 'conglomerate' to the south faulted against Goudini Formation sandstone to the north. About a kilometre further on **(geosite 3, map 4)** (GPS S 33° 39.787′, E 24° 23.446′) you get a close-up view of the younger rock, and see that it is in fact not a conglomerate at all, but a sedimentary breccia and anything but typical Enon. There is less sorting than usual, with the conspicuously angular fragments showing a dramatic range of size. This is perhaps a useful piece of evidence to show that the conglomerate with the rounded clasts is not derived from the faults but from the more gently formed downwarps opposite them to the south. The rock you're looking at here is a fault scarp breccia, undoubtedly fault-derived but, in contrast to the true tectonic breccia you saw at the mouth of the Nuwekloof, it is an example of an extremely immature sedimentary rock – meaning that its components have been transported only a short distance from their point of origin.

As you wind along you may become aware of wider expanses of water in the river not far to the south of you. This is because you have reached the point where the Baviaanskloof River, which you

Throughout the Baviaanskloof, steeply dipping folded sediments are truncated by the African Land Surface, formed during a period of prolonged stability following Gondwana break-up.

Though at first looking like Enon conglomerate, the conspicuously angular and unsorted nature of this rock is a direct reminder of the faulting that has formed the Baviaanskloof valley.

have followed for nearly 100 km, has been joined by the bigger Kouga River. To give an idea of the flatness of the old rivers in these parts, the place where you first catch sight of the Kouga is some 50 km (following the river) before reaching the dam wall. The height of the Kouga Dam wall is 81 m, telling you that in 50 km the river bed drops by this amount – in other words less than 2 m per km. And from the dam to the sea, along what becomes the Gamtoos River not far below the dam, the gradient is less still. The river itself has practically reached the base level below which it will not cut: now all that remains is for the valley to widen.

Soon after you've encountered the wider expanse of water, the road can no longer be accommodated on the flood plain and has to climb into the mountains again, up the Holgat Pass, this time to the north of the river. It will rejoin the Gamtoos, much wider by now, only at Komdomo, where one leaves the Baviaanskloof Nature Reserve to enter the citrus-orchard area around Patensie. The first part of the climb is through wooded tributary valleys, liberally dotted with big yellowwoods (*Podocarpus falcatus*) and other species well known to Cape gardeners, such as the bosvlier (*Nuxia floribunda*). Once on top of the interfluve you are rewarded with the best panoramic view to be had on this trip, where the extent and relative flatness of the African Land Surface are beautifully illustrated.

At the first hairpin bend on Combrink's Pass, which takes you back into the valley, you cross the Baviaanskloof Fault. This separates the Peninsula Formation, which makes up the high ground you've been on, from the Goudini Formation you're on now. You stay on the latter unit until you are in the valley and approaching the eastern gate of the Baviaanskloof Nature Reserve. About 2.5 km beyond the gate you start to notice grey to pale brown shale in the cuttings **(geosite 4, map 4)** (GPS S 33° 38.707′, E 24° 27.416′). These are of the Gydo Formation of the Bokkeveld Group, a

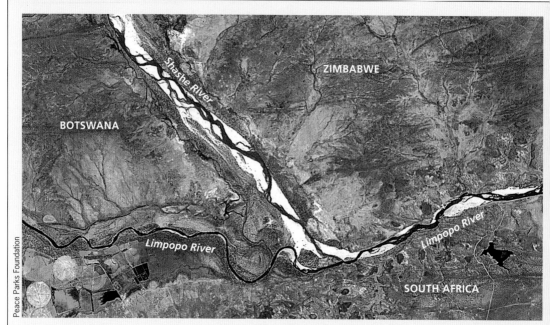

The examples of river capture in the Eastern Cape do not really show the abandoned sections at all clearly. A much more dramatic example is beyond the country's border in the north; here, various long river sections became abandoned when the proto-Zambezi cut back from the coast, capturing the headwaters of the river that had formerly entered the sea via what we know as the lower Limpopo River. What had been major rivers, such as the Shashe, were reduced, sometimes, to a trickle. In the image above, the normally dry Shashe flows after recent storms in the area, joining the Limpopo on its voyage towards the east coast.

River evolution

Having reached the Kouga River, which downstream becomes the Gamtoos, a major Eastern Cape river, now is a good time to touch on the most curious element of river evolution: river capture or river piracy. It is an aspect of geomorphology unusually well illustrated in this part of the world.

We know that rivers grow by headwater advancement. Starting as a trickle in a barely perceptible valley on a hill slope, the stream deepens the valley as it grows, cutting back endlessly, either from the coast or from a bigger river to which it is a tributary. In time it divides the hilly massif in two – and keeps going.

Assuming a river has cut through soft rocks to start with, it not only cuts back, but it cuts down too. Even if it encounters harder rock as it erodes back, it strives to maintain the base level at which it has started. Any zones of weakness, such as faults or close-spaced joints in the hard rock, will be exploited in the quest to maintain the starting base level, even if it constricts valleys into narrow kloofs or gorges.

Let's assume it has split the hilly block or ridge and emerged into lower ground on the other side, a valley formed by a contemporaneous or older river. This other river, perhaps having started at a slightly higher level or flowed over harder formations, is not as deep. The river we're following meets up with it. Being deeper it 'captures' the headwaters of the new river, channelling them into its own course – and making the term 'piracy' entirely appropriate.

In the southern part of the Eastern Cape, the main wide valleys are defined by the east-west grain of the fold belt and parallel rift faulting. We should not forget the important role played by the alternating hard and soft component formations: the Table Mountain Group being mainly extremely resistant to erosion; the

Bokkeveld Group easily eroded, and the Witteberg Group moderately resistant. Roughly perpendicular to the main tectonic fabric are tight gorges formed along secondary fault zones and joint clusters. The map (fig. 9, below) shows how river capture has drastically relandscaped the Eastern Cape.

As you are about to emerge from the Baviaanskloof, it's interesting to note how the Kouga joined the Baviaanskloof River (the 'pirate') at some stage in its history, having previously entered the sea just north of Cape St Francis as part of the Krom River system. Soon after leaving the reserve you'll drive along the Groot River. This, too, has been captured by the 'proto-Baviaanskloof River', previously having been a main part of the Sundays River system, which flows into Algoa Bay far to the east.

If you've driven to St Francis Bay you'll be familiar with the Krom River – not a particularly significant river compared with, say, the Gamtoos, whose wide flood plain and abundant irrigation water support this major citrus- and vegetable-producing area, making it an important contributor to the Eastern Cape economy. The roles of the two systems have been reversed in an ironic twist: the river you cross on the N2 between Humansdorp and Port Elizabeth, the Gamtoos, would, without its successful piracy, enter St Francis Bay as the Baviaans, no more than a stream like the Krom today, with no need for a fine, 200 m-long suspension bridge to cross it. Such is the role played by geological processes.

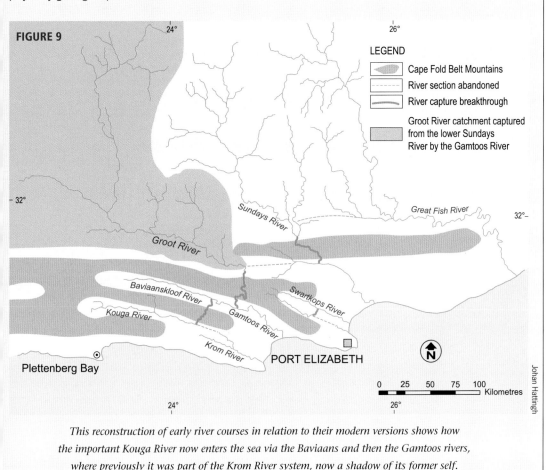

This reconstruction of early river courses in relation to their modern versions shows how the important Kouga River now enters the sea via the Baviaans and then the Gamtoos rivers, where previously it was part of the Krom River system, now a shadow of its former self.

The disturbed nature of the Bokkeveld shale is a reminder that you are in a part of South Africa that has been tectonically active time and time again over many millions of years.

formation known for its wealth of fossils in those parts where the folding is less extreme than it is here. The Witrivier on your left has been able to carve out quite a wide valley from the soft shales, which are now under citrus cultivation, with some of the farms offering guest accommodation.

After driving through farmland for 5 km, you may notice a bigger river coming in from the east. This is the Grootrivier. Just below its confluence with the Witrivier you'll notice the valley closing in; this is because you are approaching, almost head on, the quartzites of the ultra-resistant Peninsula Formation. You leave the Baviaanskloof very much as you came into it a long way back: emerging into a broad valley from a tight, vertically walled kloof cut through Peninsula Formation quartzite **(geosite 5, map 4)** (GPS S 33° 43.361', E 24° 37.193'). As before, the northern wall of the open valley – this one much wider – is defined by a fault, not the same fault that runs the length of the Baviaanskloof, but an equally important one that bounds the Gamtoos Basin.

The parallels with the Baviaanskloof, now far behind you, continue. Once again you see a half-graben (or semi-rift valley), with a fault on the northern side and a downwarp on the southern side, and again there is Enon conglomerate deposited in the trough thus formed. This is wider than the one in Baviaanskloof, though: there is substantially more Enon conglomerate, and a unit you may not have come across before, on this route anyway, called the Kirkwood Formation.

It comprises mudrock and sandstone deposited in a fluvial (riverine) environment shortly after Gondwana disintegrated and probably not long after the formation of the Enon conglomerate. In this basin there is quite an extensive area underlain by Kirkwood sediments to the north of the conglomerate and stretching up to the bounding fault. You'll see good examples of the unit up ahead: in the meantime, here in the cuttings as you approach Patensie are the best possible exposures of the conglomerate, and worth a good look.

As you entered the Baviaanskloof through the Nuwekloof, so you leave it, dramatically, through the Grootrivierpoort, carved by the power of river erosion through even the ultra-resistant Table Mountain Group. The well-bound nature of the Enon conglomerates with occasional sandy layers (inset left) is dramatically illustrated by these vertical cliffs west of Patensie. The effect of 'point-loading' is shown in the numerous cracked cobbles (inset right).

Like the Enon near the top of the Baviaanskloof, these are not significantly iron-stained, but are mostly pale brownish grey. About 4 km out of the Grootrivier gorge you pass the road to Humansdorp branching off to the right, and a few hundred metres after this is a locality celebrated in the region as Queen Victoria's Profile. It is thus named because some imaginative eye saw a resemblance between the eroded conglomerate cliff face and the monarch's profile. You're forgiven if you don't see it, but you cannot fail to be impressed by vertical cuttings edging the road that are tens of metres in height **(geosite 6, map 4)** (GPS S 33° 45.509', E 24° 41.426'), showing solid cobble to small boulder conglomerate. You won't see anything like this again, so be prepared to stop and walk about in order to take it in fully, if you can find somewhere safe to stop (not guaranteed – it was all the engineers could do to cut a road between the river and the conglomerate).

Note that a significant number of the cobbles are cracked. This not very common phenomenon is caused by 'point-loading'. A cobble with an 'overburden' or load (of cobbles and boulders) of at least 17 m above it, that comes into direct contact with a slightly softer neighbour will crack the softer cobble (or boulder). The cracking is an indication that there was no sandy matrix at any time in the formation of the conglomerate to cushion the load.

You stay close to the river for a few kilometres beyond Patensie and before leaving the citrus orchards and climbing half-way up the slope to Hankey. As you gain elevation you see good outcrops of Kirkwood Formation mudrock in the cutting to the right of the road **(geosite 7, map 4)** (GPS S 33° 47.101', E 24° 51.122'), this the only good example you see of the unit.

After leaving Hankey, you climb some more until you are on top of the watershed, noticing here and there accumulations of beautifully rounded pebbles, left on the terrace by an earlier course of the Gamtoos. Some 10 km out of Hankey, at about the turn-off to the Loerieruskamp and a fairly substantial farmstall, both on the left of the road, ahead of you in the distance is the mouth of the Gamtoos where it debouches into St Francis Bay, and you catch a glimpse of the sprawling suburbia of Jeffreys Bay. What is most striking, though, is the beautifully planar wave-cut African Land Surface southwest of the river valley and inland from Jeffreys Bay. For the last kilometre or so before joining the N2, you drive over aeolianite (fossil sand dunes) of the Tertiary-Quaternary Nanaga Formation, though, sadly, this is a soft unit that only exceptionally makes outcrop, so you won't see it in this location.

There has been no shortage of outcrop on this route. You must have enjoyed the magnificent scenery and the feeling that, as you got deep into the Baviaanskloof, you were entering a forgotten realm. You have seen how the countryside in the Cape coastal mountain belt came to be: how the mountains and valleys were shaped, how the extraordinary red and grey conglomerates formed, and how the river valleys, though carved tens of millions of years ago, have come down through the ages to carry the rivers that cut them.

Between Patensie and Hankey, alternating iron-rich and iron-poor mudrock of the Kirkwood Formation makes for a rather spectacular display.

Nowhere will you see much thicker sequences of Enon sediments than those overlooking the Gamtoos River from the west, in a natural cliff face cut by the meandering river over an unimaginably long span of time.

5 N9: Colesberg to north of George

GEOLOGICAL OVERVIEW

Upcountry holidaymakers on their annual pilgrimage to the Cape south coast will long since have discovered the N9, a merciful escape from the much busier N1. From Colesberg heading southwards you can idle if you feel like it, slow down and gaze, or maybe – now that you have it – even stop and read from this book. Along the way you can visit the Valley of Desolation, one of the scenic wonders of South Africa. You'll also see just about everything the Karoo and Cape Supergroups have to offer, including wonderful fossils from the Beaufort Group (the main component of the Karoo Supergroup), some magnificent folding, and dolerite sills and dykes injected into the sediments in the form of molten basaltic magma as the continents prepared to split. You'll see some Enon conglomerate deposited in our own rift valleys formed during the dismemberment of Gondwana, and plateaus that are remnants of flood-plains formed by ancient rivers many millions of years ago, these relics now perched well above the modern-day rivers.

Geology of the route

Colesberg to Graaff-Reinet

As you leave Colesberg on the N9, the mountains that herald the gateway to the holiday coast are still far over the horizon, as they would have been 250 million years ago if you had travelled over this surface. In those days you would have been on swampy flats. The sediments gradually forming in the rivers and on the flood-plains at this level would have been buried by similar sediments, over and over again, laying down beds of mudrock, siltstone and sandstone of the Beaufort Group. After each deposition they were buried again, deeper and deeper, until they lay thousands of metres below the surface. Then Gondwana broke up and new coastlines and river systems formed, and slowly but surely those thousands of metres were stripped off again. Today, rocks formed long ago and once deeply buried, are once more at the surface.

You've come out of the Orange River valley and are still in the High Karoo, above the Great Escarpment. As you head south towards the coast you'll go down a number of passes, losing altitude steadily even if you go up and down as you do so. The sediments you are driving over are mudrock and shale of the Adelaide Subgroup (comprising various formations), high in the Beaufort Group. These soft sediments make for gently undulating countryside. The occasional prominences consist mostly of dolerite, a boon for the upgrade of the roads in the area. This hard brittle rock, known for its durability, is used by engineers for their road aggregate, and having regular small quarries next to the road makes for good economics.

As you approach Noupoort, the first village south of Colesberg, you will see for the first time imposing flat-topped mesas and plateaus beyond it and to the west (**geosite 1, map 5**) (GPS S 31° 09.330′, E 24° 57.785′). Some layering is apparent in these slopes, with harder layers of sandstone both lower down and forming the mesas' flat tops. You've

The Valley of Desolation near Graaff-Reinet will be a highlight
of this journey, specially for those who don't already know it.

MAP 5

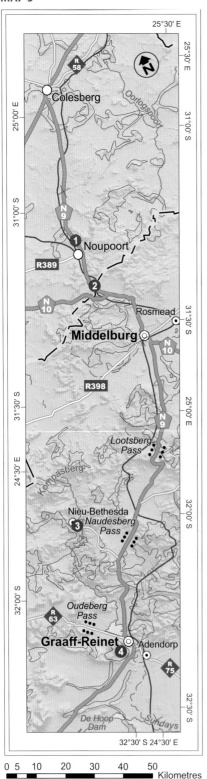

Approaching Noupoort you start to get into more broken country, with flat-topped hilly massifs as conspicuous as the resistant horizontal sandstone beds breaking their smooth slopes.

come up in the stratigraphy, and the unit making the hills and plateaus where you are now is the Katberg Formation, overlying the shale and mudrock you've been on since Colesberg. Where the Adelaide Subgroup is of Permian age, the overlying harder-wearing, sandier sediments are Triassic in age. You are looking at a major geohistorical break – between the Palaeozoic Era (Permian Period) and the younger Mesozoic Era (Triassic Period).

Heading south from Noupoort, soon after the 30.2 km marker plate, you enter a magnificent cutting through Katberg sandstone **(geosite 2, map 5)** (GPS S 31° 17.434', E 24° 57.121') (with more shown in the hill slope above it to the right (west). (The road has recently been upgraded here: let's hope when you read this the cutting has not been plastered over, as have many in the country.) You then drop down topographically, back onto open, gently undulating plains cut from the softer Adelaide shales underlying the Katberg Formation. There are still sandstone hills around and also some conspicuously higher hills to the west and ahead. These are not flat topped but irregularly crowned. They are capped by dolerite, which was intensively intruded into the Karoo sediments in these parts, with some of the sills (horizontal) and sheets (cutting obliquely across the beds they intrude) several tens of metres thick. Dolerite is very resistant to erosion, evidenced by the increasing number of road cuttings through the unbedded medium- to dark grey rock. This morphology is typical of the towering ridges and crests of the plateaus that you'll see for a while now, until after Graaff-Reinet.

The end-Permian extinction

The contact between the Adelaide Subgroup and the Katberg Formation is a major time line because the end of the Permian marks the greatest global extinction event we know of in Earth's entire history. In its scale of devastation as a terminator of species (and whole genera), this catastrophe dwarfed the end-Cretaceous extinction event that put paid to the dinosaurs, among many other living things. It is estimated that the cataclysm that closed the Permian saw global temperatures rise by 8°C, carbon dioxide levels go up to 2 000 parts per million or ppm (currently 388 ppm, and rising!) and ultraviolet radiation increase drastically. It would be 10 million years before conditions returned to 'normal'.

The Katberg Formation of the Beaufort Group, seen here south of Noupoort, consists predominantly of beige and grey sandstone, and was formed by slow-flowing rivers meandering over the wide plains of the time.

There's not much change in the geology as you head southwest past Middelburg, still mostly driving over Adelaide Subgroup with Katberg sandstone and dolerite in the hills on either side of the road. You climb almost imperceptibly back into these sandstones to the top of Lootsberg Pass – perhaps the surest reminder that you are dropping down the Great Escarpment. In the pass you'll see that the shale and mudrock, in places conspicuously maroon, are about as common as the slightly coarser-grained cream- to grey-coloured sandstone. At the bottom of the pass you are out of the Katberg Formation sandstone but stay in the Permian (Adelaide Subgroup) mudrock until you're almost in the fold mountains far to the south. This is fossil country, as you have crossed over into beds below – in other words deposited before – the end-Permian extinction.

After the N9-6: 47.4 marker plate, there is one of several well-signposted turn-offs to the west, to Nieu Bethesda and the Owl Route. Provided you're not in a hurry and don't mind travelling on a good gravel road (26.5 km), take it. You will wind through some extremely scenic country, where little has changed since ox-wagon days, deep in South Africa's history. To start with, you're on the rolling plains you've been on since the bottom of Lootsberg Pass. Soon after leaving the N9, though, you find yourself scaling a substantial ridge, the Voor-Sneeuberg. As you breast it, ahead of you and to your right, you cannot miss the very prominent peak of Kompasberg. At 2 502 m above sea level, it is South Africa's highest mountain outside the Drakensberg/Maluti highlands, and nearly twice the height of Ben Nevis, Britain's highest hill (a mere 1 344 m). Needless to say, the peak is dolerite, though much of the surrounding mountain is composed of Katberg Formation sandstone.

Once in Nieu Bethesda, visit the Kitching Fossil Exploration Centre and prepare to go deep into prehistory. The centre has been thoughtfully conceived by Wits University's Bernard Price Institute for Palaeontology. C.J.M. (Croonie) Kitching and his son James were great pioneers of South African palaeontology, partly thanks to their close association with South Africa's iconic palaeontological

The exposures of fossilized bones in the Gatsrivier in Nieu Bethesda reflect a moment frozen in time, rarely seen by non-palaeontologists.

family, the Rubidges. The remarkable collection of mammal-like reptile fossils from around these parts is celebrated – and studied – globally. So take your time, though once through the doors of the centre you won't need any persuasion. Ask a guide to take you the short distance to the mudrock bed of the (usually dry) Gatsrivier, which runs along the edge of the town, and you will see a number of remnants of fossil bones *in situ*, a rare phenomenon anywhere **(geosite 3, map 5)** (GPS S 31° 52.073', E 24° 33.073'). If you haven't done it before, this is a 'must see'.

There are several routes from Nieu Bethesda to nearby Graaff-Reinet. You can go back to the N9 the way you came, or follow an alternative road soon after leaving the village. This joins the N9 further south than from where you initially left it. Graaff-Reinet is a historical and beautifully preserved town. It has a number of excellent museums, including one with many more fossils on display, and merits a night stop-over. Plan to visit the Valley of Desolation **(geosite 4, map 5)** (GPS S 32° 15.990', E 24° 29.546'), just out of town on the Murraysburg road, preferably early in the morning or in the late afternoon. This is dolerite at its most dramatic – the epitome of how this mainly vertically jointed rock may form towering vertical faces, sometimes of prodigious height. The views are magnificent.

Spandaukop, overlooking Graaff-Reinet, is mostly composed of sedimentary sandstone – in stark contrast with the nearby Valley of Desolation, carved entirely out of hard igneous dolerite, which cut through the sandstone some time after its formation.

In the right climatic and geomorphological environment these vertical faces may occur in any rock that tends to form vertical joints, like basalt or sandstone. Consider the famous Victoria Falls plunging over a cliff of basalt. The basalt was formed by the same type of magma, but it flowed over the surface, cooling quickly, rather than being intruded and squeezed into a pile of sedimentary rocks, where it cooled slowly to form dolerite, as is the case at the Valley of Desolation. Dolerite has crystals that are visible to the naked eye, the most obvious being the elongate white feldspar crystals.

Graaff-Reinet to the N12 north of George

Even if you do not make it to the Valley of Desolation, you cannot help noticing Spandaukop, the prominent conical peak between it and the town of Graaff-Reinet. Its alternating shale, mudrock and sandstone add a pleasing dimension to the symmetrical hill, in contrast with the Valley of Desolation where the dolerite makes such a bold statement.

As you approach Aberdeen, be prepared to say goodbye to the dolerite that has surrounded you for a good while. You're approaching the northern limit of the deformed zone known as the Cape Fold Belt. As the folding suggests, huge blocks of crustal material were being pushed towards each other, contorting the sediment caught in the middle. It was an environment of intense compression and crustal thickening. Even after this compressional regime was relaxed, it was still not a crustal domain conducive to the opening of tensional cracks that would allow the ascent of basaltic magma, which would have manifested as dolerite.

This red shale south of Aberdeen is the last exposure of the continental Beaufort sediments (with their minor component of red-weathering iron) to be seen on this route, as you'll soon be on the more carbonaceous black shale (subaqueous) of the Ecca, almost entirely soil-covered.

MAP 6

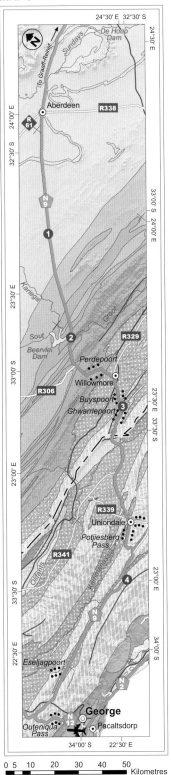

Leaving Aberdeen on the N9 southwards, you continue to drop down in the stratigraphy. Having been on Beaufort Group sediments, deposited in river channels and across wide swampy plains, since Colesberg, up ahead you are going to cross over into the offshore deposits of the Ecca Group. One of the surest signs that you're still in the Beaufort is the reddish coloration of the shales, indicating the surface deposition characteristic of this group, with any iron in the sediments oxidizing to red iron oxide. The last such shale is right at the end of a cutting after the 70.8 km marker plate, well south of Aberdeen **(geosite 1, map 6)** (GPS S 32° 46.768′, E 23° 43.709′).

Opposite the Beervlei Dam the dark blue-grey Dwyka tillite is covered with white scree of Witteberg sandstone from the cliffs above.

The fracking controversy

Graaff-Reinet is regarded by many as the jewel of the Karoo. It is not surprising, then, that the loudest protest to the notion of deep natural gas or petroleum extraction by 'fracking' of Karoo rocks has come from these parts. Perceptions here – and widely – vary only in their degree of negativity.

The great majority of the world's commercial petroleum formed from the decayed remains of microscopic or near-microscopic marine organisms in fine-grained rocks that formed in deep, still water. From there the petroleum migrated – in traditional oil fields – to permeable reservoir rocks, from which, millions of years later, it can be pumped directly. Where gas has formed in shale and never moved to accumulate in reservoir rocks like sandstone, fracturing is necessary to provide conduits to get it out. Examples of the latter are the Whitehill Formation of the Ecca Group, here in the Karoo, and the Green River Formation in Wyoming, USA, currently a big producer. In South Africa, some of the Ecca shales are potentially methane-rich, but this is only if the originally high content of decayed freshwater organic material, leanly and homogeneously distributed through the very 'tight' rock in the first place, has been preserved.

In 'fracking' ('Induced Hydraulic Fracturing'), a specialized fracturing fluid is pumped down a borehole or 'wellbore' at a rate sufficient to elevate pressure at depths to fracture the target bed, a technique requiring skill and experience. For the fractures thus produced to function as low-pressure channels accessible to any gas in the shale, a 'proppant', such as sand, has to be introduced to carry the rock pressure once the pressure of fracturing fluid has been reduced, in order to allow the gas to travel to the surface. In this way an artificial aquifer, connected to the surface, is available into which the gas, under the natural pressure of a head of rock, will feed.

The main (but not only) objections to fracking in the Karoo are, in no particular order: (a) the uncertainty surrounding where sufficient water will be sourced to pump large volumes of fracturing fluid into large-diameter wellbores; (b) what the effect would be on groundwater quality because of the significant amounts of introduced fracturing fluid; (c) what the precise composition of the fracturing fluid would be (like that of Coca Cola, it is seemingly a tightly guarded secret); and (d) what effect large numbers of drills and ancillary vehicles, driving this way and that across pristine veld, would have on the Karoo.

At the moment, and until it has been established by geological exploration that there is still sufficient methane in the target shale, protest is emotive and academic. Fracking in this part of the world may never happen. What the remonstration is all about, though, is simple: to ensure that, at best (and particularly if you live in the Karoo and if large gas reserves were to be indicated by exploration), fracking never happens; or, at worst, if it does go ahead, that every possible safeguard is put in place to minimize the impact on the environment.

Soon the high ridge ahead becomes a conspicuous part of your vista, but before getting there you cross a broad band of Ecca shale, which, because it is soft, makes little or no outcrop, and then Dwyka tillite. At 40.8 km (counting backwards), there is a road aggregate borrow-pit on your left, with good outcrop of tillite. The next tillite you'll see is on the left of the road at the beginning of the poort through the range you've been approaching, with the Beervlei Dam (which is usually empty) to your right **(geosite 2, map 6)** (GPS S 33° 04.175', E 23° 29.566'). The tillite, which marks the base of the Karoo Supergroup, here lies below quartzites of the upper Witteberg Group (pre-Karoo Cape Supergroup). Before folding, the Witteberg, which is older than the Dwyka, lay below it. (In geology the principle of Superposition has it that in a group of stratified sedimentary rocks the lowest were the earliest to be deposited.) The inversion is because during folding the Witteberg was over-folded to the north (tilted beyond the vertical, so the sequences are essentially upside down), as has happened to large parts of the Cape stratigraphy in this eastern part of the fold belt.

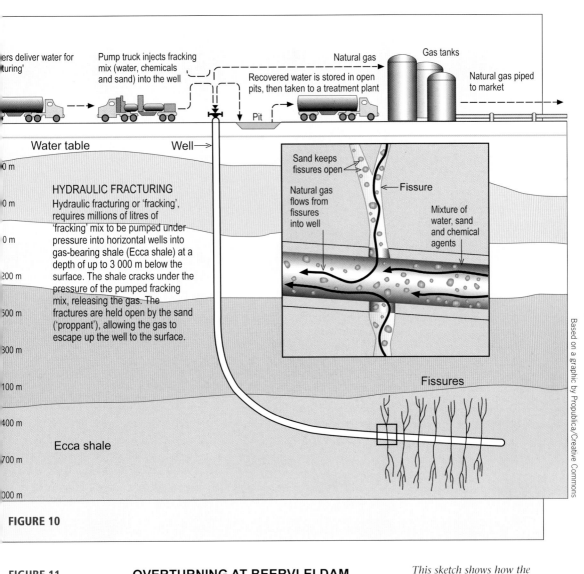

ers deliver water for 'turing'

Pump truck injects fracking mix (water, chemicals and sand) into the well

Natural gas

Gas tanks

Recovered water is stored in open pits, then taken to a treatment plant

Natural gas piped to market

Pit

Water table

Well→

HYDRAULIC FRACTURING

Hydraulic fracturing or 'fracking', requires millions of litres of 'fracking' mix to be pumped under pressure into horizontal wells into gas-bearing shale (Ecca shale) at a depth of up to 3 000 m below the surface. The shale cracks under the pressure of the pumped fracking mix, releasing the gas. The fractures are held open by the sand ('proppant'), allowing the gas to escape up the well to the surface.

Sand keeps fissures open

Natural gas flows from fissures into well

Fissure

Mixture of water, sand and chemical agents

Fissures

Ecca shale

0 m

0 m

0 m

200 m

500 m

300 m

100 m

400 m

700 m

000 m

FIGURE 10

FIGURE 11

OVERTURNING AT BEERVLEI DAM

This sketch shows how the Witteberg comes to be overlying the younger Dwyka tillite in an inversion of the normal succession, where sediments are progressively younger upwards.

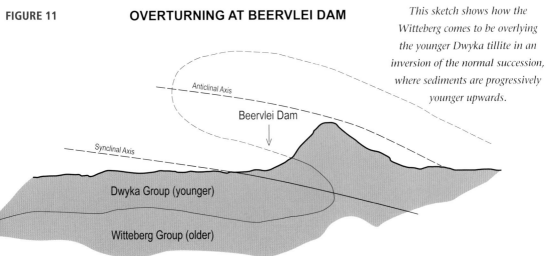

Anticlinal Axis

Beervlei Dam

Synclinal Axis

Dwyka Group (younger)

Witteberg Group (older)

Steep south-dipping Bokkeveld sediments contain cross-bedded siltstone (inset), which shows 'way-up' direction, confirming that the sediments are overturned (tilted through 90°). (See explanatory diagram, fig. 6, p. 79.)

You're well into the Cape Fold Belt now and the structure is complicated, as you'll notice if you drive slowly through the poort, or stop to get out of your vehicle. Once you're out of the gorge and opposite the turn-off to the right to Rietbron, look to your left and you'll see some beautifully sculptured folding. Another thing you should take note of about here is the flat surface higher up and straight ahead of you, stretching across much of the skyline. You may wonder how, in tightly contorted alternating hard and soft sediments, it is possible to find flat surfaces topping the folding. It's part of the very ancient African Erosion Surface, which formed during a prolonged period of stability when the rivers – and the streams and streamlets that fed them – had as long as they needed to reduce once-rugged terrain to a wide, Kalahari-like panorama. These anomalously level skylines occur widely throughout the Eastern Cape. In the many millions of years since their formation they have been uplifted relative to sea level, and deep valleys have been – and continue to be – cut into them. Expansive remnants of the original surface remain, however, now at the high level where you see them.

You continue through deeply dissected Witteberg Group rocks until you see Willowmore ahead of you, at which point you're travelling over the softer stratigraphy of the (pre-Witteberg) upper Bokkeveld Group. After Willowmore, at the end of a long straight run, the road turns to the left. Stop opposite the road to the farm Buyspoort **(geosite 3, map 6)** (GPS S 33° 21.057′, E 23° 26.176′) to see, on the left of the road, some good examples of small-scale trough cross-bedding. These show that the steeply south-dipping siltstone is overturned. After this, you're in dissected country again, tightly folded in the complex way characteristic of much of the Cape Fold Belt (CFB), and you then wind through steeply dipping sediments of both the lower Bokkeveld and upper Table Mountain Group (TMG). Note how you are dropping down the stratigraphy, into older and older sediments.

These beautifully rounded cobbles in the road cutting, seen soon after you emerge from the poort beyond Willowmore, are from Enon conglomerate, even if it is not clearly exposed here. Like the Enon elsewhere, this conglomerate accumulated in rapidly forming rift valleys during the beginning of Gondwana break-up.

After a few kilometres you emerge into open country, where, if you keep your eyes wide open, you'll see rounded cobbles and a few boulders in the cuttings. Although it's not particularly well exposed at the roadside, you're travelling over Enon conglomerate, which covers quite a large area here. The best exposures are in the reddish hills ahead, on the other side of the Olifants River.

As you emerge from the hills you have crossed a significant geological boundary, from Palaeozoic folded Cape Supergroup sediments into much younger Enon conglomerate. Notice that the quartzite hills to the left, behind and to the right, form an almost unnatural linear wall. The line of that wall marks the Kango Fault, a deep-rooted, crustal-scale fracture. It has dropped the Enon-filled sub-basin over which you are travelling by many hundreds of metres relative to the adjacent quartzites.

In the distance ahead of you are the foothill ranges of the Outeniqua Mountains, into which the town of Uniondale is tucked. Having crossed open hilly country carved out of the soft Bokkeveld sediments for some 20 km, you're about to return to the more spectacular TMG, and another fascinating aspect of southern Cape geology is soon going to present itself. As you breast

The horizontal hill tops (oervlakte) around Uniondale are remnants of the ancient valley floor, now dissected by erosion that is forming the present valley base.

Oervlakte

In Afrikaans these anomalously flat surfaces within the wide valleys are called 'oervlakte'. The older, broader valleys of the southern Cape abound with these remnants of prehistoric valley floors, from Montagu to Grahamstown. In summary, this is how the ancient valley floors have been preserved until today. Over unimaginably long spans of time, the soaking of shaly rocks by percolating rainwater has leached them of all but the basic clay minerals to which they have decomposed, mainly kaolin. Subsequently, in a much drier time, upward water movement has deposited significant amounts of silica, in places together with iron, in the uppermost soil layer. Accumulating over millions of years, there was sufficient precipitation to form a resistant hard capping, up to a couple of metres thick (called the Grahamstown Formation after the town where it is particularly well represented). You can see both the kaolin and silica cap rock as you climb out of Uniondale heading for George or Oudtshoorn, through the Potjiesberg Pass. It's a sight unusual enough to slow down for, or even stop. (See also a short explanation of prehistoric valley floors in ch. 3, p. 77.)

Leaving Uniondale, you pass close to a valley-edge plateau preserved by the hard iron-
and silica-rich capping, with the kaolin (extremely leached shale) below it (inset).

the rise with Uniondale below you, in the valley to your left you cannot help being struck by a number of remarkable flat-topped mesas perched over the valley floor. If you let your eye follow them towards the range ahead of you, you'll notice that the last one, which at its nearer end drops away into the farmlands below, continues towards the steep slope, rising gently southwards. These planar surfaces are the petrified remnants of the soil and sediments on the ancient valley floor of many millions of years ago, now standing high above the modern valleys.

From the 73 km marker plate to beyond 72 km (counting backwards, with 0 where the N9 – the road you're on – leaves the N12) are some good examples of extremely complicated but aesthetically pleasing folds.

The last extraordinary geological feature you will see on this journey is in the second long, thin valley along which you drive after the end of the Potjiesberg Pass. For a few kilometres after you enter it, the valley is traversed by the headwaters of the east-flowing Keurbooms River, which you first cross at the bottom of the pass **(geosite 4, map 6)** (GPS S 33° 46.458′, E 22° 57.428′). This river reaches the ocean at Plettenberg Bay, off to the east. Then, as one drives westward and over a low rise, the valley drops off to the west, almost imperceptibly.

This unusually elongate valley owes its existence to a narrow, tight, synclinal keel of soft Bokkeveld shale between adjacent bands of much harder TMG sandstone (imagine a dugout canoe with sides of sandstone and Bokkeveld shale in the middle). You are travelling westward, roughly down the middle of the syncline. Once past the highest point in the shale, a local watershed, you

Rivers ancient and modern

Rivers that rise near the sea, but on the inland slopes of coastal ranges, and run for hundreds or even thousands of kilometres through the hinterland before finally 'making a mouth', are not unusual: Brazil's São Francisco and the Niger of West Africa are two examples. What is remarkable about the Langkloof valley you travel along as you conclude the drive along the N9, is that the rivers cross it, seemingly spurning the chance to take the easy way down its shaly length, westward. The reason is that they are very ancient rivers. Millions of years ago they had their origin in the Kammanassie valley and cut back from there by headward erosion through the flanking quartzite before reaching the next valley floored by shale. Now, why should the Kammanassie valley have seen a river form there, long before the tight Upper Langkloof valley you're in? The reason is that the Kammanassie valley is underlain by a much wider synclinal keel of soft Bokkeveld sediments, which was open to the west; whereas the relatively tight syncline the N9 follows is, like the dugout canoe, closed by durable TMG sandstone wrapping around it at both ends.

The Keurbooms River, by contrast, runs eastward directly to the coast. The narrow Upper Langkloof syncline you're in, where the river has its headwaters, curves southwards at its eastern end, while, at the same time, the coastline turns to the north at Plettenberg Bay. In other words the two roughly linear features – the Upper Langkloof syncline and the coastline – converge. However, towards the western end of the long synclinal valley the coast and the valley are widely separated. The deeper Kammanassie valley to the north has had a more profound influence on the drainages in this section of the Upper Langkloof than any streams cutting back from the distant coastline.

On the other hand, the Keurbooms and its narrow enclosed headwaters, along which you briefly drove, is a headward extension of the network of rivers that started to cut back from the coastline formed when Gondwana broke up.

might expect water to flow westwards down the middle of the syncline, with tributaries coming in off the slopes on both sides, like a herringbone. But no – all the streams drain across the valley, from left (south) to right (north). They flow from valleys starting in the southern sandstone, down across the shale and out through deep gorges cut into the sandstone to the north. Once through this obstacle, they join the west-flowing Kammanassie River in the next valley to the north. This flows steadily westwards and northwards, away from the sea, until it links up with the Olifants River near Oudtshoorn, which flows into the Gouritz River. This, in turn, debouches into the sea well to the west of Mossel Bay.

Finally, let's look at what caused the southern curvature of the Outeniqua Mountains in an otherwise predominantly east-west Cape Fold Belt. It was undoubtedly a complex process, happening in multiple phases over a long period of time, and ending as Gondwana started to disaggregate. Before break-up, the Falkland Plate was located off the east coast of what would become South Africa. During the first part of its long drift towards South America, along the Agulhas-Falkland Fracture Zone (AFFZ), this plate tended to drag with it obliquely inclined structures adjacent to the AFFZ – like Cape folds – as it passed by.

It is bizarre to consider two of the Gondwana jigsaw pieces – India and the Falkland Islands – starting as near neighbours east of southern Africa, and finishing almost diametrically across the globe. Pliny the Elder, Roman author and naturalist for whom there was always something new out of Africa, would have smiled. It is indeed a strange world we live in.

FIGURE 12

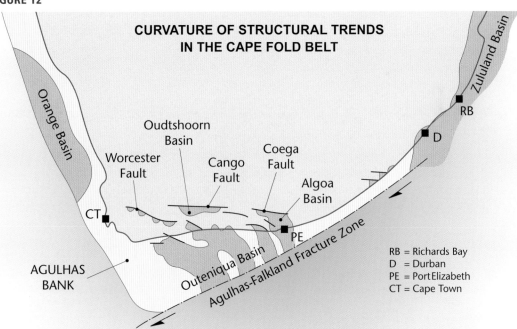

The westward slide of the Falkland Plateau caused fractures to develop along the southern Cape coast. The crust on the southern side of these fractures dropped downwards, creating depressions in which sediment, eroded from the higher-lying side, was deposited. Note the curvature of structural trends towards the Agulhas-Falkland Fracture Zone. (The locations of major cities are shown for reference.)

6 N10: N2 to the Namibian border

GEOLOGICAL OVERVIEW

This journey along the N10 is the longest described in the book. It takes you along a broadly southeast-northwest diagonal, from the small settlement of Ncanara, which is just to the northeast of Port Elizabeth, all the way up to the Namibian border, traversing countless geological formations along the way. It's as diverse as any road you'll cover. You start near the eastern end of the Cape Fold Belt, but soon leave the folding behind you as you move into a long stretch underlain by horizontal Karoo units. You leave these near Prieska and move into excitingly varied Precambrian geology in the Orange River valley. Finally, beyond Upington, you cross into the vast Kalahari 'thirstland'.

Across the centre of this route you'll see good examples of a range of horizontal Karoo sediments, though near the beginning and towards the end you'll see some spectacular folding, in this photograph of the Transvaal Supergroup near Prieska.

MAP 7

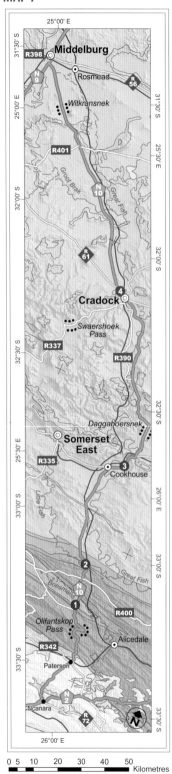

Geology of the route

Ncanara to Middelburg

You start this route along the N10 in the Eastern Cape at the Ncanara cloverleaf. From the intersection, you leave the N2 and the coast behind, and climb slowly through farmland and Eastern Cape thornveld, with the fossil dunes of Tertiary and Quaternary times not far below the surface. The dunes were formed on Cretaceous-aged sediments, mainly mudrock and sandstone, of the Algoa Basin. Just north of Paterson you leave this basin, quite soon encountering the first hard rocks along this route as you start the climb over the Zuurberge. These rocks are much older, Palaeozoic-aged folded quartzite, sandstone and shale of the Witteberg Group.

Before long, you are on the steep Olifantskop Pass, notable for the unusual strip of indigenous forest along the face of the ridge to the left of the pass. There is plenty of folded, brown-weathered Witteberg sandstone in evidence near the top. Here the uppermost part of the Witteberg has quite a large component of siltstone and mudrock. Just after passing the marker plate N10-1: 51.0, you cross from the Witteberg Group (at the top of the Cape Supergroup) to Dwyka tillite at the base of the Karoo Supergroup. In a cutting 1 km further on you will see an excellent display of dark grey deep-water shales of the Ecca Group, overlying the Dwyka **(geosite 1, map 7)** (GPS S 33º15.044', E 25º 53.547').

Once over the Boesmans River and past the Alicedale turn-off, you're back in Dwyka tillite again, and then into the mixed mudrock and sandstone of the Witteberg. It shows asymmetrical syncline-anticline pairs in places, a reminder that you're still in the Cape Fold Belt.

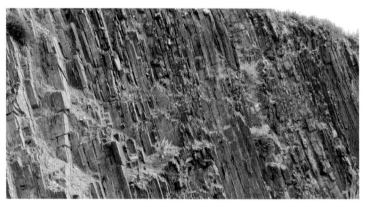

The near vertical Ecca shale at geosite 1 offers a cross-section through this unit – unusual exposure of a sequence that is mostly either covered by soil or overlain by younger Beaufort sediments.

You will not find many better examples than at this locality of the contact between the Witteberg sediments and the Dwyka Group, here well bedded (darker bands in main photo, and inset). Both groups of sediments have been overturned during Cape folding (see 'overturning' diagram on p. 109).

With high country just to the west of you and a broken ridge ahead, you'll see the railway line close by on the right as both it and the road prepare to emerge from the hilly country to the plains ahead. At the beginning of the flats (after the 70.0 marker plate) you cross, for the second time, from Witteberg sandstone and shale onto Dwyka tillite. Here, this once horizontal contact is almost vertical, even slightly overturned, with the Witteberg sediments pushed over the younger tillite. It is an unusually clear contact and you should stop to look at it. There is about a 30° divergence in dip between the bedding of the Witteberg sediments and that of the Dwyka, as the photograph above shows **(geosite 2, map 7)** (GPS S 33° 06.243', E 25° 52.540'). Don't forget that this is a contact between two supergroups – not something one sees every day. As such, there is a major break between the Cape Supergroup (Witteberg Group) and the Karoo Supergroup (Dwyka Group), which geologists call an unconformity, so to find a divergence such as is seen here is not surprising. (The angular difference may well have been exaggerated by the Witteberg being thrust over the Dwyka.)

Further north, in the far distance, you can see what looks like the escarpment, but for now you continue over gently rolling terrain, crossing the Little Fish River some 2 km after the contact just described. The occasional cuttings show mudrock and shale with subordinate sandstone. As you head northwards, the higher ground on both sides, particularly ahead, becomes more dominant in the landscape. Finer-grained sediments still predominate, but fine-grained sandstone, 1 m thick or more in places, is conspicuous.

With a new set of numbering having started at the Middleton turn-off, stop in the cutting after the N10-2: 12.2 marker plate to look at some beautiful examples of trough cross-bedding to the left (west) of the road, with beds unusually clearly defined. At this cutting, you're in the top fossiliferous Permian formation in the Beaufort Group, the Adelaide Subgroup. Above this unit and still to come, is the Triassic Katberg Formation, which postdates the cataclysmic end-Permian mass extinction (see ch. 5 on the N9, p. 103). You'll see only a small part of the Katberg around

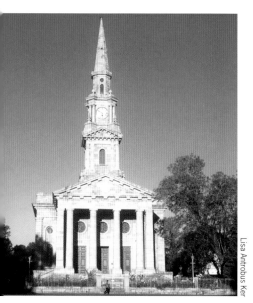

The Dutch Reformed 'Mother' Church in Cradock, modelled on the famous St Martins-in-the-Field in London, is built from locally quarried Beaufort sandstone.

Middelburg; if the conditions were more conducive to finding them, you might be looking for fossils here. But you're in the Eastern Cape grasslands with a soil profile well developed over the underlying rock, and the rivers are mostly muddy water flowing between sandy or muddy banks. It's a far cry from the part of the Karoo that is the fossil hunter's mecca.

You're reaching the end of the wide plains as you approach the escarpment. The transition from low to high country is undramatic, with spurs separated by deeply penetrating valleys. Soon after passing the turn-off to Cookhouse (where the next set of road marker numbering starts), you cross the Great Fish River and start climbing. Between road markers 6.4 and 6.6 is a cutting of which the eastern wall shows another striking example of trough cross-bedding in channel sandstone **(geosite 3, map 7)** (GPS S 32° 42.730′, E 25° 51.730′). Some 5 km later (11.2 marker), you see the first dolerite on this drive, in cuttings on both sides of a little stream. The dolerite shows that you're moving onto the Karoo Igneous Province.

From here onwards and mainly to the east (the Great Fish River valley runs far below you to the west), much of the high ground is capped by or thickly impregnated with dolerite. You continue to gain altitude, crossing the Tarka River at 58.8. There are still higher dolerite-capped prominences around, but to all intents and purposes you have left the escarpment behind as you approach the regional centre of Cradock.

As you leave Cradock, heading northwards, you'll notice a large quarry above the town's small industrial area, excavations very much in operation in 2012. To your right, close to the road, you'll see a smooth, rounded, dome-like outcrop, somewhat reminiscent of Paarl Rock in the Western Cape **(geosite 4, map 7)** (GPS S 32° 09.808′, E 25° 36.279′). This dome is part of the same dolerite body as the one quarried across the valley.

As you climb out of the bowl in which Cradock nestles, the lower hills around you are mostly dolerite-crowned shale and mudrock of the Adelaide Subgroup. In the far distance to the right and ahead, though, are peaks and ridges of Katberg Formation rocks. These have a higher proportion of resistant sandstone and they, too, are liberally intruded by dolerite. You stay on undulating plains interrupted here and there by hills composed mostly of dolerite, until you cross the Great Fish River again. From here, the high Katberg Formation hills start to form a prominent component of the topography. By the time you pass the 'Middelburg 50' board, you can clearly see where the road makes its way up the high ridge ahead. Some 10 km on, you climb the ridge. In the cutting to your right beautiful banded shales and mudrocks accompany the sandstone. Note that they are horizontal; by now you are well out of the Cape folding. Once you're over the top of the ridge, the sandstone beds stand out clearly in the slope to your left.

You then drop into a wide basin dotted with koppies, some quite high, and make your way towards Middelburg, which lies towards the northwestern corner of the plain. Before you reach it, you cross one of the very long and thin, late intrusive dykes that extend for many tens of kilometres southeastwards, back past Cradock and down towards Cookhouse.

Pegmatoid dolerite

This is a good opportunity to look at some igneous processes and their effects. Thick sheets of dolerite show smooth, gently domed weathered surfaces like this because, like the granite seen in Paarl Rock or Rio de Janeiro's 'Sugar Loaf', they cooled slowly. Because the bodies of igneous rock are big and came up from the fiery depths with a great store of heat, they imparted large amounts of heat to the intruded sediments and also stayed warmer longer within themselves. The fact that they could attain this sort of equilibrium with their environment means that they formed only very widely spaced joints as they slowly cooled off. Considering that weathering is concentrated along joints, if these are spaced many metres instead of centimetres apart, the rock is spared the intense weathering that the thinner, quickly chilled – and consequently more closely jointed – bodies are subjected to. Smooth, gently rounded outcrops covering wide expanses are often the result.

The granite of Paarl Rock is an example of a group of igneous rocks that formed pegmatites in their top parts, normally the last part of the body to have crystallized. Near the roof of the rising magma, steam and other hydrothermal fluids collected, which, cooling slowly, permitted crystals to grow to much greater size than in the surrounding granite. Rarely, the same process happened in dolerite, so it is gratifying to see little veins of pegmatoid dolerite in the first low cutting on the right of the road on the very outskirts of Cradock, as the inset below shows. (True pegmatite forms from silica-rich rock such as granite.)

The dome shape of this dolerite outcrop at Cradock and the pegmatoid veinlets (inset) are both rarities in one of the most common rock types in the Karoo Basin, suggesting the dolerite is unusually thick here.

MAP 8

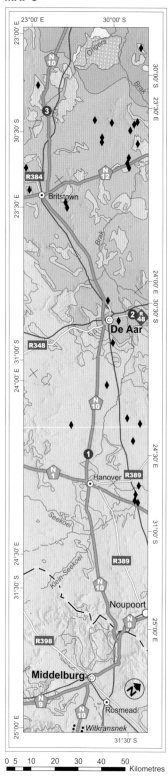

Middelburg to northwest of Britstown

On leaving Middelburg, you follow the N9/N10 northwards, climbing slowly for 24 km until you leave what has been a doubled-up N9/N10 and head to the northwest, the N10 once again its own road. Between distance marker plates N10-5: 4.0 and 8.6 you see a good representation of the Triassic Katberg Formation, with some dolerite intruded, particularly as you ascend the Winterhoek Pass. Then you go down again, having crossed, incidentally, the country's main watershed. After a few cuttings (mainly with dolerite) you're back on the wide plains shaped from the shale and mudrock of the Adelaide Subgroup. Quite soon you reach – and cross – the N1 at Hanover, such topographic relief as there is provided by dolerite **(geosite 1, map 8)** (GPS S 31° 00.167', E 24° 21.031').

TOP AND ABOVE: *Though harder than the sediments they intrude, dolerite dykes and sills commonly show close-spaced joints, with horizontal joints being more conspicuous sometimes, and vertical ones at other times.*

Leaving the N1 behind, you're in a world more dominated by dolerite than the one you've left behind. All the relief in the landscape is made by irregular bodies of the characteristic Karoo dolerite that form sheets inclined to the bedding, and by some conical bodies with a roughly rounded expression on the surface. The dolerite is harder than the mudrocks it intrudes and stands as low, usually quite well-vegetated ridges. Only to the east and northeast of your direction of travel do the horizontal sills, conformably squeezed between beds of sediment, cap large low plateaus. You see them in the far distance to your right. As you approach De Aar, you can't miss the group of high mesas to the north of the town, some quite extensive **(geosite 2, map 8)** (GPS S 30° 34.117', E 24° 03.881'). They are the most conspicuous feature of the topography you'll see for some time. Drive on past De Aar, and expect no significant change in the scenery for a while as you head west towards Britstown.

Leaving Britstown, you get onto the N12, which doubles up briefly with the N10 as you head northwards. A few kilometres north of the town your road leaves the N12 to turn westwards again. Refer to the marker plates along the road: just after N10-8: 30.0, you cross the bridge over the usually dry Ongers River **(geosite 3, map 8)** (GPS S 30° 23.528', E 23° 16.696'). With its barely noticeable effect on the landscape today, this river illustrates how climate has changed over millions of years. In earlier, wetter times it flowed permanently, a tributary to the Brakrivier, which joins the Orange River east of Prieska.

Northwest of Britstown to north of Groblershoop

From 43.2 km you cross a rise through a shallow cutting in dolerite. The only noteworthy feature of yet another dolerite cutting is that it's the last one you'll see on this trip, as you approach the edge of the main Karoo Basin. Because you're well onto the great interior plateau of South Africa, the landscape is ultramature, with none of the softer formations visible. You're therefore not aware of going from the Beaufort Group onto the Ecca and then the Dwyka, but that's what is happening.

FIGURE 13   **CRUSTAL ARCHITECTURE OF SOUTHERN AFRICA**

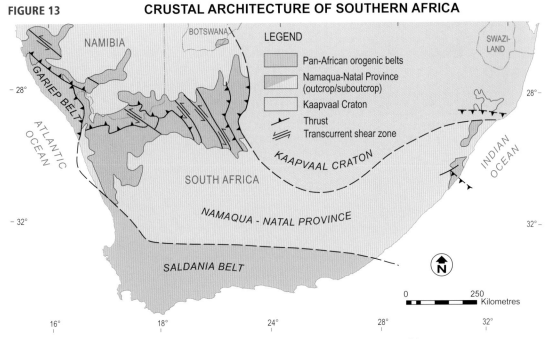

This simplified map shows the major basement units you cross on this route.

MAP 9

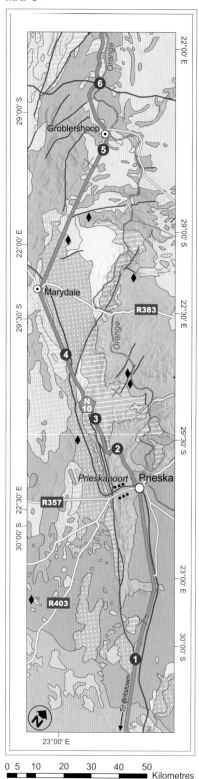

0 5   10   20   30   40   50
                                          Kilometres

Earth's crust and what lies above it

The oldest basic building blocks of Earth's crust are ancient Archaean continental nuclei, called cratons, that were stabilized billions of years ago. Then, in the stretches of ocean between them, sediments were deposited and lavas poured over them too. The resulting formations were folded and metamorphosed in a process that was repeated again and again. The folded formations between the cratons are called Mobile Belts or Metamorphic Provinces, among other names. At various times, 'supracrustal' formations were formed in basins floored by these primitive building blocks (supra is the Latin for 'above'). The Ghaap Group is an example of a supracrustal unit, as are the Karoo formations on which you've been for most of the trip so far. They were all deposited on top of the crust.

The next hills you'll see anywhere near the road are of the Proterozoic Ghaap Group **(geosite 1, map 9)** (GPS S 30° 05.506', E 23° 03.022'). This is a new name on this route, and as you'll continue to encounter unfamiliar units, now is a good a time to look at some regional geology and stratigraphy.

In a while you're going to cross a major geological crustal divide, from the Kaapvaal Craton to the Namaqua Sector of the Namaqua-Natal Province. But first you're going to see the sediments of the Transvaal Supergroup spectacularly folded at the edge of the craton. Perhaps you've seen Transvaal sediments on the Kaapvaal Craton in Mpumalanga or even along the N18 between Warrenton and Vryburg where they are horizontal or nearly so. However, as you approach Prieska, to the west and not far ahead you'll see the well-banded rocks – iron formation and carbonates – folded into the most dramatic shapes. Just southeast of Prieska, as you drop into the Orange River valley, you'll see bedded Karoo sediments (as well as unbedded Dwyka tillite) which, although they're deeply weathered and the bedding is not easy to see, are horizontal. This is because they were laid down long after the folding of the Transvaal sediments.

At about the N10-8: 73.0N marker plate you cross a low rise that continues to the northwest (to your left), remaining a notable feature of the landscape from here towards Prieska. The hills and ridges consist of dolomite and chert of the Ghaap Group (of the Transvaal Supergroup).

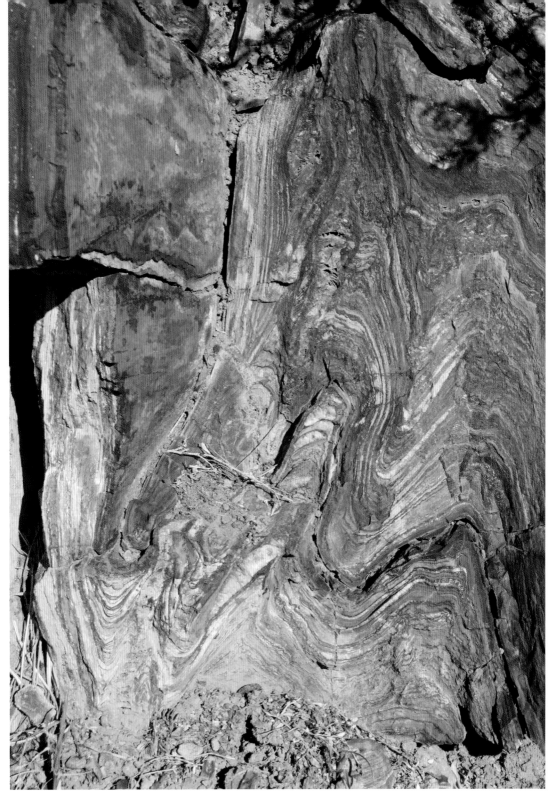

Chemical sediments like these iron- and silica-rich beds of the Asbestos Hills Subgroup
(Ghaap Group, Transvaal Supergroup) lend themselves to intricate folding without rupturing.

The dolomite of the Ghaap Group shows the 'elephant-skin' weathering characteristic of these rocks.

They lead into the very rugged hill country that persists some distance northwestwards from Prieska and through which you'll drive. Having had your first view into the Orange River valley at about the 115.0 marker plate, you're now approaching Prieska. You'll see some Dwyka shales and tillite in low road cuttings and then just about at the turn-off into the town, you see the Transvaal sediments at close quarters, here flaggy ('slaty') iron formation.

Soon after passing Prieska, you start climbing into the hills, encountering many cuttings. They mostly expose flaggy iron formation and generally iron-rich sediments and you'll start to see rocky, well-bedded 'reefs' on the hill slopes, stained dark red-brown, almost black, by the

Asbestos and tiger's eye

Prieska was an important asbestos-mining centre in the days before the serious negative consequences of exposure to blue asbestos (crocidolite) fibres became known. The crocidolite (one of the amphibole family of minerals), unique to this part of South Africa, is a more dangerous form than the chrysotile asbestos (fibrous olivine, a different mineral) found in greenstone belts around the world, sometimes in economic quantities. After crocidolite has been silicified during prolonged periods of exposure to the atmosphere, with the fibres now tightly bound and the colour changed to gold (more rarely red or remaining blue), it becomes the well-known ornamental stone tiger's eye. As you go into the first major valley after Prieska, look around and you will see dwellings – mostly disused now – and diggings in the hills, the latter for tiger's eye. Tiger's eye would not have been so valuable were it not restricted to this small part of South Africa where the 'mother mineral', crocidolite, occurs.

iron. The cutting from N10-9: 12.8N to 13.2 is a good high one with excellent exposures of folded banded iron formation (BIF) of the Asbestos Hills Subgroup (of the Ghaap Group, Transvaal Supergroup) **(geosite 2, map 9)** (GPS S 29° 38.193', E 22° 36.807').

After the cutting at the 24.2 beacon, you will start seeing some dolomitic limestone in the cuttings, which are still numerous **(geosite 3, map 9)** (GPS S 29° 36.355', E 22° 30.233'). It's not immediately obvious as limestone, but the characteristic elephant-skin weathering on top of the cuttings reveals its identity at once. Then you go through a couple of cuttings that show good sequences of normal clastic sediments, mainly sandstones, including quartzite and impure brownish varieties and some white-weathering arkose, a sandstone rich in the mineral feldspar.

You are now moving from ruggedly hilly country to a more gently undulating topography. After the 37.0 marker plate there is an extensive, quite high cutting where you can see a long sequence of homogeneous dark grey lava of the Ventersdorp Supergroup. This unit is older than the Transvaal sediments you've been seeing for a while and underlies it stratigraphically. Before the folding that tilted the formations into their near-vertical positions, the Ventersdorp Supergroup lay below the Transvaal Supergroup. If you stop to have a close look at these rocks, do so near the beginning of the cutting where you will see some beds of white quartzitic sandstone situated at the base of the Transvaal sequence.

After a couple more cuttings showing the same uniformly dark grey Ventersdorp lavas, at the 47.8 marker plate you're in the first of a few cuttings where the Schalkseput Granite, of Archaean age, is exposed. Stop at the next cutting (48.8 marker plate) if you want to see an exceptionally

The homogeneous texture of the Schalkseput Granite, with no banding evident, is typical of Archaean granites where their stable cratonic setting has protected them from deformation after their intrusion.

The presence of iron explains why these Kalahari dunes are tinted a strikingly attractive red.

handsome rock, carrying both common varieties of mica – biotite and muscovite **(geosite 4, map 9)** (GPS S 29° 30.981', E 22° 18.660'). You've crossed from the lava onto granite because you've gone over a fault, one of many in this highly disturbed zone along the major divide between the Kaapvaal Craton and the Namaqua Sector of the Namaqua-Natal Province mentioned earlier.

You have crossed from that beautifully homogeneous granite into another kind, this one distinctly streaky or gneissose, called the Draghoender Granite. It's also Archaean, so you're still on the Kaapvaal Craton, but getting steadily nearer its edge. In the first few cuttings where you see this new rock type, from the 55.6 marker plate, it's quite weathered. Stop at 61.2 to see a good example of fresher granite-gneiss.

Quite soon you pass Marydale, the country flattening out as you go, now that you're some 20 km away from the more broken Orange River valley. There are a few more cuttings with weathered granite and granite-gneiss of the same unit, but on the surface you see mostly calcrete, the white secondary limestone that forms from the underlying lime-bearing bedrock. You also see red sand gathered up into dunes in places, a reminder that you're on the edge of the Kalahari **(geosite 5, map 9)** (GPS S 28° 55.847', E 22° 00.237'). After quite a distance of no outcrop at all, immediately after the N10-10: 28.8N marker plate, is an exposure in a road cut of well-bedded grey quartzite. It belongs to the Brulpan Group, which is the first part of the Namaqua-Natal Province to be seen on your route.

Between the last gneiss outcrop and this quartzite, you have passed over a key fault, called the Dabep Shear Zone or Dabep Thrust. ('Fault', 'shear zone' and 'thrust' are all terms that describe major breaks in the crust and its supracrustal covering, quite commonly separating blocks of radically different geology.) For a long time – since about Britstown – you've been travelling over the Kaapvaal Craton, even if it has mostly been far below the surface. Now you're onto the Namaqua-Natal Province (NNP) – and not for the first time. Between the end of the Cape folding, around Cookhouse and Britstown, the Namaqua-Natal Province was deep below you. Now it's at the surface and, as you approach Groblershoop, you get to see it up close. This is an area of enormous complexity, often without much outcrop. It has been divided into a number of distinct 'terranes' or subprovinces on the basis of stratigraphy and the age and grade (or intensity) of metamorphism and tectonism.

Groblershoop is close to the Orange River where it winds across relatively flat terrain with plenty of calcrete at or near the surface, but with little outcrop. After passing through Groblershoop, you can look at a good exposure of sediments of the Groblershoop Formation of the Brulpan Group (part of the NNP) in the cutting just before the road passes under the Sishen-Saldanha railway line. Notice that the sediments here are less quartz-rich than the quartzite you saw a little further back, and they are conspicuously schistose, with plenty of flaky mica **(geosite 6, map 9)** (GPS S 28° 47.515′, E 21° 52.169′).

North of Groblershoop to the Namibian border

After Groblershoop various units of the NNP are exposed, but not particularly well in what remains gently rolling terrain for some distance, with white surface limestone obscuring bedrock for much of the way. Not far before Upington, you're out of the rolling riverside plains and into much hillier country. The last stop scheduled before Upington **(geosite 1, map 10)** (GPS S 28° 26.086′, E 21° 21.508′) is just after the 102.6 marker plate, where you get a good idea of the high grade to which the older sediments of this part of the NNP were metamorphosed. Here the strikingly banded sedimentary gneiss, quartzite and amphibolite are part of another unit in the NNP called the Vaalkoppies Group.

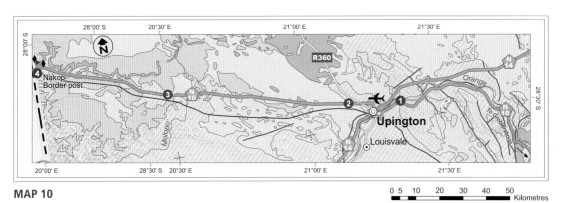

MAP 10

0 5 10 20 30 40 50 Kilometres

LEFT AND ABOVE: *The banded metasediments of the Vaalkoppies Group are well displayed in this road cutting in the Orange River valley.*

In the last section of the N10, from near Groblershoop to the Namibian border, the first low cutting after Upington, at the N10-12: 11.4N marker plate, is of hornblende-biotite gneiss and quartzo-feldspathic gneiss. These rocks are of volcanic origin but were later subjected to high-grade metamorphism, which changed them completely **(geosite 2, map 10)** (GPS S 28° 24.687', E 21° 10.636'). Soon after this cutting, you emerge from the valley onto wide, barely undulating plains with scattered inselbergs dotted about. What little vegetation the red Kalahari sand supports is low enough not to obstruct the panoramic view and, from the 21.0 marker plate onwards, low 'fixed' sand dunes are evident on the northern skyline. Most of the suboutcrop below the sand is in the process of being replaced by calcrete – a good example can be seen in a borrow pit between the 25.8 and 26.0 beacons.

At 49.4 you breast a low rise of horizontal Nama Group sandstone. From here, the flat tops of this unit are a dominant feature in the landscape, both ahead and to the right (north), the panoramic views now gone. These sediments are another example of a supracrustal formation, of end-Proterozoic to Cambrian age, therefore somewhat younger than the Precambrian rocks on which you've been since leaving the Karoo Basin. Soon after signboards to Keimoes (to the south) and Noenieput and Rietfontein (to the north) is a cutting with biotite schist and quartz-muscovite pegmatite of the Biesje Poort Formation. By now you are into the heart of the NNP and, moving on, you'll notice that there are many low koppies of the basement formations around, though the flat tops of Nama sediments are still prevalent.

These gneisses 11.4 km northwest of Upington are typical of the high-grade metamorphic rocks to be found widely in the Namaqua-Natal Province.

Blue-green chrysocolla and green malachite in this Nama sandstone tell of minor amounts of copper that found their way into the Nama sedimentary environment.

At 67.0 you cross the dry Molopo River, a major river of earlier, wetter times that forms the southern border of Botswana with South Africa for hundreds of kilometres. Now rarely flowing, it links with the Orange River not far south of this crossing.

When you go through the cutting around the 80.0 marker plate, keep a lookout near the beginning of the cut for conspicuous green (malachite) and blue-green (chrysocolla) copper staining on rocks on both sides of the road. The sandstones and mudrocks that are host to the copper mineralization were laid down in a fluvial to shallow-marine environment **(geosite 3, map 10)** (GPS S 28° 16.093', E 20° 29.968').

Soon you will notice scattered koppies of smoothly brown-weathered rock, somewhat reminiscent of the granite koppies characteristic of the lowveld of South Africa and large parts of Zimbabwe. In places you'll see quite tall vertical columns of rock. At 85.2 there is a cutting through this rock where you can see it freshly broken – a dark grey, coarsely crystalline igneous rock. It is biotite-rich (hence the dark colour) granitoid. The rock shows little or no banding, meaning that it was intruded into the well-banded metamorphic rocks of the NNP after they had been deformed and metamorphosed.

As you approach the Namibian border, you'll notice ridges of red sand not far south of the road – in fact, low dunes. These and higher dunes on the southern skyline are a reminder that when the climate is dry enough, the finer sand washed down rivers and into pans during storms will be blown far across the landscape by the prevailing wind.

Even closer to the border are koppies to the left of the road that have been partially cut through for road-building, offering you a good idea of the NNP rocks at this end of the country. It's a metamorphosed sedimentary succession, here consisting mainly of an unusual dark-coloured, high-grade metamorphic rock called kinzigite, containing the minerals garnet and sillimanite, and with some pegmatite intruded into it **(geosite 4, map 10)** (GPS S 28° 05.402′, E 20° 01.044′). The flat Nama sediments are as ubiquitous as ever.

Enjoy Namibia, because you probably haven't come this far just for the geology. I hope, though, that a drive that might otherwise have been flat and featureless for much of the way has given you a glimpse deep into our geological past, to a time when land masses were colliding, some (the craton) resistant, others (the NNP) subjected to forces that crumpled them into bizarre shapes and heated them intensely, even melting them in part. Before, during and after this process, magma – granitic and other – welled up from the depths to add further heat, and form the complex substrate on which life has taken root. As you approach the border post, you prepare to slow down and stop; for Earth there is no such rest.

The conspicuous red colour of these Nama shales and mudrock indicates deposition in a shallow-water environment, where small amounts of iron in the sediments were quickly oxidized.

7 N6: Bloemfontein to East London

GEOLOGICAL OVERVIEW

The N6 national highway takes you up close to the rock formations that cap the 'Roof of Africa'. The national road joins Bloemfontein to the coast at East London by the shortest possible route, so apart from the grandeur of the journey itself, the cuttings in the various passes give you an incomparable window into the geology of the southeastern part of the country. Other than across the Beaufort Group, the road takes you through the overlying Molteno and Elliot formations. Soon after starting your journey along the N6, you will skirt an area of the Beaufort Formation which,

for quite a few years, appeared to promise deposits of economically recoverable uranium, and which buzzed with excitement. You will pass through Aliwal North on the Free State/Eastern Cape border, an important fossil centre, and near to some early alluvial-diamond diggings. Again, in the line of energy, the country's only known coalfields – before serious reserves were found on the Highveld and in KwaZulu-Natal – were situated around Molteno-Indwe, along this route just north of Queenstown.

Geology of the route

Bloemfontein to Jamestown

The N6 branches off the N1 on the southern outskirts of Bloemfontein and gradually swings southeastwards away from it, towards Lesotho and the Eastern Cape highlands. This new departure offers a glimpse of rarely seen sedimentary units overlying the Beaufort Group, which is what you'll find across most of the Karoo; and also an escape from heavy-truck traffic. Until you get near the top of the Beaufort, though, you stay in gentle central Free State topography, with only scattered, low, dolerite-capped hills and ridges breaking the rolling highveld.

This environment was laid down during the Palaeozoic Era, which lasted until some 230 million years ago. The landscape of that era was characterized by featureless plains stretching in all directions. Between low-lying scattered islands no more than a few metres high, wide rivers meandered sluggishly. Some had their headwaters in a high mountain range far to the south, others from hilly country in the direction of present-day Botswana. All brought water – and sediment – to the low-lying Karoo swamps and river flood plains. Sand deposited in the river channels was left behind, forming extensive sand horizons or sheets as the channels migrated laterally. From time to time, surges of water spilled over the channel banks and onto the intervening flood plains, carrying fine mud and clay in suspension, which then settled out, covering wide areas. This process continued for many millions of years. Over time, more and more sediment piled up on top of those layers (now exhumed around you). And as the load of sediment in the vast basin grew correspondingly heavier, the crust slowly subsided. At the same time, erosion was stripping material – and weight – off the mountains, which steadily rose, just as an iceberg rises as the surface ice melts. In this way, perfect balance was maintained for millions of years, so that the sediments at any level are not very different from those a thousand metres above or below them.

Around Bloemfontein the topographic prominences are usually composed of dolerite, such as in this photograph, since the intruded Beaufort sediments – mostly soft mudrock – are easily flattened by erosion in an area of mature topography.

Over time, the water was squeezed out of the sediments and depth-induced pressure and heat compacted and solidified them, in a process geologists call lithification. Then, as forces deep in the mantle began to stretch Gondwana, which had been stable for so long, basaltic magma came surging up into the resulting tensional cracks. (The sustained tension would ultimately break the supercontinent Gondwana into a mosaic of less gigantic plates – Africa, South America and others.) Much of the magma reached the surface, where it flowed far and wide and cooled, producing the basalt that makes up the 'Roof of Africa' to the east of where you are. Some of the magma, however, never saw the light of day, squeezing instead between beds of sediment or just chilling out in the feeder conduits. These sills, sheets and dykes are what you see around you, intruded into the Beaufort Group sediments.

Not far west of Reddersburg, the first town you pass through after leaving the N1, a major exploration venture was mounted in the late 1970s by Rio Tinto. This was to evaluate new discoveries of high-grade bodies of uranium ore, which were ultimately to prove too limited to be developed economically.

Although most of the hills in these parts are capped by dolerite the sandstone ledges on the slopes of this plateau are conspicuous.

Getting back to the scenery, you will note that over much of the Karoo the high ground is composed mainly of dolerite. This intrusive igneous rock is clearly much harder and more erosion-resistant than the soft shales that predominate in the landscape. After Reddersburg, a very prominent massif capped by dolerite is visible some distance to the left of the road. There is a similar, slightly less imposing feature closer to the road, starting behind the farm 'Bougainvillea'. Horizontal sandstone ledges are also evident on the lower slopes of the hill. As you approach Smithfield, a popular stopover point for travellers *en route* between the Highveld and the East London coast, the country becomes more varied and you drive through a number of low cuttings **(geosite 1, map 11)** (GPS S 30° 11.670', E 26° 31.376'), mostly dolerite intruded in mudrock.

A hint of uranium

The farm where the first occurrence was investigated was just over the horizon from Reddersburg. The discovery led to Rio Tinto's mounting a concerted campaign to secure all potentially mineralized ground over an area of hundreds of square kilometres. As a Rio Tinto geologist at the time (in 1978), I clearly remember the rush of adrenalin on walking over the 'discovery outcrop', and the sustained excitement that followed. Similar occurrences of uranium had been found by other companies hundreds of kilometres away, near Beaufort West, five years earlier. As at Beaufort West, and later at Laingsburg, the individual bodies were found to be too small to be developed economically, despite occurring in fairly numerous clusters.

Like that of oil, the distribution of uranium in sandstone is controlled first and foremost by the architecture of the sedimentary environment of the time. So it is essential to understand the environment in which the fluvial deposition took place, and the processes that occurred subsequently – first to introduce the uranium-bearing fluids, and then to fix the uranium in the sediment. To evaluate the uranium deposits, mining companies explored the whole of the western outcrop area of the Beaufort Group (at least 100 000 km²) for a decade or more, deploying teams of geologists who compiled a detailed geological data-base of the area, which has significantly enriched our knowledge and understanding of the region's geological history.

You may wonder how the uranium found its way into the Karoo rocks. During lithification of the Beaufort Group sediments – a process that could have taken millions of years – water trapped between grains of sand and clay was squeezed out of the water-laid sediments and moved up the pressure gradient from deeper to shallower (lower pressure) parts. As they moved, the fluids took with them soluble components from the adjacent rock and hardening sediments through which they travelled, like uranium and, in the southwestern Karoo, molybdenum too. These minerals were then precipitated in permeable sandstone bodies whose chemistry was reducing. The uranium present in the original sediments, as well as in some volcanic ash, was in almost undetectably low concentrations, i.e. a few to a few tens of parts per million (ppm). (The worldwide average for concentrations of uranium in shale is 4 ppm.) These beds comprised sediment eroded from the Cape Fold Belt mountains to the south and west, and other highlands surrounding the Karoo Basin. Given enough time and a large enough catchment area, what had started out as almost undetectable concentrations became upgraded to be potentially minable – in the case of uranium, this may mean a grade as low as 0.02 per cent uranium, or 200 ppm.

Uranium is used as a raw material for the production of nuclear fuel used to run nuclear power plants, like Koeberg Nuclear Power Station, which is situated along the west coast, just north of Cape Town.

MAP 11

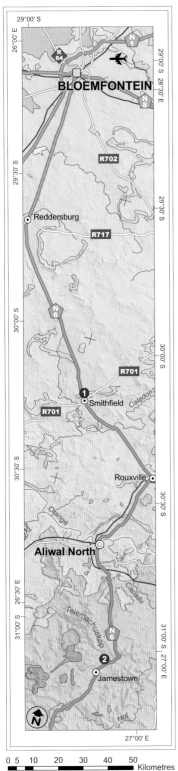

As you approach Smithfield, keep a lookout for this inclined dolerite sheet cutting through the sediments in the road cutting.

Some 7 km after passing through picturesque Smithfield, you breast a rise and find the wide Caledon River valley spread out below you. You'll notice that the sediments in the cuttings are similar to those you've seen so far, namely beds of pale buff to grey sandstone with conspicuously maroon mudrock above and below. With the Thaba Putsoa and Drakensberg mountain ranges forming the country's high watershed not far east of the N6, the eastern countryside is distinctly higher than that to the west. After crossing the Caledon River, look for two particularly high massifs to your left. Both of these have South Africa's highest extensive sedimentary unit, the Triassic (i.e. post-Permian) Elliot Formation, on their slopes. The more distant of them, again dolerite capped, forms the backdrop to the local centre of Zastron, far off your route.

Next, you pass Rouxville, another old farming town. Driving on through the same gently rolling countryside, 10 km after the town you start the gradual descent into the Orange River valley. Dolerite, sandstone and mudrock make up the higher ground, but this is only occasionally evident in road cuttings. Before you know it, you've reached the river and have crossed into the Eastern Cape, entering the town of Aliwal North on its southern bank. This is a town full of history and prehistory. There is plenty of good accommodation, and if you've chosen to break your journey here and you have the time, try and visit the Aliwal North Museum (not to be confused with the Kerkplein Museum), where you will get an insight into events in these parts, both in the recent and very dim-and-distant past.

Smithfield and archaeology

To students of archaeology Smithfield is more than a lovingly restored Victorian village in beautiful surroundings. It is where, in 1877, pioneer geologist George Stow, while excavating a cave in the district, found a comprehensive collection of Late Stone Age tools dating roughly from 18 000–2 000 years ago. They were distinctive in size, style, raw material used and the shape of the 'flake blanks'. When the European terminology for South African Stone Age cultures was discontinued in 1926 the name 'Smithfield' was adopted for artifacts with these particular characteristics. In 1926 and 1927 it was decided to subdivide the implement manufacturing industry into Smithfield A, B and C cultures.

Most of the tools were scrapers, pounders and grinders, all of stone, though bone tools, ostrich shells for carrying and storing water and for ornaments, pottery and even glass have been found in Smithfield sites. Although the full age of the industry is not known, there is no doubt it was still active when the first Europeans arrived in the 17th century.

The Smithfield industry was later expanded to include Smithfield N and P, though they were from further afield, as far as Weenen in KwaZulu-Natal – acknowledging that many broadly contemporaneous sites were found over a wide part of east-central South Africa. The name Smithfield has found its way into archaeological reference books, where it is immortalized for students of our relatively recent prehistory.

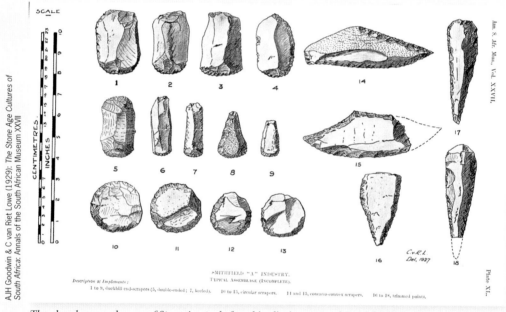

The abundance and range of Stone Age tools found in diggings around Smithfield led to the town's being immortalized among palaeontologists, even if the name has to a large extent been superseded.

Our particular interest is in the fossils, in which the area abounds. Their discovery is the more remarkable when one considers that the proportion of outcrop is substantially less than, say, around Graaff-Reinet. The obvious difference is the exposure: grassveld versus the comparatively arid and well-exposed Karoo. In addition, Aliwal North is topographically a lot higher than Graaff-Reinet. With the sediments of the Karoo Supergroup lying mostly horizontally, this means it is stratigraphically higher, too. So, remembering that sediments get older as you go down in

Image detail: Tobie Beele, Iziko Museums of South Africa Natural History

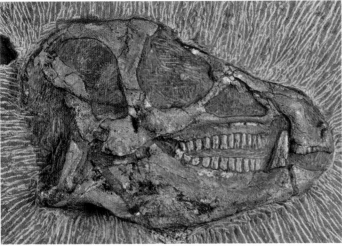

Billy de Klerk

ABOVE: Euparkeria africana *was a reptile approximately 1.2 m long, which just preceded the dinosaurs. The first specimen was discovered in a quarry near Aliwal North. In this illustration, it is shown pursuing a dragonfly.*

LEFT: *This specimen of* Heterodontosaurus, *in the process of being dug out of the rock when this was written, was found near Barkly East, not far from Aliwal North. It was a small, beaked, plant-eating dinosaur found in Jurassic sediments in the Eastern Cape.*

the stratigraphic column, the sediments at Graaff-Reinet are older than at Aliwal North. There the Beaufort sediments are Permian in age; here they are Triassic, just before the Jurassic, heyday of the dinosaurs. Between the Permian and the Triassic was an event – no-one knows exactly what it was – that brought about the greatest mass extinction of all time. So it is not hard to imagine that the numerous fossils found around Aliwal North are quite different from those that have been dug up in profusion around Graaff-Reinet.

N6: Bloemfontein to East London **141**

'Gogga' Brown's legacy

Born in 1834, Alfred 'Gogga' Brown arrived in Aliwal North as a young school teacher, becoming in due course the town's postmaster and librarian, and later on the de facto curator of its little museum. For most of his life, Brown's passion was the collection, identification and documentation of fossils. He became friendly with one of South Africa's foremost palaeontologists, country GP Dr Robert Broom, as well as with the celebrated British palaeontologist, Professor TH Huxley, to whom he sent many specimens. Another associate was Dr Daniel Kannemeyer, also a GP, based in the neighbouring town of Burgersdorp, and after whom the mammal-like reptile Kannemeyeria was named in honour of its discoverer.

Brown was a remarkable and somewhat eccentric character. He discovered an extraordinary number of fossils – amphibians, dinosaurs, fish and plants, often enduring conditions of extreme hardship to do so. One of the secrets of Brown's success as a collector was his easy access to the Late-Triassic Molteno Formation, which he visited time and again, travelling by ox-wagon – if this can be called easy!

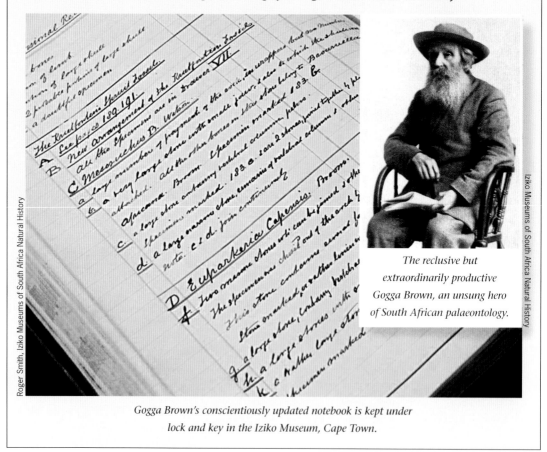

The reclusive but extraordinarily productive Gogga Brown, an unsung hero of South African palaeontology.

Gogga Brown's conscientiously updated notebook is kept under lock and key in the Iziko Museum, Cape Town.

The Late-Triassic Molteno Formation is well represented east and south of Aliwal North. It has been said that the '… Molteno Formation provides an unrivalled window onto Late Triassic plant and insect communities close to the time of origin of the mammals, dinosaurs and possibly the flowering plants', and further, that this 'remarkable diversity reflects the acme of the Triassic explosion following the end-Permian extinction' (*Towards Gondwana Alive*, p. 74).

An artist's impression of the creatures at large in these parts during Triassic Molteno times: (a) Euskelosaurus; (b) Massospondylus; (c) Heterodontosaurus; and (d) coelurosaurs.

Maggie Newman

Among the fossils to be seen in the Aliwal North Museum are *Uranocentrodon*, a Triassic amphibian that lived some 230 million years ago, and *Euskelosaurus brownii*, a dinosaur from approximately the same period.

The rich legacy of discoveries of reptilian and dinosaur remains found on farms around Aliwal North is thanks to the passion of an early collector, 'Gogga' Brown. The fossils from around here are as important in these parts as the Kitching and Rubidge family collections are around Graaff-Reinet to the southwest.

Back on the road, nothing much has changed for a while since leaving Aliwal North, but it's going to change soon. You're not only climbing out of the Orange River valley, you're taking important steps up the stratigraphic ladder, out of the Beaufort Group and into the Molteno Formation. Apart from its fossil wealth, remember that the Molteno is the unit that hosts the coal burned in the fires and furnaces of the early settlers of these parts. Crossing from the mudrock-dominated uppermost Beaufort to the overlying, relatively sandstone-rich Molteno is less dramatic than the next transition – from the Molteno Formation into the Elliot Formation, previously known as the 'Red Beds' for their characteristic coloration. You will catch your first glimpse of these beds ahead and to the right as you pass the 'Jamestown 30' signboard, and then again 4 km later on, much closer to your direction of travel and to the left of it. The Elliot Formation could be described as 'assertive', since the hard sandstone beds liberally present in its section tend to give it the highest parts of the landscape. Farmers are careful not to leave their livestock on its slopes in the winter.

The unbedded Jurassic-age pyroclastics, or volcanic sediments, in these two 'knobs' north of Jamestown bridge the gap between true sediments and the volcanic lavas of the highlands in and around Lesotho.

With Jamestown about 13 km ahead of you (according to the marker plates along the road), you enter more broken country heralding your descent into the town. To your right you can't help noticing a high conical peak, the dolerite-capped Telemachuskop, which, at 2 080 m above sea level, is considerably higher than Johannesburg.

Closer to Jamestown you will see to the west (right) of the road two pale knobs **(geosite 2, map 11)** (GPS S 31° 04.894', E 26° 48.764') making quite prominent features in the topography. In this environment of predominantly horizontally layered slopes, these completely unbedded features are particularly distinctive. The knobs are two plugs of pyroclastic material, a fragmentary explosive-related volcanic rock. Magma from deep below the crust can reach the surface in two ways. By far the most common involves the so-called tholeiitic or flood basalts, such as those of the Karoo Igneous Province. Very fluid lava spills out from fissures – cracks in the crust – and flows over great distances, burying or flowing around everything in its path. Much less commonly, if the source magma is gaseous and under pressure, it may explode up as froth, to make pumice or fragmentary ash. Think of a fizzy drink bottle suddenly being uncapped and depressurized; it foams and shoots out of the bottle. Having been blasted out of the pipe that gave it access to the surface, the ash – sometimes very fine-grained – may filter down and be washed into sedimentary basins; or it may remain where it fell, in which case it will appear 'massive' (not showing any bedding), or show only very faint bedding. It is amazing that such a volatile process can leave little trace of its origin

MAP 12

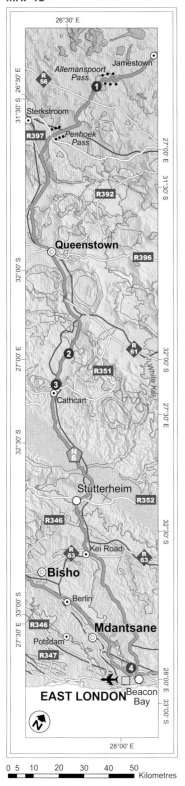

detectable to the untrained eye. This seems to have been the case around Jamestown, where there's a lot of it dotted around, with the biggest expanses lying not far west of the town.

Jamestown to East London

After Jamestown you travel in a valley cut into the relatively softer Molteno sediments, with plateaus of the overlying Elliot sediments on both sides of the road. Just after the Dordrecht turn-off you drop down to lower terrain via the Allemanspoort Pass. To begin with, the cuttings show shale and mudrock, with little sandstone. Then you're into dolerite, which, after a stretch with no outcrop, appears to the left of the road again, just after

The dolerite at the foot of Allemanspoort Pass
shows some good columnar jointing.

You get a closer view of the pyroclastic rocks on the
flats between Allemanspoort Pass and Penhoek Pass.

Rebirth of South Africa's first coalfield

Deep below your feet lie Ecca shales. In the deep-water conditions of Ecca sedimentation it is supposed that masses of micro-organisms may have left a legacy of exploitable methane in the shales. Continuously and ever so slowly, conditions change. During the times of Beaufort sedimentation the Ecca basin shrank and filled until the flanking coastal plains had widened to cover the entire basin from horizon to horizon. Ferns flourished and reptiles romped. The climate grew drier and hotter, alternating with milder, wetter times. Over time, sediment supply dwindled. By Molteno times the hinterland was being elevated by tectonism so that rivers sourced there had gradients steep enough to transport cobbles, pebbles and coarse sand to the distant plains where they were deposited as fluvial energy waned. There were still prolonged periods of stability when river gradients diminished and their sediment load-carrying capacity dropped. At these times the bedload comprised mainly finer sand, while the suspended load of mud and clay spread far across the flat floodplains. Periodically, and where swampy conditions prevailed, vegetation grew profusely enough for peat beds to form, and it was these that, over time, would mature and harden to seams of black coal. With the modern imperative to track down energy sources, there is a minor boom in the mining and exploration of coal around Indwe, bringing in much-needed foreign currency to South Africa. These days coal-mining need not be messy, and – for the public – it carries none of the imponderables of fracking.

Elitheni Coal (Pty) Ltd has resurrected the once buoyant coal-mining industry in the Eastern Cape, where South Africa's first coal mines operated from 1860 to 1915. As the only developers, owners and operators in the Eastern Cape coalfields, Elitheni has proven over 266 million tonnes on only 6% of its rights area, with a further 1.5 billion tonnes estimated. The mine site is situated between Dordrecht and Indwe about 100 km from Queenstown, making it only 300 km from the underutilised port of East London and the deep-water port of Coega. Elitheni will commence exports of its coal in 2013 and retain a focus on serving the local market as well. An estimated 500 direct jobs will be created in and around the mine community during the initial period, rising to a potential of approximately 2 000 direct jobs within five years. Elitheni is the Xhosa for 'the place of new beginnings', a name that will surely bring hope to the community.

Elitheni Coal (Pty) Ltd

The Elitheni mine gets under way early in 2013, signalling the resurrection
of an industry that last flourished in these parts many decades ago.

*As you ascend Hobbs Hill, just before Cathcart, bright maroon mudrock breaks
the sequence of beige sandstone, which dominates the sequence here.*

the turn-off to the right towards Burgersdorp. The dolerite has been quarried here, leaving faces that show quite well-developed columnar jointing, formed during cooling of the magma, and this is also conspicuous in the cutting to the right of the road. After the curves at the bottom of the pass you're on a long, straightish section of road, to the left of which you'll see a ridge of the unbedded pyroclastic material first seen approaching Jamestown **(geosite 1, map 12)** (GPS S 31° 19.512', E 26° 42.053'). After passing under the Molteno-Dordrecht road, you'll see another shapeless knob on the skyline to your left, the last you'll see of these pyroclastics.

Soon after you've passed the pyroclastic knob you're at the top of the Penhoek Pass. Spread out below you, in a magnificent panorama, is some of the most attractive scenery South Africa has to offer. The last of the sandstone-striped slopes of the Elliot Formation extend a short distance on your right, but most of the high ground that embraces the wide rolling lowlands at your feet is dolerite-capped Molteno, the unit below the Elliot. Around here, in times gone by, one would have seen a number of small coal-mining operations. Undulating plains alternate with corridors between high dolerite plateaus, more plains and then the hilly country around Queenstown. You've been slowly but surely losing altitude, and by the time you reach Queenstown, you have travelled over sediments of the Beaufort Group for a while. Since these rocks are shaly for the most part, there is little outcrop.

After crossing the Black Kei River 25 km from Queenstown, and 5 km after it the Waqu River, cuttings are mostly composed of massive to faintly bedded pale mauve-grey sandstone of the Beaufort Group **(geosite 2, map 12)** (GPS S 32° 09.474', E 27° 07.239'), inter-bedded with varying amounts of mauvish mudrock. Past the turn-off to Whittlesea you're at the foot of Hobbs Hill, which the road and railway line ascend side by side; both have cuttings with magnificent exposures of bright maroon mudrock and paler mauve, well-bedded sandstone **(geosite 3, map 12)** (GPS S 32° 15.874', E 27° 08.552'). At the top of the Hill you're practically in Cathcart, which lies just below the eastern end of a high ridge of dolerite called the Windvoëlberg. The sediments intruded by the dolerite are still of the Beaufort Group and will persist until you're in East London.

As you approach the coast, a conspicuous feature of the landscape is the very flat surface you travel over. Half-close your eyes and look to your right: the skyline is as flat as a billiard table. Open your eyes again and you will see, at a distance, tributary valleys in which rivers are heading towards the coast, and that the country is in fact quite dissected. But the fact remains that the surface being incised is remarkably – almost unnaturally – level. This very ancient surface, called the African Land Surface, was the base level attained some 50 million years ago, formed as rivers cut back from the newly formed coastline as Gondwana disintegrated. Valleys widened as they grew longer, and in front of the retreating escarpment, hills and plateaus shrank until finally there was nothing more to strip away. A vast flat coastal plain had been formed, with only a very gentle seaward slope. Inland, above nick-points in the main rivers, the same levelling and flattening happened, creating a surface

Despite the valleys closer to hand, the very level skyline as you approach the coast is a sure sign that you are looking at the African Land Surface of erosion.

Road cuttings in the descent into East London are a fitting end to a trip that has shown you so much Beaufort sandstone, here brightened by colourful Tecomaria *cascading down the cutting.*

that was the same age and as level, just more elevated. There is a pleasingly ironic inversion at play as you consider the valleys currently being cut into the African Land Surface, like those to your left as you approach East London: while it is now the 'top level' being dissected, it only acquired its near-perfect flatness by being the 'base level' in an earlier cycle of landscape evolution.

As you make the final descent into East London, through some quite high cuttings, you'll see the last geology of the trip – brown sandstone and mudrock of the Adelaide Subgroup, at the lower part of the Beaufort Group **(geosite 4, map 12)** (GPS S 32° 57.512', E 27° 54.950').

The N6 has offered an exercise in getting to know the Beaufort better, with a fairly brief excursion into the overlying Molteno and Elliot formations. In the Beaufort you've seen the sort of sediments that, in a perfect world, might have hosted important uranium deposits; and in the Molteno you've been transported back to a time when conditions were suitable for the formation of the peat that would lithify to form the coal seams first mined in South Africa. You have seen an interesting kind of rock, probably new to many: the pyroclastic associated with Stormberg volcanicity. And the route finished off on a land surface that was formed as the continent of Africa took shape. I hope you'll agree it was anything but boring.

8 R72: East London to Ncanara

GEOLOGICAL OVERVIEW

Apart from the fact that this is such a scenic drive, traffic-free for most of the way and not much less direct than the road you would normally take between East London and Port Elizabeth, there is much else on offer. Along with some good patches of indigenous forest and a number of wonderful birding spots, this eastern part of the Sunshine Coast also has plenty of excellent geology. The R72 mostly stays quite close

to the beach, so that the continuous exposures of rock on the beaches in places like Kidd's Beach and Port Alfred are great places for the geologically minded to spend an hour or two. On this drive you get glimpses of a large spectrum of South African Phanerozoic stratigraphy, from the Devonian Witteberg Group to the Tertiary-Quaternary Nanaga Formation. You will see a magnificent unconformity, and a boulder beach that strains credulity. Whether a resident of these parts or a holidaymaker, your eyes will be opened.

The Woody Cape dunes are a dramatic example of geology in progress, especially on a windy day.

Geology of the route

East London to Ncanara

There's a more scenic way of getting from East London out onto the R72 than just driving straight down Settler's Way until you're out of the industrial areas. Soon after you've crossed the Biko Bridge over the Buffalo River, take Nuffield Road to the left and head down towards the harbour. At the railway marshalling yard, turn right and head out along the coast, and keep going. Boards indicate that you're on the M18W. After about 2 km you reach the end of the golf course on your right. You'll notice some low but conspicuous outcrop within and beyond the golf course property and not far above the road, as well as along the rocky beach just to the left of the road. A close look would show you that the outcrop is dolerite. It goes below the road and along the beach for some 200 m, after which the coastal outcrop is Beaufort mudrock and sandstone.

At the head of the beach below the end of the golf course property and extending for a few hundred metres is a remarkable phenomenon. It's not really evident unless you stop and get out, but even then the scale of the beachhead boulders is not immediately evident **(geosite 1, map 13)** (GPS S 33° 02.624', E 27° 53.528'). However, compared to the occasional patches of pebbles, cobbles and sometimes boulders (up to the size of a rugby ball, say) found in places on our beaches, these boulders are gigantic. Few weigh less than a tonne, some a few tonnes. Not only are they impressive in size, they also show an almost bizarre degree of rounding, here and there almost perfect spheres.

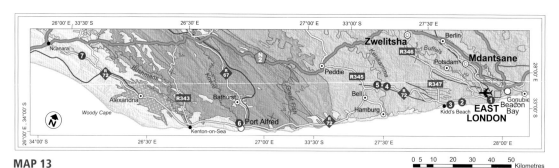

MAP 13

The boulder beach opposite the West Bank Golf Course in East London is remarkable, both for the size and the rounding of the boulders.

'Cordon dunes' can be seen as one heads westwards out of East London wherever the terrain slopes gently down to the beach.

These boulders are dolerite, blocks that in the geological past came to lie on the beach. Once there, their enormous size prevented them from moving very far up or down the beach, rolled by violent storm-wave action. This may have been the main agent of their rounding or it may merely have perfected a 'pre-rounding' by the spheroidal weathering so typical of dolerites, and seen in many parts of the Karoo. Either way, this beach is a wonder of geology.

To get back onto the R72, continue for a few kilometres along Prince George Street, which turns away from the beach when you get to the Grand Prix Circuit. It meets Settler's Way (the R72) not far inland.

Some misleading geological terms

In the description of the dolerite boulders above, it is suggested that the concepts of **rounding** (or roundness) and **sphericity** are not synonymous – for good reason. The two terms are used to describe the shape of sedimentary clasts, but they are subtly different. Roundness is generally a measure of the extent to which clasts have moved, a process that 'knocks the corners off' what might have started as very angular fragments. There is a recognized – but not strictly measurable – gradation in the description of clasts:

- very angular
- angular
- sub-angular
- sub-rounded
- rounded
- well-rounded.

very angular   *well-rounded*

But a well-rounded clast may still have the shape of an elongate 'lozenge', and is nothing like spherical. The degree of sphericity has less to do with transport and more with the original shape of the fragment concerned, say an elongate block compared to an equidimensional one, a sausage as opposed to a meatball.

Another term that crops up now and again when describing sedimentary rock, and that may seem strange, is **massive**. The origins of the term are obscure, but it has nothing to do with mass or size – an approximate synonym would be 'unbedded' or 'without layers'.

Back on the R72 for a while, you may notice the low ridge to your left, irregular but not varying much in height **(geosite 2, map 13)** (GPS S 33° 05.627', E 27° 45.116'). The patches of sand peeping through the coastal scrub here and there indicate that these are dunes. The dunes fringe the coast discontinuously from East London all the way through to Wilderness. They are found only where the coastal strip slopes gently down to the beach, normally on softer, easily eroded rocks. In contrast, where the coastline has been carved from hard quartzites and sandstones of the Table Mountain Group, for example along the 100 km stretch east of Plettenberg Bay, the beach is backed by steep rocky sea cliffs, allowing no space for sand accumulation between their base and the high-water mark. Those beaches are practically devoid of sand and dunes.

Kidd's Beach is a charmingly unspoiled coastal village **(geosite 3, map 13)** (GPS S 33° 09.290', E 27° 41.769'). The rocky beach in front of most of the village is a good place to see Katberg Formation sandstone. In these parts, the Katberg forms the uppermost unit in the predominantly mudrock-dominated Beaufort Group, towards the top of the entire huge Karoo Supergroup. The sandstone is quite coarse-grained with scattered pebbles of various rock types, mainly of quartz and quartzite. The pebbles indicate derivation from Cape Supergroup rocks in a part of the Cape Fold Belt to the southeast of you that was being actively uplifted and eroded at the time, and is now below sea level.

The Triassic-aged Katberg Formation (Karoo Supergroup) occupies the centre of a shallow syncline, southwestwards of which the formations you cross are steadily lower in the stratigraphic column, and so are older. This continues until you come onto Early Devonian-aged Bokkeveld Group (Cape Supergroup) sediments around Kenton-on-Sea. You've crossed about 150 million years (Ma): from 230 Ma in the Triassic, shortly after the devastating end-Permian extinction, through which only a few species such as the mammal-like reptile *Lystrosaurus* survived, going way back to 380 Ma in the Devonian, when the invertebrates that had ruled the oceans were being joined by the first vertebrate fish, the placoderms.

Occasional pebble 'runs' are quite characteristic of the Katberg Formation (upper Beaufort Group),
this one separating well-bedded sandstone below the pebbles from massive sandstone above the pebbles.

*At Kidd's Beach sedimentary effects (ripple marks) in today's beach sand
can be seen alongside sandstone beds over 200 million years old.*

Moving away from Kidd's Beach, looking inland across most of the synclinal core of the Katberg sandstone and beyond, away from the coast, you'll notice the smoothly peneplained African Land Surface **(geosite 4, map 13)** (GPS S 33° 09.886', E 27° 25.282'). (For an explanation of the genesis of this surface, see ch. 7 on the N6, p. 148.) This ancient plain is deeply dissected by many rivers and their tributaries, but it nevertheless forms a beautifully planar surface on the areas between the drainages. As you drop into river valleys such as the Tyolomnqa (Chalumna), the Keiskamma, or the Great Fish, there are cuttings in which the sandstone and mudrock of the upper Beaufort Group are showcased. The rocks are mostly brown to beige, with pale grey variants in places. The sandstone beds vary from massive to bedded, although the bedding is not usually very marked. Maroon mudrock is occasionally conspicuous, a diagnostic feature of the Beaufort Group. Bedding dips are commonly quite gentle, becoming steeper southeastwards as you progress towards the core of the fold belt to the south.

Where for hundreds of kilometres along the main length of the fold belt, the beds dip mainly north- or southwards, here the bedding dips predominantly to the northeast or southwest. That is because during the rupturing of Gondwana, a major transform fracture zone (or 'tear-fault' – a more descriptive term), called the Agulhas-Falkland Fracture Zone (AFFZ), formed offshore, close to the southern KwaZulu-Natal coastline and along the northern part of the Eastern Cape, before heading out seawards to curve around to the south of the extensive Agulhas Bank. The previously perfectly east-west Cape Fold Belt reacted to the major shearing force that dragged the Falkland Islands platelet southwestwards past it, by curving the fold belt southwards towards the AFFZ. (See the diagram on p. 115.)

Although dissected by the river valleys of today, the ancient, remarkably level African Land Surface of erosion is conspicuous in these parts.

The relatively minor Keiskamma River has a wide floodplain because, when sea level was lower than it is now, the
base of the V-shaped valley was commensurately lower, and has been filled, or 'drowned', as sea level has risen.

Incidentally, since East London where you started, there has been only a relatively minor amount of dolerite outcrop evident, most conspicuously at the top of the pass going down into the Keiskamma River valley. Keep in mind that the compressional regime that preceded most of the Karoo sedimentation and the subsequent break-up of Gondwana led to folding and thrusting and substantial crustal thickening – not a favourable environment for dolerite intrusion.

Looking far left towards the river mouth as you drop into the Keiskamma valley, you'll note a couple of things **(geosite 5, map 13)** (GPS S 33° 11.342′, E 27° 23.740′). Firstly, look at the over-steepened part of the river bank where it has been undercut from top to bottom – suggesting a really major collapse. Secondly, note the tremendous width of the flood plain for what you'll see is not a very big river. This can now be explained by virtue of the fact that some 21 000 years ago, when the Last Glacial Stage was at its peak (maximum polar icing), sea level – and the Keiskamma River valley – was 120 m lower than at present. Then, as glacial ice melted worldwide, and sea level rapidly rose, the valley became filled with alluvial, littoral and marine sedimentary detritus transported mostly by the river from inland, but also by longshore drift along the coast. Essentially, the river now meanders over sediment it previously deposited in the valley.

Having crossed this regionally important river, you'll find more cuttings *en route* back up to the flats, one with the bright maroon Beaufort mudrock referred to earlier. There are also good views of the estuarine part of the Keiskamma floodplain, showing its exaggerated width.

You travel off the Beaufort Group sediments onto those of the Ecca without being aware of it as there is no outcrop at or near the contact. The first you know of your descent down the stratigraphic column is when you see a fairly conspicuous exposure of Dwyka Group tillite (stratigraphically below the Ecca), about 5.5 km after crossing the Mpekweni River. The outcrop is, however, somewhat disguised by black manganese oxide that coats some of it.

Being massive (unlayered) and genetically quite different from other sediments, the tillite usually does not weather and decompose as easily as other fine-grained, bedded sediments and therefore generally tends to be present as outcrop. The mudrock and fine-grained sandstone of the underlying Witteberg Group – like the Ecca shales – are not as easy to see. Other than exposures coming up in Port Alfred, which soon looms ahead, you generally only find thin strips of Witteberg outcrop in the intertidal zones of the coastal reaches and along the banks of bigger rivers that you will cross.

There is a 'must see' geological exposure in Port Alfred that will take you only five minutes out of your way. Once you know what to look for and where, you can view it as you drive past, but the first time you should stop and give it a more measured appraisal. What you are going to see is an unconformity: a contact between two rock units of drastically different age, the two of them formed under very different circumstances. Unconformities rank high among the pinnacles of geological experience, especially when they are as well exposed as this one.

Immediately after you've crossed the Kowie River, turn left, and then, after a matter of metres, turn right into a grassy park area, backed by a conspicuous vertical scarp **(geosite 6, map 13)** (GPS S 33° 35.782', E 26° 53.198'). It's in this scarp that you'll find what you're looking for. Park in

Like Kidd's Beach, Port Alfred has magnificent outcrops along the beach where sedimentary features, such as 'overturned' cross-bedding resembling typical tectonic folding, can be seen (see inset).

the shade and walk around to get a feel for what you're seeing. The lowermost three quarters of the face consists of well-bedded, almost vertically standing quartzite of the lower Witteberg Group. It doesn't go to the top of the face, though. The uppermost part of the exposure is horizontally bedded, and in a few places you can see the flat-lying softer sandstone in direct contact with the near-vertical beds below it. This is the unconformity: it's between mid-Devonian, i.e. mid-Palaeozoic quartzite below (380 million years old), and much younger overlying sandstone, of Late Miocene to Pliocene age (late Cenozoic, approximately 5–6 million years old). The contact between the two units is so well defined it could be drawn as a pencil line on the outcrop. Consider that between deposition of those two sequences of sandstone, a towering range of fold mountains was built where you stand, and then removed by erosion – and the whole Karoo Basin, covering more than half of South Africa, was formed. After that, and still well before deposition of the overlying upper sandstone, the most dramatic chain of events in South Africa's recent geological history took place: the break-up of Gondwana. It's a telling pencil line. It is not always the volume of rock that reflects the time: the missing parts in between (i.e. hiatuses) sometimes tell of much longer intervals.

In the part of the face nearest the river you can see a basal conglomerate capping the steeply dipping beds, just below the horizontal upper sandstone. This is a sure sign that you are looking at the start of a new sedimentary cycle, where high-energy rivers flowed down steep gradients from freshly uplifted terrain, carrying coarser material than possible when flowing over gentler slopes. There's an even more dramatic example of the Port Alfred unconformity back across the river and north of the road, behind the police station and municipal workshops. Go and see this for yourself – it's difficult to do justice to these features in a photograph.

From Port Alfred to Ncanara you'll see no basement (really hard rock) geology, but you will have glimpses of coastal aeolianite, or dune rock, far inland, out of sight of the sea. If you stopped to look at the unconformity in Port Alfred, you saw boulders quite high in a cliff face that are related – albeit distantly – to the modern shoreline. This is a good time to review the recent geological history of the coastal strip of this part of South Africa.

The unconformity between nearly 400 million-year-old Devonian sandstones and the much younger (5–6 million years old) sandstones that overlie them is most easily photographed immediately northeast of the Kowie River, but more easily accessed across the river on the southeast side.

FIGURE 14

SEA LEVEL CHANGE IN SOUTH AFRICA

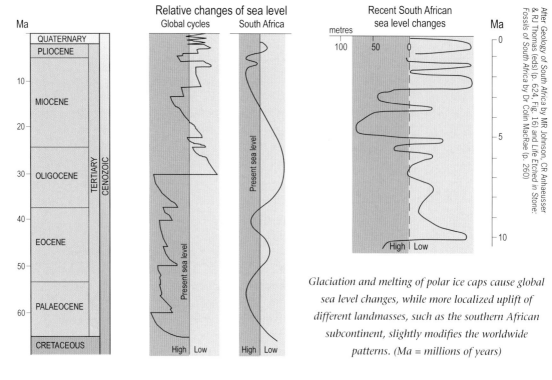

Glaciation and melting of polar ice caps cause global sea level changes, while more localized uplift of different landmasses, such as the southern African subcontinent, slightly modifies the worldwide patterns. (Ma = millions of years)

After Geology of South Africa by MR Johnson, CR Anhaeusser & RJ Thomas (eds) (p. 624, Fig. 16) and Life Etched in Stone: Fossils of South Africa by Dr Colin MacRae (p. 260)

After the break-up of Gondwana, east-west, fault-bounded valleys were eroded back from where they met the northeast-southwest coastline, and rivers quickly found the zones of softer rocks and exploited them. The Cape Fold Belt mountains shed vast amounts of coarse material into the streams running off them and into the kind of alluvial fans that can be seen on lower mountain slopes today – only bigger. In flood times pebbles, cobbles and boulders were washed into large rivers that carried them across the subsiding valley floors, giving us the conglomerate of the Enon Formation.

Later, as conditions stabilized and slopes decreased in pitch, rivers accumulated mainly sand and mud, depositing their load on the flats and thereby creating the Kirkwood Formation. Further from the mountains, along the interface between land and sea, the material deposited in coastal and marine environments was even finer-grained. These marine sediments are known as the Sundays River Formation. Together, the three formations are grouped as the Uitenhage Group, and as you drive towards Ncanara, directly ahead of you is the most extensive area underlain by these sediments. The sediments were deposited from the late Jurassic onwards into the Cretaceous. A large number of dinosaur remains have been recovered from the Early Cretaceous Kirkwood Formation, some of which can be seen on display in the world-class Albany Museum at Grahamstown and in the Port Elizabeth Museum.

Stability was short-lived: a Cretaceous meteorite impact in faraway Mexico brought about years of unremittingly wintry and gloomy conditions that put paid to the dinosaurs. Along the Eastern Cape coast in those times – the late Cretaceous and early Tertiary – relative tectonic stability had been reached, the rugged post-Gondwana break-up landscape had been toned down and, after the temperate to humid Cretaceous, the climate was drying.

Pines and firs

Diplodocus

Yellowwood trees

Cycads

Dicraeosaurus

Ancient crocodile

Horsetails

Paranthodon africanus

Ferns

Dinosaur nest with eggs and hatchlings, found in 2009

Nqwebasaurus thwazi

Careful collecting of fossils has enabled assembly of this 'rogues' gallery' of dinosaurs that frequented these parts during the time the Uitenhage Group was deposited.

Dune formation

The four prerequisites for the formation of dunes are:

- Low-lying country behind the beach,
- A generous supply of sand to the beach environment,
- A regime of strong wind in a prevailing onshore direction, and
- A relatively dry climate.

From Hamburg at the mouth of the Keiskamma to where the Sundays River reaches the coast at Colchester, northeast of Port Elizabeth, a variety of geological factors make for low relief inland of the beach, so the first criterion is met. The Sundays River is an ancient river with an extensive catchment generally comprised of geologically young formations. These yield huge amounts of sand, meaning that the second of the above requirements is satisfied. For the last two factors, strong winds and relative aridity at the southern end of the continent are a natural consequence of the emergence of planet Earth from a comparatively recent Ice Age. Along with the winter cold fronts that sweep relentlessly along the coast from west to east, the wind howls, first from the southwest and then from the east as the fronts pass. Although the wind sometimes brings rain, most often it is dry, always blowing onshore. Not for nothing is Port Elizabeth called the Windy City. With all dune-building criteria met, a substantial dune field, unique in South Africa, forms in the region of the Sundays River mouth.

However, along the coastline you have already travelled, back in the direction of East London, the wind regime drops and the sand supply is less. Consequently, only a narrow dune cordon, immediately adjacent to the beach and now vegetated, has formed.

The day on which this photograph was taken the wind was easterly, and tonnes of sand were being moved.

Far inland, the dunes that formed this sandstone were stabilized millions of years ago.

Towards the end of the Tertiary, the relative sea level was as much as 375 m higher than at present. That is why a basal conglomerate comprising mainly marine oyster shells can occur high in the hills and out of sight of the sea in the general area of your route. The boulders you saw above the unconformity in Port Alfred are part of a river mouth section of that former beach (or near-beach). You won't see any of the oyster-shell conglomerate on the drive, but in cuttings as you approach Ncanara you will catch glimpses of the dune rocks that followed the beach as it moved towards the ocean in response to the falling sea level.

The coast south of Alexandria is dry enough and the wind locally aggressive enough for seeds that might alight on the most recently formed dunes to be blasted away with the dune-top sand before they can germinate and take root. If you want to see the Alexandria Dune Field, head south from Alexandria towards Woody Cape along a good road that goes back to Cannon Rocks and Boknes and, ultimately, to the R72 again. Call in at the Woody Cape Section of the Addo Elephant National Park (along this road), where there is basic accommodation and you can get a permit and directions to the beach. A short walk westwards along the shore will bring you into the active dune field. It's particularly impressive if there's a wind blowing, which is most of the time. Then, with the sand stinging the backs of your legs, you really see a geological process at work. It's worth the detour.

The active dunes reach inland to the interface with the vegetation cover, where the wind is no longer sufficiently violent to stop the settling and germination of seeds and subsequent plant growth. Below the surface and over time, the shelly material in the sand releases some of its calcium carbonate to mingle with the slightly acidic rainwater. The carbonate is then precipitated elsewhere in the stabilized dune as cement around the sand grains. In this way, dunes are fossilized almost as one watches, though the dune rock you see in occasional cuttings as you approach Ncanara is 5 million years old or more **(geosite 7, map 13)** (GPS S 33° 35.953', E 26° 06.025').

From the giant dolerite boulders at East London to the tiny, cement-bonded grains of seashell and quartz, the R72 has been a useful laboratory of Earth-shaping processes, big and small! I hope you have enjoyed it.

9 R66/R34/R33: Gingindlovu to eMkhondo

GEOLOGICAL OVERVIEW

The road that turns off the N2 close to Gingindlovu and heads inland to rejoin the N2 at eMkhondo (Piet Retief) offers a substantially more direct route from Durban or Pietermaritzburg to Mpumalanga than the N2 – and it showcases a wealth of geology.

You start in the coastal lowlands, climbing quite quickly to cooler climes around Eshowe. From here you stay close to the escarpment, at times traversing rolling uplands, at others crossing wide river valleys or seeing them close by to the east as you head northwards. By the time you approach the end of this short route, at eMkhondo, you're far inland as you've driven almost due north, whereas the coastline trends in a northeasterly direction. From Vryheid until you join the N2 again you're on high ground underlain by the core of the old Kaapvaal Craton. Not far over the eastern horizon towards the last stretch of the journey lies the southern end of the Lebombo range, which forms a defining topographic feature along the eastern border of Swaziland and in Mpumalanga.

For most of the route the large flat-topped plateaus that dominate the skyline comprise horizontal cover formations of the 500–450 million-year-old Natal Group in the south and somewhat younger Karoo Supergroup in the north. These cover formations are also called supracrustal formations, referring to the fact that they were deposited 'on top of the crust'. One of the most important features in the wide valleys is the much older White uMfolozi Inlier – comprising the first formations to be deposited on the primitive basement or crust. Near the beginning and end of the route you'll see small 'windows' into this crustal geology, all in all a good cross-section of the Earth's history, some of it exceptionally beautifully exposed.

Well-bedded sandstone of the Vryheid Formation (Ecca Group, Karoo Supergroup), seen a short distance north of Vryheid, reflects deposition at the outer edge of a coastal delta. The railway line carries coal to the coast from mines in the same geological unit, mostly in Mpumalanga.

Geology of the route

Gingindlovu to Glückstadt

As you set off on the R66, surrounded by coastal sugar-cane lands, the deep soil means that you don't see much outcrop, most road cuttings being well grassed over. Flat-topped bluffs far to the south are made by the hard horizontal sandstones of the Early Ordovician Natal Group.

The first striking exposure occurs as you head out of the Nkwalini valley after Eshowe **(geosite 1, map 14)** (GPS S 28° 41.834', E 31° 31.325'). Stop near the top of the pass out of the valley at the Thuthukani Tuck Shop with its fruit sellers, 3 km after the major turn-off to the right to Empangeni and Richards Bay. From here you can walk a short distance up or down the road where you'll be able to have a close look at relatively unweathered vertically banded Archaean granitic gneisses. With these rocks in front of you, it's a good time to consider that you've crossed from one of the two main parts of South Africa's basement geology onto the other. Earlier on you were in the Tugela Terrain of the Natal Metamorphic Province (of the Namaqua-Natal Province). Though hardly seeing them, you drove across gneisses of this geological unit as you headed up the pass into Eshowe. Now you're moving onto an older and fundamentally different part of the crust, the Kaapvaal Craton, which will be below you, either directly or beneath cover formations, for the rest of the trip. The rocks in this cutting and in boulders up the slope are quite typical of the craton.

About 5 km further on you reach the top of the watershed ridge you've been climbing and get glimpses of the pale mauve to beige horizontal Natal Group sandstones. You can't stop here but there's better to come, where you can do so. Some 10 km further on, the spur on which the road has travelled starts to broaden and you find yourself in flatter country covered with timber plantations and practically no outcrop. Although you still don't see any outcrop as you approach the next town, Melmoth, it is on Dwyka tillite, which overlies the Natal Group sandstones and is represented here in part of a down-faulted graben.

MAP 14

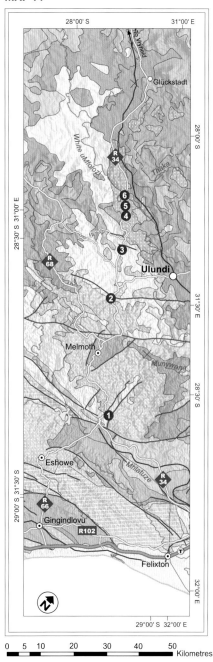

Granitic gneiss of the Kaapvaal Craton makes scattered outcrops in the rolling green hills across the road from the Thuthukani Tuck Shop. The banding typical of this rock type is exposed in the nearby cutting (inset).

For the next stop, look out for the Mtonjaneni turn-off to the left. Soon after this point, you come to the edge of the White uMfolozi valley. From 1.7–2 km after the turn-off, with enough space to pull off the road, is a beautiful example of the sedimentary features to be seen in Natal Group sandstone **(geosite 2, map 14)** (GPS S 28° 27.580', E 31° 20.045'). It's a stack of cross-bedded pale mauve sandstone with minor darker mauve mudrock, showing dewatering structures (which were conduits of water escape formed as the sediments were consolidating), and some soft-sediment overfolding. Imagine this sedimentary overfolding forming, much as a new load of sand deposited down an ever-so-gentle slope deforms the top parts of the semi-consolidated beds below it, dragging the beds over on top of themselves. The photographs opposite show these phenomena clearly and will help you find examples in the cutting. Earthquake shocks during sedimentation, well-documented events, may trigger the formation of such structures.

As you pass the turn-off to Ulundi, perhaps even before, you'll notice a single high plateau standing conspicuously above the general skyline far in the distance ahead of you. It is the dolerite-capped Nhlazatshe, which you'll see more closely and read about in a while.

In the meantime you drop into the valley where, before crossing the White uMfolozi itself, you go over several of its tributaries. About 12 km after the Ulundi turn-off, the second of two closely spaced streams is the Mphaphoma (clearly labelled), where you will see plenty of outcrop upstream (to the left) of the rather fine bridge. Soon after the crossing there's a track turning to the right where you can park. It's worth stopping here and walking down to the river upstream of the bridge – there are established paths **(geosite 3, map 14)** (GPS S 28° 20.586', E 31° 15.668'). Have a good look at the Archaean granite that forms the basement to the overlying sedimentary successions such as the Pongola Supergroup – the granite conspicuously homogeneous, pink and coarse-grained with, here and there, narrow veins of fine-grained granite called aplite, which characterize the basement granites of the Kaapvaal Craton.

As you climb out of this valley you will see quite a prominent ridge to your right – it is formed by the basal quartzite of the Archaean Nsuze Group (see photograph on p. 177). At nearly 3 billion years, these are the oldest sedimentary rocks you'll see on this route, having been derived from erosion of the underlying granites. About 1 km after a turn-off to the left to Babanango, keep a lookout for the sign pointing to the right and marked 'Denny Dalton 4 km'. It's best not to use

Beautiful cross-bedded Natal Group sandstone in this cutting shows dewatering structures (left inset) and sedimentary overfolding (right inset).

In the bed of the Mphaphoma stream is an excellent example of Archaean granite of the Kaapvaal Craton.

The Dwyka tillite in this climatic environment shows very well-developed spheroidal or 'onion-skin' weathering.

this road to get to the gold mine of this name, partly because it's the longer road, through the Denny Dalton village, and partly because there's good rock exposure in the cuttings along the R66/R34 before you get to the alternative 'mine' road. The first cutting shows well-bedded Archaean sediments, mostly sandstone with minor mudrock, and some dolerite at the end of the cutting. After this there are amygdaloidal lavas that overlie the basal quartzites of the Nsuze Group.

Then you're out of the basement and into Dwyka tillite of the younger cover. The tillite shows the best spheroidal weathering you're ever likely to see, of aesthetic appeal more than geological importance. In certain climatic environments, this kind of weathering characterizes internally massive or unbedded rocks that have never been disturbed by tectonism. (During tectonism – or orogeny, or mountain-building – the 'massiveness' a rock might initially have had is destroyed and replaced by a metamorphic 'fabric'. This results from minerals that re-orient themselves in response to the Earth's movement, leading to a banded or cleaved rock. During weathering, such a rock breaks up along the banding or cleavage, often quite finely, and this is evident in outcrop.)

For those intrigued by Dwyka tillite, the parts around Denny Dalton are a good locality. Take the next turn-off ('Denny Dalton 2 km') to the mine. Some 1.3 km down this road, look for a slab of smooth rock in the shallow gulley to the left of the road, where it's easy to see the glacial scratches or striations on the 'pavement' roughly perpendicular to the road. These formed where hard fragments caught up in the ice sheets scoured the underlying surface, while the finer material in the ice polished those same surfaces. Around 300 m further, and with a convenient shade tree just beyond it, look for a place to the left of the road where you can see that the fence is regularly climbed through, with a path leading away from the fence down the slope **(geosite 4, map 14)** (GPS S 28° 17.071', E 31° 13.434'). This path will take you to the Denny Dalton Mine. The fairly large stone mine buildings are to your right. At the sharp left turn in the path, a small cliff is evident

In the gulley running past the mine are wonderful exposures of Dwyka tillite on a very uneven basement floor. In places, direction of the glacial striations is evident, as indicated by the dotted lines (see inset).

Denny Dalton – the Witwatersrand that was not to be

The fortune hunters of old were nothing if not resolute. Where there were streams and rivers, they panned them, ever hopeful that at the end of the swirling of a shovelful of dirt there would be some glistening flecks of gold in the bottom of the pan. Occasionally they were rewarded. Then they looked up the slopes of the valleys searching for a white quartz 'reef' (geologists call them veins) that might be the source, or for anything that stood out from the surroundings and might be carrying gold.

Around 1893, five years after the conglomerates on the 'Ridge of White Waters' – by then being mined on a growing scale for their gold – had been assigned to the Witwatersrand Series, similar rocks were found in a tight valley deep in the interior of Zululand, where a stream had yielded exciting amounts of gold. By then farms had been laid out and surveyed and in that year Thomas Denny, John Dalton and Scott Paulsen bought the farm Tusschenby and set about commissioning a gold extraction plant.

The men were not deterred by the extreme hardness of the Archaean (Mozaan Group) conglomerates; after they had worked what ore they could in a small opencast operation, they drove adits into the hillside to excavate more ore. By June 1895 the Denny Dalton Gold Mining Company had crushed 682 tonnes of ore, from which 4.5 kg of gold was extracted (6.6 grams per tonne). It was a tantalizing result, though they must have hoped for better to come. But it was not to be. The next record we have is after the Dennys had withdrawn from the mine. From 1 772 tonnes processed in 1905 and 1906, only 5.6 kg of gold was recovered, an even more disappointing outcome. The last known production was in 1926, when improved extraction methods allowed the recovery of some gold from the tailings dumps. Since then, interest in the area is intermittently reawakened when the gold price spikes but it soon falls back to dormancy. Hopes of a new gold belt are a thing of the past.

Thomas Denny was a skilled and innovative engineer. One of the improvements he introduced in the plant was a rotating iron mesh drum through which the soft matrix binding the conglomerate gold-bearing pebbles could fall and be collected, so that the sterile (i.e. gold-free) pebbles did not have to be crushed, as they were on the Witwatersrand. Sons Harry and George Denny worked as Mine Secretary and Mine Manager respectively. However, not even that degree of family involvement and father Thomas's ingenuity could get more gold out of the ground than streams had put there 3 billion years ago. In 1895 the family withdrew from the business. Both Harry and George went on to distinguish themselves on the mines of the Witwatersrand and the name Denny is a proud one in the annals of gold mining in South Africa, perpetuated in the street name Denny Dalton Road in Johannesburg.

on the left of the old constructed mine road, with a path below it. Follow the path up this gulley to where you will find the adits into the hill from which the gold ore was once extracted. (See above text box on Denny Dalton.)

If you want to see how irregular the basal contact of the Dwyka tillite can be, find your way to the base of the nearby gulley and walk up it for a short distance. You will see how the tillite was directed by the pre-existing topography over which the ice sheets flowed. You'll also see the size of material the ice could transport, dramatically illustrated by clasts of up to 1 m in diameter and by no means locally derived. There is, furthermore, a locality (GPS S 28° 16'49.22", E 31° 13'30.57") where you can see a fault that has juxtaposed sediments and volcanics of the Pongola Supergroup, capped by unfaulted tillite. This is a worthwhile locality at which to spend some time.

Back on the main road, head on for another 4 km until you come to a secondary road off to the right (GPS S 28° 15'8.29", E 31° 11'49.86"). It is used for, among other things, maintenance

The mouth of an adit at the Denny Dalton Mine shows conglomerate similar to that mined on the Witwatersrand.

of the Eskom power lines through these parts, which you will see clearly from the road. Follow the good gravel road for a few hundred metres to under the lines and walk to the low ridge ahead of you. After crossing some gritty sandstone, you will see what is thought to be the oldest Superior-type banded iron formation (BIF) in the world (see text box on BIF on p. 173), lying stratigraphically not far above the gold-bearing conglomerates further south **(geosite 5, map 14)** (GPS S 28° 15.132′, E 31° 12.048′).

Once you have returned to the R66/R34, at the next cutting look out for calcareous (mainly dolomitic) sediments of the Nsuze Group that underlie the banded iron formation and gold-bearing conglomerates of the Mozaan Group. This area is interesting in that the older Nsuze Group strata dip to the northeast at about 20° while the overlying Mozaan Group dips northeast at 10°. This difference suggests that the older Nsuze rocks were slightly tilted and then levelled by erosion before the first Mozaan sedimentation started.

*This banded iron formation of the Mozaan Group (see geosite 5)
is thought to be the oldest of its type in the world.*

After crossing the White uMfolozi bridge, pull over on the small grass verge next to the 120 km/h sign **(geosite 6, map 14)** (GPS S 28° 14.067', E 31° 10.610'). On your right, in the large cutting across the road, Nsuze Group volcanic rocks that overlie the calcareous sandstones of the previous road cutting are exposed. The base of the volcanics consists of a rather remarkable type of rock called lapilli tuffs, which one doesn't get to see too often. These are formed during certain volcanic eruptions when molten 'blobs' of magma, ejected into the freezing atmosphere, are chilled almost instantly to form little spherules (from less than 1 mm up to 3 mm in diameter). These spherules, called lapilli, then rain down like small hailstones, and the bed formed where they 'land' – usually in the water – is a lapilli tuff.

Further on in this cutting, ordinary lavas that were extruded over the surface were full of gaseous bubbles, which released steam as the lava cooled. The resulting pockets, or amygdales, were filled with secondary minerals such as calcite. It's worthwhile taking a walk back onto the White uMfolozi bridge and looking upstream to see the thick succession of sandstone, calcareous sandstone and dolomite (hosting well-preserved stromatolites). If you cross the bridge and look downstream, the contact between the sandstone and the overlying lavas can be seen on the northern bank of the river. These Nsuze Group volcanics also contain amazing structures, such as blocky lava (also known as 'aa') and ropy lava ('pa-hoi-hoi'), somewhat similar to the structures seen in lava flows in Hawaii, which explains the strange names!

Banded iron formation (BIF)

'Superior-type' banded iron formation is thus named because its 'type area' is in the iron mines of the Lake Superior area. Between them, these iron mines produce the bulk of the USA's supply. The other main type of iron formation is the 'Algoma-type', which is found in Archaean belts and generally makes smaller deposits than the Superior-type. Genetically, they differ markedly.

Beautiful examples of Algoma-type can be seen around Barberton, where they are intimately associated with volcanics, this association being their main distinguishing characteristic. The iron-rich sediments formed in Archaean times in oxygen-deficient or anoxic seas fringing the volcanic island arcs that were the precursors to the first cratons.

The younger Superior-type banded iron formations were formed later, during the late Archaean and Palaeoproterozoic. As the greenstone belts amalgamated to form the beginnings of the cratons, and with topographic relief on the planet's surface still subdued, broad continental shelves evolved. Below the level of tides and waves, the environment was still relatively anoxic, and formation of finely layered iron oxide-silica precipitate continued, but on a drastically larger scale than earlier and with little or no volcanic input and still not much land-derived clastic sedimentation. Examples of the resultant Superior-type banded iron formations can be seen in the Mozaan Group (Pongola Supergroup) near the White uMfolozi River, as well as in the Contorted Bed in the Witwatersrand sediments (exposed in Jan Smuts Avenue close to Wits University).

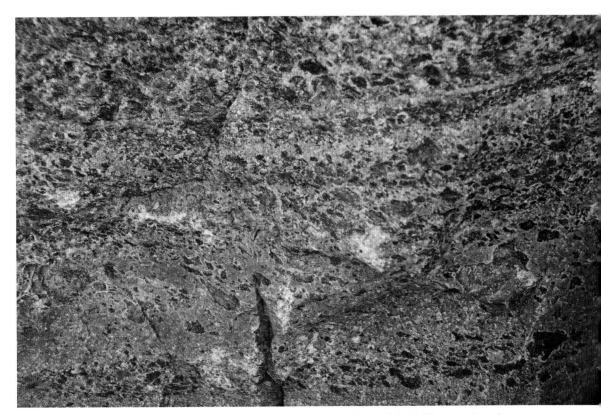

Lapilli tuffs, such as are found in the Nsuze Group near the White uMfolozi bridge, were formed from molten lava blasted into the atmosphere, congealing and falling to Earth as hailstones do.

You'll soon be out of the White uMfolozi valley and off the Archaean White uMfolozi Inlier, with the approaching uplands mostly underlain by Dwyka tillite. To your right, look out for the Nhlazatshe plateau, which you first saw from the southern side of the valley. It is one of the high, dominant, dolerite-capped massifs with slopes of sandstone of the Vryheid Formation of the Ecca Group, the unit above the Dwyka in the Karoo Supergroup. You drive for a while along the edge of these cover formations, with basement rocks to the left, Karoo to the right.

Now the tributary valleys of the White uMfolozi are shallower and, reminiscent of your ascent out of the much deeper Nkwalini valley earlier on, you find the country flattening out. The closeness of the Richards Bay railway line is a reminder that you're approaching the coalfields of northern KwaZulu-Natal and neighbouring Mpumalanga. In fact, you're not yet quite cut off from the lowlands, as soon after passing under the railway line you'll note the country dropping away to your right. The land slopes down into the valleys of the Black uMfolozi and its tributaries, its White counterpart out of sight but still not far to the west. But soon there's level ground on both sides of the road; you're back in farming country. You'll pass just to the west of the settlement of Glückstadt, where you can buy cold drinks from the little shop if the sightseeing has made you thirsty. Next stop will be Vryheid, some 30 km ahead.

Dolerite-capped Nhlazatshe, visible from tens of kilometres to the south, has prominent outcrops of Vryheid Formation sandstone on its slopes.

Glückstadt to eMkhondo (Piet Retief)

About 8.5 km after the Glückstadt turn-off, you'll see a more direct reminder of the approaching coalfields: conspicuous black dumps to the left of the road, with the railway line just beyond it. In the not-too-distant past, this was presumably a coal-loading station from the small Vryheid collieries nearby. Dolerite in cuttings after this is a sign that you're well into the eastern part of the Karoo Basin.

You're approaching Vryheid, and from this town to the next, Paulpietersburg, you're going to deviate from the main R33 road to take a more direct, more easterly road. It skirts the deeply incised Bivane River gorge for a distance and, apart from offering access to a dramatic and extremely

174   Geology off the beaten track

MAP 15

*One can imagine sand being deposited from the north (above the
tunnel) onto the fronts of deltas building out from the coastline,
to leave this fine legacy in Vryheid Formation sandstone*

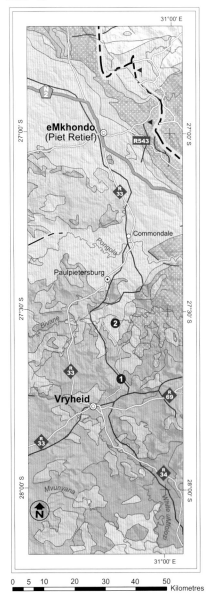

worthwhile exposure of Vryheid Formation sandstone just outside Vryheid, it allows you a last good look at the basement granites that formed the building blocks of the Kaapvaal Craton. This road leads to the Natal Spa resort and is well marked as such.

To get onto the detour, turn right onto the R69 (Louwsburg) as you enter Vryheid, follow this to the T-junction, turn left towards Vryheid town and then, after 750 m, first right towards Paulpietersburg. Follow this road for a few kilometres until you get to a T-junction where you turn left towards Natal Spa. Soon you'll cross the bridge over the Richards Bay railway line, immediately after which turn left up the Transnet gravel service road. When you reach the straight section of this road, next to and above the railway line (here in a cutting), you'll see black Ecca shale in the railway cutting below you **(geosite 1, map 15)** (GPS S 27° 41.893', E 30° 52.240'). This is typical of the deeper, still-water sediments of the Ecca Basin well known to KwaZulu-Natal residents. What you've really come to see, though, is another type of sediment completely – delta-front sandstone, magnificently displayed on the slope above the railway line over quite a long section before the tunnel. To find this worthwhile spot, drive to the end of the service road. There can be few better examples in a single exposure where the cross-stratification that characterizes delta fronts can be seen on such a grand scale. (See text box on sedimentary processes in ch. 2, pp. 52–53.)

Back on the tar road, you are soon in timber plantations again. Some 300 m after a 'Kruger Gate' turn-off to the left, you'll start to see blocks of granite among the trees, the blocks becoming bigger and more plentiful as you go. Just over 1 km further on you're out of the trees and starting to drop into a major east-facing valley, with plenty of granite around. It's worth taking the short drive to Natal Spa with its hot springs, even if it's just to see majestic masses of granite of the Archaean Anhalt Granitoid Suite **(geosite 2, map 15)** (GPS S 27° 31.632', E 30° 51.987'). The granite blocks persist as you head north from the spa to Paulpietersburg.

Hot springs

Natal Spa exists because of an unusually strong thermal spring in the Bivane River valley at that locality. It is the hottest and strongest of a line of tepid (23.8°C) to hot (40.7°C) springs stretching for about 130 km northeastwards from here. The resource has been exploited as the focal point of a substantial tourist resort in this remote area. There are 11 springs (or groups of springs) on an arcuate line, all discharging heated, alkaline water rich in sodium bicarbonate. The Bivane River hot spring was reported by a local farmer in around 1888 and then scientifically described by State Geologist Dr Molengraaff the following year. He noted a distinct 'rotten egg', i.e. hydrogen sulphide, odour. However, it becomes less noticeable when the water is pumped from the ground. Other than the main spring, there are two others at the spa and additional water is brought to the surface via boreholes.

All except one of the line of warm to hot springs are in Archaean granite. The line does not show as a feature on aerial photos or satellite images and may reflect deep-reaching fracturing with practically no displacement related to subtle up-arching of the crust. This, in turn, is thought to be due to convection cells in the asthenosphere. The fracture zones would act as conduits of heat from deeper levels in the crust. Together with the surrounding body of rock through which descending waters pass, the zones would contribute soluble components, such as hydrogen sulphide, which would reach the surface as the water ascends.

To reiterate the point made in respect of the hot-water springs at Montagu (ch. 3): the main requirement for thermal springs is good 'plumbing', to allow water heated at depth by the natural geothermal gradient to be returned to the surface fast enough for the heat not to be dissipated – as is the case here.

A brief detour to the Natal Spa is worth the minutes it takes to see the fine example of Archaean granite in the Bivane valley at the spa.

Now is a good time to make the point that not all the topography we know is sculpted by the rivers of today: some is … well, as old as the hills. Before the start of sedimentation in the Karoo Basin, there were highlands around its edge and they have survived, even if in somewhat modified form. For example, some way to the north of where you are now, the towering slopes of the Mpumalanga escarpment and the hills behind it were high ranges long before the cover formations – like the Karoo – were laid down.

Just after Paulpietersburg, where you rejoin the R33, note the turn-off to the right to Hartland. If you were to follow that road, it would take you down into the Pongola River valley where the sediments and volcanics of the Pongola Supergroup are most widespread. Keep in mind that the conglomerates that carried the gold at Denny Dalton are part of this unit, which can be traced far into Swaziland as well as into equivalent units in the Witwatersrand. You cross the Pongola River 13.5 km north of Paulpietersburg and are now in Mpumalanga. Soon after entering the province, the very weathered outcrops you see on the side of the road are the southern margin of the Commondale Greenstone Belt, which forms a fragment of the proto-crust (3.3 billion years old) into which the granite basement intruded 3.1 billion years ago. The greenstone belt is made up mainly of mafic to ultramafic volcanics (iron-, magnesium- and calcium-rich, silica-poor), with some sediments that form part of the basement to the Pongola sediments. After the greenstone belt outcrops you're on granite, with some dolerite intrusions, until you reach the N2 just east of eMkhondo.

Now you know that eastern Zululand is not only scenically magnificent and full of fascinating history; its geology is every bit as good a reason to choose this route from KwaZulu-Natal to Mpumalanga. Apart from some wonderful exposures of Karoo sediments, it is the extremely ancient geology that makes this much more than just a trip from A to B. The 3.3 billion-year age of the greenstone belt you've just seen is quite extraordinary. At that time in most other cratons, primitive greenstone belts were still being intruded by the first granites. Here, by contrast, the early crust had been formed and was ready to accommodate the first supracrustal formations: the nearly 10 km-thick Pongola Supergroup of lavas and sediments, aged from 3 billion years to slightly younger, was already forming. Consider yourself privileged to have seen it.

One of the geological highlights of this route is the White uMfolozi Inlier, the large area of very ancient formations exposed where the Karoo sediments have been stripped off. The white ridge in the photograph consists of basal Nsuze quartzites near Denny Dalton, deposited very nearly 3 billion years ago.

10 Barberton

GEOLOGICAL OVERVIEW

The oldest rocks in the world are found in and around greenstone belts, and geologists everywhere agree that Barberton is the greenstone belt *par excellence*. They visit Barberton from far and wide, not only for the quality of its three-dimensional exposures, but more particularly for the uniquely complete story it tells and for the remarkable state of preservation of the rocks. In countless instances around the world, far younger rocks have been changed beyond recognition: here you will see aspects of formation so fresh and clear that it is hard to believe their enormous antiquity.

Barberton is situated in an easily accessible part of South Africa, with a benign climate and magnificent scenery. The area boasts the oldest continuously operating gold mines in the country. Many of the names – of mines, creeks and mountain peaks – resonate with history. The natural history is unusually rich and well endowed with endemic species. At the time of writing, an application is being considered for the Barberton Mountain Land (BML) – also known as the Makhonjwa Mountains – to be declared a World Heritage Site (WHS), based mainly on its geological value; let's hope that its status has been resolved by the time you read this.

MSc students from Rhodes University Geology Department examine an iconic outcrop: spinifex texture in komatiite just above the confluence of Spinifex Creek and the nKomati River.

Geology of the route

Before going out to see the amazing geological sites that Barberton offers, let's set the scene by going right back to the very beginning of our planet's history. Around 4.6 billion years ago, nearly 9 billion years after the Big Bang, dust and gas in the outer part of the Milky Way galaxy gathered to form our solar system: the Sun and its planets. Our solar system formed more or less during the last third of 'Universe Time'. Back then, 4.6 billion years ago, the planets were only very approximately as we know them today. Earth was forming by gravitational attraction, pulling smaller bodies together, so that for a while near the beginning it was in a stage of growth. It was solid to start with, but the constant bombardment by other celestial bodies – asteroids and meteorites – generated enough heat by kinetic energy to melt the proto-Earth. Our planet's own internal gravity caused it to separate out into a denser core at the centre and a less dense mantle floating on the outside of the core.

In the chaos of those early times, collision occurred with another very large astral body, possibly about the size of Mars, which was of such force that it vaporised part of the mantle. This vapour went into orbit around the Earth, gradually condensing as it was pulled by gravity into a

The old aerial cableway is still evident in places, which was used for transporting asbestos from the mine at Havelock (now Bulembu) in Swaziland to the railhead in Barberton.

single body, the Moon. It is still by far our nearest neighbour in the galaxy, bound to the Earth by gravity just as we are bound to the Sun. In the context of our solar system, Earth's moon is large compared to its parent planet.

The mantle of the Earth started to solidify as it slowly cooled. Gases were released from the interior of the planet, mainly carbon dioxide, water vapour, methane, carbon monoxide, nitrous oxide, argon, hydrogen and nitrogen; if there was any oxygen present originally, it was a minor component. For the first time the Earth had an atmosphere. As the cooling continued, the water vapour in the atmosphere started to condense and the Earth became encircled with water, a global proto-ocean, in which the very first sedimentary rocks could be deposited. However, we know of such a formation only from a single locality in Greenland.

The still extremely hot and fluid mantle was unstable. Around the globe convection cells brought red-hot mantle material to the surface, where it gave off great amounts of heat before sinking to the depths of the mantle again.

Around 3.5 billion years ago, at what is now Barberton, submarine lavas with an unusual chemical composition erupted from fissures that formed as the mantle's very thin solid skin ruptured – and plate tectonics got under way. These komatiite lavas formed the Earth's first oceanic crust (basal Onverwacht Group, Barberton). The name komatiite is applied to such rocks wherever they occur around the globe, not just within a stone's throw from the river after which they were named.

An artist's impression of Barberton 3.5 billion years ago shows elements referred to in the chapter: (a) a much closer moon rising, (b) felsic volcanic cones, (c) stromatolites, (d) pillow lavas (basalts), (e) black carbonaceous and white chert chemical sediments, (f) siliceous sinter cones and hydrothermal vents, and (g) a shower of meteorites.

MAP 16

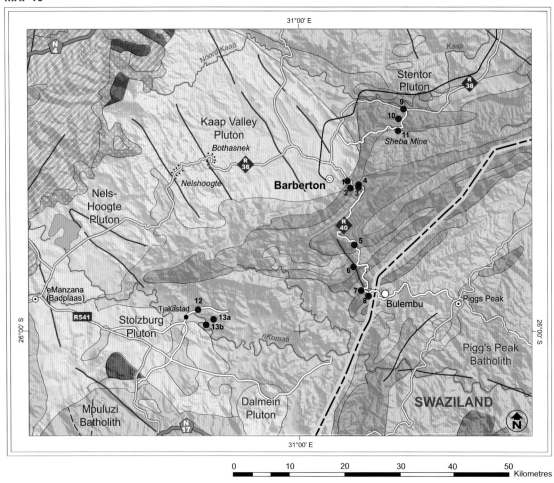

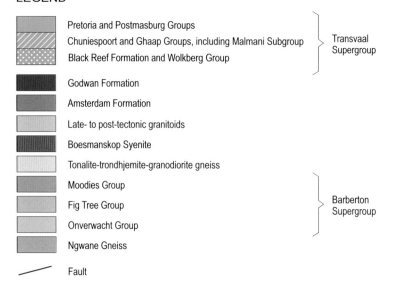

LEGEND

	Pretoria and Postmasburg Groups	
	Chuniespoort and Ghaap Groups, including Malmani Subgroup	Transvaal Supergroup
	Black Reef Formation and Wolkberg Group	

	Godwan Formation
	Amsterdam Formation
	Late- to post-tectonic granitoids
	Boesmanskop Syenite
	Tonalite-trondhjemite-granodiorite gneiss

	Moodies Group	
	Fig Tree Group	Barberton Supergroup
	Onverwacht Group	
	Ngwane Gneiss	

	Fault

As spreading of the sea floor forced the early mantle and thin crust of one plate beneath another, a string of volcanic islands (called an island arc) was formed. Lava poured down the island slopes, and ash and volcanic dust were blasted out, only to shower down as pyroclastic flows. The process went on and on, building substantial thicknesses of material, which we know as the Onverwacht Group. In the mantle, differential melting of minerals with different melting points gave rise to granitoid magma. Being lighter than the surrounding material, this magma rose to form the first plutons around Barberton. (Its component minerals are lighter, the density of granite being 2.8 tonnes per m³ compared with 3.3 of komatiite.) Clastic sediment, formed by chemical weathering and physical erosion of exposed crust, was shed from the first land above the proto-ocean into its near-shore region to build the Fig Tree Group. In the turbulent near-surface environment that still prevailed about 3.2 billion years ago, the first island arcs and associated plutons were pushed together by convection in the mantle to form the earliest microcontinent. Though very different from the vast continents spread over the Earth today, the first semblance of the environment as we know it was coming into being.

BML strata are divided into three subdivisions or groups, which together form the Barberton Supergroup:

Group	Age: old to youngest (Ma = Million years)	Composition and Formation
Moodies	3 225 – 3 215 Ma	Mudrocks, sandstones and conglomerates in alluvial, fluvial, deltaic, shoreline and tidal environment
Fig Tree	3 255 – 3 225 Ma	Sandstones, shales and conglomerates, mostly deposited in deep water; chemical sediments, including chert, banded iron formation, baryte; some volcanic strata
Onverwacht	3 550 – 3 260 Ma	Komatiites and basalts; occur as fine-grained tuffs, pillow lavas, lava flows, breccias; some chert

Nonetheless, it was a very different world from the one we live in. Meteoric bombardment continued unabated in a universe much fuller of diverse debris than today. Volcanic and meteoric dust was thick in the atmosphere, to the extent that you would barely have seen your hand held out in front of you. On an Earth that had not had a solid exterior for very long, oceanic temperatures were still far higher than at present – an estimated 70°C during 'Fig Tree' times. The Moon was only half as far from the Earth as it is now, meaning that tides were much more extreme. The lunar month is estimated to have been a brief 15–18 days.

Barberton Makhonjwa GeoTrail

As you leave your air-conditioned environment, cast your mind back to much, much earlier times, before there were clear blue skies and four-week months. The following route was initially described by the local branch of the Geological Society of South Africa and later by those who prepared the World Heritage Site application – it's called the Barberton Makhonjwa GeoTrail, for which a guide book has been produced. Give yourself a day to do the GeoTrail, reserving another to see some sights for which Barberton is celebrated among geologists around the world, and that are not to be found on the trail.

Herringbone cross-bedding in tidally formed sandstone or tidalite, as seen here, can be used to estimate the length of the lunar cycle at the time the rock was formed.

Your route starts as the R40, so you need to get to the Sheba Road intersection where it crosses the R38, then follow the R40 out of town. Bulembu, where you're heading, is just across the Swaziland border. It's the name given to the old Havelock Asbestos Mine. Higher up the pass, you'll see the by now dilapidated cableway once used for hauling the product from the mine down to Barberton.

In an ironic inversion, as ancient geology and recent geomorphology intersect, the granitoids, which would normally be the most resistant to erosion, have been levelled by erosion and now form part of the Lowveld, leaving the sediments and volcanics of the Barberton Greenstone Belt (BGB) as the imposing hills that tower over Barberton.

The granite of the De Kaap valley in which Barberton is situated is called the Kaap Valley Tonalite and you can see it at 2.5 km out of town **(geosite 1, map 16)** (GPS S 25° 46.208′, E 31° 03.965′). The pale-coloured crystalline tonalite forms the lower part of the cutting, separated from the fine-grained grey volcanic rock of the basal part of the Onverwacht Group by a roughly vertical line that is interpreted as a fault. Keeping in mind that the Onverwacht is the lowest of the three groups that make up the Barberton Sequence, this is a good place to start, especially as the Kaap Valley Tonalite next to it is one of a number of granitoids that for millions of years continued to rise through the crust around the BGB. This contact marks the definitive boundary of the Barberton Supergroup, the geological start of the Archaean greenstone belt rocks.

The next geosite at which you're going to stop is a further 4.4 km along the road, called 'white tidal sandstone' **(geosite 2, map 16)** (GPS S 25° 47.672′, E 31° 05.026′). The sandstone is part of the Moodies Group (the youngest member of the sequence) and the outcrop is well worth the stop. The beds will show you a phenomenon that geologists seldom, if ever, get to see. The beds over which you walk – and look down onto – have been tilted, so you see them side-on, because the folding has turned them through 90° from the horizontal attitude of their deposition. They are beautifully cross-bedded, but most of the bedding is planar and uni-directional, meaning that the direction of flow of the water that deposited the sand was constant. If you look hard, though, here and there you'll see 'herringbone' cross-bedding, where two sets of beds were evidently deposited by water flowing first in one direction and then in the opposite, providing a pattern like a fish skeleton. It is well accepted that the mechanism that produced this result was the ebb and flow in a very ancient coastal lagoon. Such sandstones are given the very descriptive name of 'tidalites'.

The genesis of conglomerates

The white low-lying outcrop stretching back from the road shows tidal sandstones or tidalites. Lower down, in the cutting just before you reach the sandstone, is a good exposure of a very different rock, a conglomerate. Geologists familiar with the environment of formation of the Barberton Greenstone Belt wondered how such a rock had formed. We know that conglomerates are formed in a high-energy milieu. Mostly these are raging rivers from distant highlands, such as deposited the Witwatersrand reefs; less commonly, they are gale-force wind-driven currents like those that gave us our conglomerate-hosted diamond beaches of the Sperrgebiet in Namibia.

Those geologists knew that these most ancient Barberton rocks were formed at a time when the first islands were emerging from the primaeval global ocean, too small for raging rivers, too new for mountains. The conglomerates in this cutting could only have been formed by mega-tides. The moon was much closer and the ocean unimaginably vast, so the tides of those days would have had energy beyond our comprehension, fully as great as the flooded rivers and surging currents of today.

*The angular shape of many of the cobbles in the Moodies Group conglomerate
is a good indication that they have not travelled far from their source.*

Olive Pigeons have been observed scratching kaolinised sediment here with their beaks and duly consuming the 'medicine', thought to counter the toxic effects of bugweed, their preferred food.

Tides exist thanks to the lunar pull on the Earth. Going back 3.5 billion years, lunar months would have lasted just 15–18 days. What is more, there was much less land and much more ocean, so the tidal 'bulge' in the ocean would have been correspondingly greater. What land there was, was flatter, and ranges between high and low tides were substantially greater. Considerably larger areas of land would have been affected by tidal wash than today, particularly during spring tides.

The sandstone here is quite soft, as you can see from the way it is being eroded, and brilliant white; both these characteristics result from the fact that when it was deposited, it was rich in both quartz, which predominates, and the mineral feldspar. Given enough time and the right environment, feldspar weathers to kaolin, a clay mineral prized for its whiteness. In a valley to the east, at a locality you'll visit on a separate drive, similar sediments, in this case unkaolinized, show the same phenomenon with a significantly higher proportion of herringbone cross-bed sets.

After 1.15 km you come to a spot (GPS S 25° 47.692', E 31° 05.659') where Olive Pigeons (*Columba arquatrix*) have scratched the surface of the cutting for the clay it exposes **(geosite 3, map 16)**. They have been observed using their beaks to scrape grooves in the clay, which they eat. Considering that kaolin is used medicinally for its capacity to absorb a wide variety of substances, it is speculated that its ingestion by pigeons may counter toxic effects of bugweed (*Solanum mauritianum*) berries, one of their preferred foods. Bugweed, a declared weed, occurs widely around South Africa, including in the Barberton hills, and human fatalities are known to have occurred after consumption of the berries. Look for the scratchings: they are not difficult to see.

About 150 m on you come to a stop which is another good reason for coming to Barberton **(geosite 4, map 16)** (GPS S 25° 47.640′, E 31° 05.698′). Here, in a piece of the mountain that had to be moved from it's *in situ* locality because there was no place where vehicles could park anywhere nearby, you will see the earliest evidence of life on Earth visible to the naked eye – again in the 3 200–3 150 million-year-old Moodies Group. (The spot is well marked and there is more than adequate parking.) Like the tidalites, the biomats (formed by the settling out of thin layers of algae, or microbes), or algal mats, here are not visually breathtaking. It's what their presence means, though, that cannot but fill you with wonder. Compared to stromatolites in the Transvaal dolomites, a mere 2 500 million years old, these biomats are substantially older.

Like the tidalites, the sediments in which the biomats are found have been tectonically tilted from their original horizontal attitude into a near-vertical position. Look for roughly vertical green-black 'crinkly laminations', which appear quite regularly across the exposure. They may

not look like much, but if you were to see them under a high-powered microscope lens and had the right expertise, you would see that they consist of 'amorphous carbon'. Specialists have shown beyond any doubt that this has been formed by microbes. These organisms would have grown in a hot-water environment incomprehensibly hostile by today's standards, with little or no oxygen and a mix of other chemicals one would hardly expect to support life of any sort, even the most primitive.

Another 4.9 km on **(geosite 5, map 16)** (GPS S 25° 52.683′, E 31° 05.289′) you will see something that's visually more dramatic – the so-called 'Painted Quarry', exposing multi-coloured banded iron formation (BIF) folded into intricate patterns. Unlike the clastic sediments of the Moodies Group seen at the last two geological stops, these chemical sediments belong to the older Fig Tree Group, where precipitated iron oxide and silica (forming chert) are an important part of the unit. The precipitation was in deep water, below the reach of waves and currents, the colours telling of different mineral composition. The red represents iron-rich material; white indicates silica; black shows iron again, as well as some manganese oxides or carbon; and the grey contains volcanic ash or clay.

The very regular alternating of layers seems to indicate that their deposition was seasonal. Their wide extent without significant variation in layer thickness implies that the source of the metals was freely circulating oceanic waters, still acidic enough to be able to hold substantial amounts of metal in

The black layers in this sediment can be seen under very high microscopic magnification to be organic, whence their name 'biomats' or 'algal mats'.

It's not difficult to see why this locality is called the Painted Quarry, where the alternating iron-rich and iron-poor layers have been contorted by tectonism that affected the sediments and volcanics making up the Barberton package.

solution until their precipitation. The extent of lithification when they were folded from their original horizontal attitude is not possible to establish with certainty: apparently they were in a transitional soft or plastic state, to have perfectly preserved their banding without showing significant fracturing.

A remarkable outcrop occurs 4.1 km beyond geosite 5 **(geosite 6, map 16)** (GPS S 25° 54.375', E 31° 05.463'), apparently as restricted in its occurrence as the BIF is widespread. It was only quite recently exposed and identified for the first time during road widening and is the only example known of such a rock type. It requires further study to be adequately explained and understood. In the meantime it is referred to as the 'tsunami deposit'. Considering the unstable character of the Earth, particularly in its early days, events such as tsunamis were probably more commonplace and more powerful than today and would have left traces.

Back to bed

We continue to borrow terms from the bedroom: beds of sandstone, sheets of dolerite, now pillows in lava. When molten lava erupts from fissures on the ocean floor, it happens quite slowly and not in a continuous flow. As a 'pulse' of lava is pumped out, its exterior chills instantly in the cool deep-sea environment, forming a glassy casing around the entire pulse, or 'pillow'. The interior part of the pillow, now shielded from the cold, chills more slowly. Many – perhaps most – of them are about the size, and very roughly the shape, of the pillow on which you rest your head at night. The pillows pile up on top of each other, like marshmallows. As with many geological processes, we don't have to speculate about pillow lavas: we can watch them today forming from active submarine volcanoes off Hawaii and New Zealand. Among these ancient pillows at Bulembu are some monsters, up to over 2 m high, which is bigger than usual. Whatever their size, though, their overall appearance and mode of formation are the same. Once you've got your eye in, they're easy to spot (see image on p. 194).

From here, for a while you continue to see good examples of finely banded chemical sediments in recent road cuttings: BIF and banded chert, in places enriched with the black carbon that was quite a common component of the Archaean oceans. However, it's the lapilli tuff 8.9 km along the road that is the next 'must-see' **(geosite 7, map 16)** (GPS S 25° 56.750', E 31° 06.508'). You've been out of the pine plantations for a while, seeing some spectacular views: now look out for the freshly exposed face of hard dove-grey rock made up of a collection of spherules ranging from the size of a pea downwards. These are called lapilli (from *lapillus*, the Latin for 'little stone') and form from

Primitive tsunamis?

The 'tsunami deposit' is a conglomerate of slabs of banded chert that show no significant rounding; the rock shows no layering but a chaotic distribution of material that, because of its lack of variety, must have been quite locally derived. Nonetheless, the material was transported sufficiently for the original bedding to have been obliterated, but not enough for much reorientation of the broken fragments. It does not look like fault scarp breccia as seen adjacent to a fault exposed to the atmosphere, where there is random orientation of breccia fragments. Nor is it in any way reminiscent of sedimentary conglomerate or pyroclastic agglomerate (a 'conglomerate' formed from solid material derived from a nearby volcano). Its provisional label of 'tsunami deposit' must therefore suffice until fuller geological investigation provides a more plausible explanation. Circumstantial evidence of 'tsunami deposits' has come to light elsewhere in the Fig Tree Group. Such units that appear to capture a specific moment in time rather than the usual continuum are called 'event beds'.

This extraordinary rock has invoked an extraordinary explanation as to its genesis: geologists have postulated that it was formed by the chaotic forces of a tsunami.

Lapilli tuffs are a relatively unusual type of volcanic rock, reflecting the uncommon phenomenon of molten material (either from volcanoes or from meteorite impacts) falling to Earth – or, as in this case, into the ocean – like a cloud of hailstones.

molten material, usually acidic to intermediate in composition, blasted into the atmosphere mostly from volcanoes (less commonly from meteorite impacts). Cooling suddenly, the molten lava solidifies, in exactly the same way as water would freeze in clouds and fall to Earth as hail. Lapilli, being heavier than ice, are not carried up by storm currents to accumulate more material, but grow as hailstones do (in some cases reaching the size of golf balls or bigger). Though spherical (like hailstones), the concentrically banded lapilli are invariably small and quite uniform in size.

In the rock at this locality the lapilli fell into the ocean; this would have resulted, to some extent, in their becoming sorted by size, even if this is hardly perceptible (the water would have been deep and still, with none of the flow necessary to accomplish the sorting seen in, for example, river-borne sediment). The lapilli were subsequently engulfed in chert. This particular unit is called the Msauli Chert and is located in the upper part of the Upper Onverwacht Group.

Even though this is the only locality where you'll see lapilli tuff, it is widespread in the BGB. The GeoTrail is a wonderful route and gives a uniquely valuable insight into the BGB as a whole. It would be too much to expect, though, that the different groupings within the total sequence would be proportionately represented in a single cross-section through the belt. You saw the Lower Onverwacht at the first stop, up against the Kaap Valley Tonalite, and you get a tantalizing glimpse of the Upper Onverwacht as you approach the Swaziland border, but for the rest you have travelled through the Moodies and Fig Tree Groups. These groups between them represent less than half of the whole Barberton succession.

Barberton gold

The Sheba Gold Mine is the area's biggest, having produced a very respectable 120 tonnes of the metal over the 127 years of its operation. The Golden Quarry in the footwall of the Sheba Fault was a super-rich mine, discovered by Edwin Bray in 1885. Over the years there have been 330 mines of all sizes that have produced gold in the area, so there is every reason to associate Barberton with gold mines, whether they were the small pick-and-shovel operations of 140 years ago or the modern, highly mechanized high-tech mines of today.

By the time you reach the Swaziland border you will have seen a good enough sample of the BGB to understand why it is compulsory viewing for students of the Archaean Eon. There is still one remarkable outcrop to see, though – the last geological stop on the Barberton Makhonjwa GeoTrail, 250 m beyond geosite 7 **(geosite 8, map 16)** (GPS S 25° 56.800′, E 31° 06.622′). In the cutting above the road here is a good example of another phenomenon for which Barberton is famous: its pillow lavas, usually of mafic to ultramafic composition, that erupted on the ocean floor.

'Pillows'

As along most of the Barberton Makhonjwa GeoTrail, the road engineers are to be thanked for giving us wonderful exposures we wouldn't otherwise have had, in this case of giant pillows in basaltic lava.

Barberton – Sheba – Spinifex Creek – Barberton

You start again from the Sheba Road intersection, but this time you follow the R38 in a northerly direction towards Kaapmuiden, which is on the N4. Before long you're next to the Suid Kaap River with the railway line close by and, although you stop at two level crossings, you stay south of the river. Quite soon the river is joined by the Noord Kaap to become the Kaap River, before joining the Crocodile a little way down the valley.

The first thing to look at is a conglomerate of the Moodies Group **(geosite 9, map 16)** (GPS S 25° 41.053′, E 31° 09.983′). The road is narrow, so park where there is space to pull off (GPS S 25° 41.076′, E 31° 09.918′) and walk the short distance to the part of the cutting where the conglomerate appears. Conspicuous in this exposure is the elongation of the pebbles and cobbles, all aligned in parallel fashion: this is because all the formations in this part of the fold structure were squeezed against the gneiss of the Stentor Pluton just across the river. The pluton acted as a solid buttress during the folding, causing severe compaction of all units close to it.

Carl Anhaeusser

The compaction and alignment of cobbles seen in the Moodies Group conglomerate in this cutting are caused by squeezing against the solid buttress of the nearby Stentor Pluton.

The same conglomerate as was seen close to the Kaap River, but further from the Stentor Pluton, has not been compressed. This picture was not taken there, but there is a good outcrop at geosite 11.

A little further on, take the Sheba Mine turn-off to the right. Drive exactly 2 km along this road, park under a spreading acacia on the right of the road (GPS S 25° 42.024', E 31° 09.993'), and walk about 100 m down a well-marked path to the river (the Fig Tree Creek). On the opposite side of the stream and easily reached by stepping stones, is a magnificent exposure of the same unit of tidalites you saw in the hills **(geosite 10, map 16)** (GPS S 25° 42.028', E 31° 09.908'). This outcrop, though, has not been intensely kaolinized, apart from which it shows a much better example of herringbone cross-bedding. It is an outcrop to fix in your mind forever.

Another 2.1 km up this road is an outcrop to the left where you can see the same conglomerate you saw on the R38 **(geosite 11, map 16)** (GPS S 25° 42.708', E 31° 09.645'). Note, though, that the clasts show no significant flattening: the reason for the difference between the two outcrops of conglomerate is that this one is well away from the contact with the resistant pluton, and the folding could be accomplished in an unconfined environment – a good example of the infinitely fascinating geological narrative.

Some 2 km further up the road there is a great view of the Sheba Fault and the Eldorado anticline, worth seeing as they're so close. To the right of the road at this spot, look for three pale near-vertical stripes on the slope of the hill: the two on the left mark the anticline, the one on the right the fault, which separates older Fig Tree and Onverwacht Group rocks (to the left of the fault) from Moodies Group formations (to the right).

Now you head back to Barberton and out on the R40 towards Nelspruit, turning left onto the R38 not far out of town. You drive through some wonderful scenery before reaching eManzana (Badplaas), where you should look for the signboard to Tjakastad, which is where you're heading. Drive straight through this village and on the dirt road across the nKomati River, turning right soon after the crossing and following this track for about 1.4 km, or until you get to a spot with GPS co-ordinates S 25° 58'19.96", E 30° 50'09.08", where you can park your car. It's a short walk down to a little stream to the right (south) of the road, which is where you will see some very picturesque pillow lavas in the basalt along the rocky river banks **(geosite 12, map 16)** (GPS S 25° 58.352', E 30° 50.210'). Not all 'pillows' are as well defined – or as photogenic – as these, which is why it's a recommended stop.

To get to a spot that, for some, will be the climax of the whole Barberton journey, drive on along the track for approximately 3.6 km to a little group of houses on the right. There's quite a well-used

The outcrops of tidalite in the bed of the Fig Tree Creek are some of the best to be seen anywhere.

These pillows, seen from above, are a good example of the sort of rock that gave them their descriptive name, well-rounded and of the sort of size you might have on your bed.

track leading between the clusters of buildings to the south, which you take and follow for about 300 m until you find a subsidiary track leading off this to the right (GPS S 25° 58' 33.00", E 30° 52' 18.74"). You can either drive or walk along this track, but it will take you to your destination. About 2.4 km from where this last stretch of track turns off, pick your way down to the stream at the bottom of the valley to your left.

About 1 km further on, this creek joins the nKomati River, so it might not surprise you to find that what you're going to see here **(geosite 13a, map 16)** (GPS S 25° 59.315' 33.00", E 30° 51.502') is komatiite – Earth's first oceanic crust – in its type locality. It was here that it was first encountered and subsequently described by twin brother geologists Morris and Richard Viljoen as they mapped the BML nearly 50 years ago. But it's not only to see a world-famous rock type in such a historical setting – and within a stone's throw from the nKomati River from which it takes its name – that you've hiked down the valley.

The other, more important reason is to find out why this stream is known among geologists as Spinifex Creek. You've come to see what is arguably the most famous texture known to geologists. Spinifex texture not only distinguishes komatiite from any other rock: it tells us a great deal about the conditions under which komatiite formed. There are two localities on the creek where the texture can be seen, the better example about 900 m down the valley **(geosite 13b, map 16)** (GPS S 25° 59.559' 33.00", E 30° 51.091') from the first and higher one.

nKomati River meets Spinifex Creek

While the name of the lava at this locality comes from the big nKomati River not far below you, the texture so beautifully shown in the Spinifex Creek outcrops was named by Australian geologists when it was first encountered at an exposure in Western Australia. The long olivine crystals that give the rock its characteristic appearance reminded them of the growth form of spinifex, a type of spiky Australian (and Indonesian) grass, and they called it 'spinifex texture'.

Komatiites may have this unique texture (they don't all show it) because they are unique rocks. Whereas basalt, when erupted, normally has a temperature of 1 100–1 250°C, komatiite has been calculated to have erupted at a fiery 1 600°C. As a consequence, it would have been extremely fluid, forming very thin layers except where it accumulated as pools in depressions in the surface over which it flowed.

The effect you see on a weathered surface is usually the most dramatic, because the olivine crystals have been weathered out of the rock, leaving casts of negative relief, often quite deep and exaggerating the effect. That is why it is distressing to see so many examples of broken surfaces in Spinifex Creek, the damage done either by collectors wanting a specimen or by photographers in search of a better picture. A picture of a really remarkable patch of outcrop is better than any sample, and the weathered surface gives the most pleasing picture. Don't vandalize these famous outcrops any more than they have already been damaged.

So, with memories of spiky-grass texture from Earth's first oceanic crust fresh in your mind, the whirlwind tour through Barberton and its environs is brought to a close with the hope that it has etched impressions into your memory that will be with you forever. You have been back to the beginning of Earth's recorded time. You've had a glimpse of phenomena, deep in the Archaean, that set the stage for later developments, and were never to be repeated. After its infancy, the planet would start to show how a few geological themes would repeat themselves again and again.

The locality on the slope above the confluence of Spinifex Creek and the nKomati River provides some wonderful examples of the texture that gives the creek its name.

11 R572/R521: including Mapungubwe

GEOLOGICAL OVERVIEW

Most readers open at this page are probably *en route* to the Mapungubwe World Heritage Site, a fine destination, and there's plenty of geology worth seeing too. The route offered here takes you off the N1 just north of Musina, proceeding westwards until you get to Mapungubwe, from there carrying on to the west, then south and back on the R572/R521 via Alldays to the N1 at Polokwane. Up near the Limpopo River you'll see highly deformed and metamorphosed – and very ancient – rocks. You'll also see a river confluence that is testimony to an extraordinary geological phenomenon as young as the rocks through which it cuts are old. Almost from start to finish you'll catch glimpses of sediments and lavas from a far-flung outlier of the Karoo Supergroup that are strikingly different from the exposures of Karoo sediments and lavas you are used to seeing further south. There are mines to be seen, too. You'll get a distant glimpse of South Africa's biggest diamond producer, De Beers' Venetia Mine, and you'll travel near some monster coalfields, whose proximity to the hallowed Mapungubwe site is problematic.

With its rich historical legacy and some fascinating geology, the Mapungubwe World Heritage Site, symbolized by the golden rhino that was found there, will be a highlight of the trip.

Geology of the route

Musina to Polokwane

To get from Musina to the World Heritage Site, you take the R572, travelling in a westerly direction. This way, you will continue across the Limpopo Belt (formerly known as the Limpopo Mobile Belt), which you crossed as you approached Musina on the N1. The Limpopo Belt is sandwiched between the Kaapvaal Craton in South Africa and its northern neighbour, the Zimbabwe Craton.

Immediately after you've turned off the N1 onto the R572, you will see quite prominent koppies to your right that look like the typical granite or granite-gneiss koppies in the lowveld, or like those commonly seen in Zimbabwe. You drive through some low cuttings, and koppies of gneiss – both small and not-so-small – are quite common to start with. The Bulai Gneiss, particularly, makes conspicuous barren, dark brown exfoliation domes and whaleback koppies, mainly to the north of the road.

The first noteworthy change is just after 60 km from the turn-off, where, in contrast to the rounded shapes you've been seeing, the koppie 50 m to your right has a flattish top and appears horizontally layered. That's because it's Karoo sandstone. It's a far cry, though, from the Karoo sandstone that makes up the mesas in the Karoo or on the Highveld. This is not surprising: you're a long way from those places, in a different sedimentary basin called the Tuli Basin. The Clarens sandstones you're looking at here are not very different from those around the Drakensberg far to the south, with bedding not easily discernible and tending to make caves and overhangs. Wherever they occur, Clarens sediments reflect deposition in conditions of extreme aridity (as prevailed at the time of deposition), not unlike in the present-day Sahara, and immediately precede the widespread eruption of basalt.

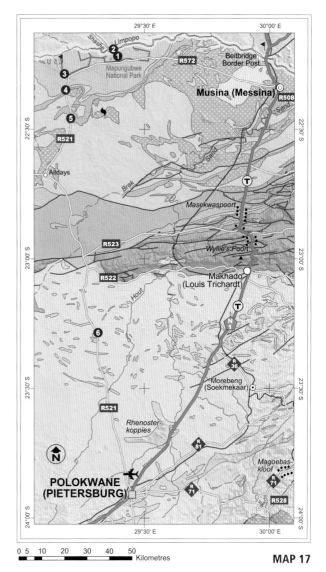

MAP 17

Mapungubwe

For many decades South Africans visiting Zimbabwe (the former Rhodesia) wandered wide-eyed, cameras clicking, around the Zimbabwe Ruins, now known as Great Zimbabwe, little dreaming that there was a historical site of equal importance in our own country: Mapungubwe.

It is held that the finely designed and more elaborate structural remains at Great Zimbabwe were a consequence of their having been built later than those south of the Limpopo, where you are now. Between the occupancy of Mapungubwe and Great Zimbabwe, building skills had been honed, it is argued. That's very conceivably only part of the reason: another was that the later builders had access to far more suitable building material. Igneous rocks, like the granite that was used in Zimbabwe, have the convenient tendency to exfoliate in the right climatic and geomorphological environment. You see them 'peeling off' in big, slightly curved slabs, a few to a few tens of centimetres thick, and can be easily broken to make excellent building blocks. The sandstone used in earlier, more southerly Mapungubwe offered no such facility, even if it was found to be soft enough to be easily bored into for anchoring purposes.

Mapungubwe has produced the most prolific archaeological gold collection in sub-Saharan Africa, now kept in the Mapungubwe Collection in the Museum at the University of Pretoria. Like most cratons, those of Zimbabwe and the Kaapvaal have been well endowed with the yellow metal and even in prehistory were important producers.

After the Stone Age hunters of the game herds that frequented the Limpopo valley, came those of the Iron Age, estimated to have been in the area around 500 AD. The earlier hunter-gatherers left us their stone tools and etchings; from the Iron Age people we have iron tools and clay pots. Some hundreds of years later, well-organized and apparently sophisticated farming communities established themselves in the valley. It is estimated that the nearby valley site, known as K2, was occupied first between AD 1030 and 1220. Mapungubwe itself, strategically located on a prominent small plateau, was inhabited after that until about AD 1290.

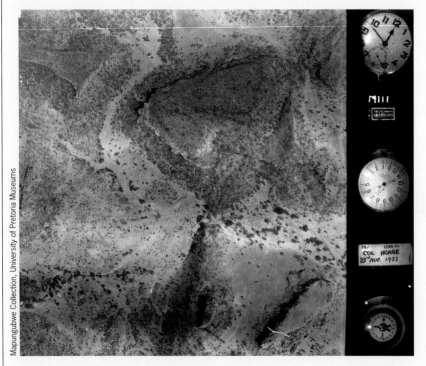

Mapungubwe Hill is in the bottom right of this historic air-photo, taken over 80 years ago as part of an aerial survey flown by the RAF. At the time, Jan Smuts was campaigning to have the area included in what we today would call a Transfrontier Park.

From exotic relics such as glass beads one gets a tantalizing glimpse of an active trade with countries such as Egypt and India, whose main interest would have been in ivory. Bones of cattle, sheep, goats and dogs have all been found here, these animals brought southwards over the centuries from North Africa and, earlier still, from the Fertile Crescent in and around Mesopotamia. It is known that the Mapungubwean diet included sorghum, millet and beans, and that the people harvested wild cotton. Apart from the most highly prized gold, copper and iron were also mined and smelted in outlying areas. Ivory was worked into beads and other ornaments. Clay was moulded and fired into pots as well as into ornamental figurines of people and animals, including a giraffe, and into useful small household items such as spoons and funnels. There is abundant evidence of a highly evolved civilization. It's not clear what happened after the move to Great Zimbabwe to have thwarted its continued development.

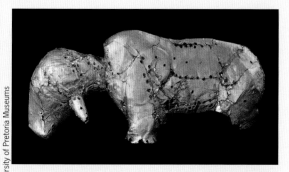

LEFT: *Among the many gold artifacts found was this gold foil-covered bovine, reminding us that then, as now, cattle were a powerful symbol of wealth.*

BELOW LEFT: *These glass beads, from the Indies, Arabia or North Africa, attest to international trade actively under way 1 000 years ago and penetrating deep into the subcontinent.*

BOTTOM LEFT AND BELOW: *The Clarens sandstone offered the early settlers easy opportunity for scraping holes in it for both practical and recreational purposes.*

Both photographs: Mapungubwe Collection, University of Pretoria Museums

Low whalebacks of gneiss like this are a common sight in the basement country of these parts.

A most unusual belt

To simplify Precambrian geology, one could say that the continental crust comprises cratons separated or surrounded by mobile or orogenic belts. The Limpopo Belt is unusual in that it's by no means a classical mobile belt – hence the name change from Limpopo Mobile Belt. It's narrower than is usual, it's older, with some sediments laid down 3.4 billion years ago or even earlier, and it's much more complicated. Typical orogenic belts, such as our Namaqua-Natal Province, consist of wide expanses of metamorphosed and tectonized sedimentary, volcanic and intrusive rocks, where the geological history can mostly be successfully worked out, although sometimes with considerable difficulty. By contrast, the grade of the metamorphism in the Limpopo Belt is extremely high and the trends of the fold patterns defy explanation using normal criteria. However, geologists continue to study the phenomenon, and are sure to find an explanation for the processes involved in due course.

The sandstones found in the main Karoo Basin belong mostly to the Ecca and Beaufort Groups. Here in Limpopo Province, rocks of equivalent age are barely evident. By far the majority you'll see, the Clarens sandstones, are younger, further south only preserved under the basalt or where the basalt has recently been stripped off. The flat-topped koppie referred to above is the first suggestion of something younger than the Limpopo Belt metamorphics. Once in the Mapungubwe National Park and World Heritage Site, you'll be on the slopes leading down to the Limpopo River with plenty of outcrop close by **(geosite 1, map 17)** (GPS S 22° 12.701', E 29° 23.231').

At the Heritage Site, the outcrop comprises almost entirely buff-coloured, fine-grained sandstone of the Clarens Formation that you've been seeing for a while, with flattish-topped koppies persisting. The most conspicuous of these is at the mesa that is the focus of the World Heritage Site. This, strictly, is Mapungubwe, though the name tends to be used to describe the wider area occupied by the early indigenous settlers who left such a rich legacy of their craft.

Don't spend too much time looking for bedding in the sandstones here: just accept that it's barely discernible.
In the exposure shown in the inset, close-up viewing shows that there is, in fact, bedding to be seen.

From the northern edge of this small plateau, you cannot help noticing a prominent black wall a few hundred metres to the northwest – it will most likely be pointed out to you. Although it's difficult to believe, this narrow vertically sided wall is not man-made – it is a dyke of Karoo dolerite, standing quite a few metres above the valley floor. Back near the main road, there is more dolerite between the parking lot of the Visitors' Centre and the centre itself. Make sure you have a look at it because it is truly an unusual manifestation of Karoo igneous activity, with large phenocrysts of plagioclase giving the rock a very unusual eye-catching texture.

The strategic value of Mapungubwe Hill in the Limpopo valley is clear. It was regarded
as a sacred place by early inhabitants, and many artifacts were found there, indicating
the existence of a flourishing civilization in the region some 1 000 years ago.

Mapungubwe Collection, University of Pretoria Museums

If you have time to drive around the park, make sure you visit the lookout decks down on the Limpopo River for an extraordinary geological phenomenon **(geosite 2, map 17)** (GPS S 22° 11.804′, E 29° 22.289′). The Limpopo, immortalized by English poet and story writer Rudyard Kipling, may indeed be a 'great grey-green, greasy river' where one crosses it a little way downstream at Beit Bridge. The lookout decks here show you the point at which it becomes great. What you see from the decks is, in fact, the confluence of two rivers: hard on your left, the grey-green perennial stream of the Limpopo in its 100 m-wide sandy bed hardly seems to warrant the name 'river'; but coming in from the north and continuing its bed after joining the Limpopo is a ribbon of sand four times as wide. This is the Shashe River but, unlike the Limpopo, it is dry most of the time. It comes out of the Kalahari, known for its expanses of sandy savanna rather than its mighty rivers.

So the Limpopo River below its confluence flows on a bed and in a valley created by the Shashe. Although now flowing only after sustained heavy rain in its headwaters, the Shashe River was once part of a system that collected its supply of annual rainwater from a vast part of Central Africa. It did so via the Upper Zambezi, after it had been joined by the Kafue and Luangwa rivers. Only recently, in geological terms, did the Lower Zambezi, entering the Indian Ocean in far northern Mozambique (as it still does), capture the headwaters of those giant Central African rivers. Cutting back a deep valley from the coast, the Lower Zambezi penetrated deeper and deeper into Central Africa until it intercepted the shallower valley of the Upper Zambezi, leaving what we now know as the Shashe River high and dry. In much more humid geological times, central Botswana was an area of great lakes. The palaeo-Lake Makgadikgadi was never as deep as the Great Lakes of Central Africa today but comparable in surface area, and for a long time the water from these parts entered the ocean via the Limpopo River.

The dolerite dyke conspicuous to the north of Mapungubwe Hill is extraordinary both for its steep sides and the extent to which it stands above the surrounding terrain, especially considering how narrow it is.
INSET: *The rock itself is also remarkably unlike the normal Karoo dolerite, showing an atypical porphyritic texture with plagioclase phenocrysts of 1 cm long that give it a very striking appearance.*

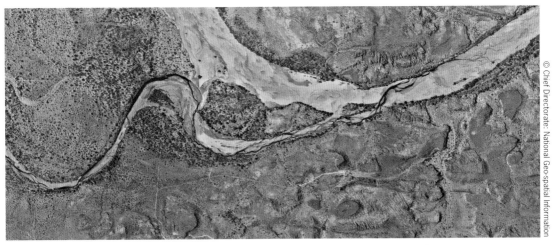

This aerial view of the Shashe-Limpopo confluence vividly illustrates the relatively junior status of the latter river in (geologically) bygone times.

Though more difficult to capture photographically, the vista from the riverside makes the point that the Shashe River is a shadow of its former self, when it was fed by a vast catchment area, and carved out an impressively wide valley.

Once out of the park and continuing westwards along the R572, for a short while you get good views down into the Limpopo valley before you're past the tributary valley. You still see high-standing bluffs of sandstone for quite a distance, all the way to the R521. Some 9 km west of the gate of the Mapungubwe National Park you enter a broad valley with prominent sandstone mesas. About 8 km further is the Little Muck Lodge Gate to the De Beers Venetia Nature Reserve on your right, soon followed by the Hilda Gate to your left, these the first of a number of entrances to the company's 33 000-hectare reserve that you'll see for a while.

If you haven't stopped at Mapungubwe, this picnic site (just up the R521 from where the R572 joins it)
offers an excellent close-up look at Clarens Formation sandstone (formerly the Cave Sandstone).

Less than 5 km past these gates you're at the R521 T-junction, where the road heads north to the Botswana border post at Pontdrift or south towards Alldays, which is the direction you'll be taking. If by any chance you didn't go into the Mapungubwe Park and want to see the Clarens sandstone close up, you could turn right here to the rest-stop point 750 m north of the T, where there is a very fine tor of sandstone **(geosite 3, map 17)** (GPS S 22° 17.503′, E 29° 11.692′). Otherwise, turn left and head south along the R521. Some 500 m south of the T-junction is a low cutting under a sandstone koppie where the basal part of the Clarens Formation, the Red Rocks Member, is well exposed. It shows diagnostic calcareous concretions ranging in diameter from around 1–10 cm. They're unusual in sometimes having fine crystals of calcite in the centre. The grey to mauve sandstone is very fine-grained and devoid of any visible bedding.

From here, keep in mind that the numbering of the kilometre marker plates runs from south to north and that as you travel southwards, the numbers get smaller. To get a good idea of some of the different kinds of sediment found in the so-called Tuli Basin (of the Karoo sedimentary domain), in which you are now, examine the low cutting on the right at 88.5 km **(geosite 4, map 17)** (GPS S 22° 20.130′, E 29° 11.880′) for some good examples of a thin bed of pebble conglomerate, a rarity in Karoo sediments. You can see more of it across the road reserve fence.

After this, you're on gneiss of the Limpopo Belt for a while, which forms the basement to the Karoo sediments. There is an exposure of it to the left of the road in a cutting at 83.3 km and a good exposure of swirling pink and dark grey gneiss immediately after you've crossed a large bridge over a sandy river bed, at 82.1 km. About 4 km after the conspicuous Evangelina Game Lodge entrance and the De Beers Regina Gate on the left, just as you come out of a gentle curve to the right, you will see all the superstructures of the Venetia Mine on your left.

At the 75.8 marker plate, note the massive to faintly bedded brown-weathering sandstone in and above the low road cutting **(geosite 5, map 17)** (GPS S 22° 26.784′, E 29° 12.792′). You're back in Karoo sediments, these of the lower part of the sequence, which you haven't seen before on this trip. This part of the Karoo sequence contains coal seams south of the Limpopo River, immediately east of the Mapungubwe National Park. At the time of writing there had been no final definitive ruling by the government as to whether mining of what are apparently viable deposits of coking coal would be allowed to continue. The huge and unique historical significance of the World Heritage Site has to be balanced against the implications for job creation and the revenue stream that would make a vast difference to the treasury of one of the country's poorest provinces. The two interests appear to be in direct conflict: time will tell whether an imaginative solution is found.

Soon you're back travelling over basement with gneiss koppies and loose blocks occasionally evident, and then you're in Alldays. After this you're on the home straight to Polokwane.

Just over 4 km out of Alldays you start the descent into a wide valley with a high hilly massif on the horizon ahead of you. This is the western end of Soutpansberg, the major mountain range of the Limpopo Province. Its resistant, roughly 1.8 billion-year-old quartzites and basalts overlie the tectonic boundary between the Limpopo Belt (which you are leaving now) and the Kaapvaal Craton. A little later the road swings round to pass south of the hills. After another 5 km you leave the higher thorn scrub for much lower vegetation and you can see another high massif to your right: this is Blouberg Mountain, comprising mainly Soutpansberg Group sediments overlying those of the older, steeply dipping Blouberg Formation (2 000–1 900 million years old).

Some 400 m after you have passed the 27 km post, there are blocks of very dark basalt in the road reserve near the fence on the left. If you look hard, you'll see tiny chips of agate, evidently from amygdales in the lava. You're travelling over the Letaba Formation, the local representative of the

Conglomerates, even small-pebble conglomerates, are a great rarity in the
Ecca Group elsewhere in the country, which is why these are worth seeing.

Venetia Mine

This is South Africa's biggest diamond producer and the main De Beers operation in the country, for over three decades a growing open-pit mine. Today it's no longer cost-effective to continue stripping waste to get down to the deep kimberlite ore, so mining is continuing underground.

The Venetia Mine, named after the farm on which it is located, is unusual in several respects. It was discovered only recently, in 1980, in a not very remote part of a country intensively explored for diamonds, some time after Botswana's Orapa had been found in a far more difficult environment, logistically and geographically. And, at 520–530 million years, the rocks are far older than most southern African diamond-bearing kimberlites. Nevertheless, young or old, it yields a steady stream of beautiful diamonds.

If you could get close to the Venetia Mine this is the view you might get of the plant.

lavas that cap the Drakensberg. As is common when travelling over basalt in the central plateau of southern Africa, the countryside is extremely flat. Some kilometres beyond that first sighting you will see more basalt blocks to the right (south) of the road and in the lands where farmers have cleared the rocks for crops. Some quartzitic sandstone, interbedded with the lavas, is quite common in the heaps.

After passing through the village of Vivo, keep an eye open for the regular 200 m-distance marker plates (still counting down) along the R521, which will see you to Polokwane. From a little before R521-2: 27.4N you will see large blocks of rock strewn over the surface to the right of the road. If you're not in a hurry, stop to look at a particularly handsome coarse- to fine-grained black to grey metapelitic gneiss. It persists to the Schiermonikoog turn-off and comes from a slice of the so-called Bandelierkop Complex folded into the Goudplaats-Hout River Gneiss (part of the Kaapvaal Craton), which is the predominant rock in the area, even if you don't see much of it.

Opposite the 7.6 marker plate and directly across from the 'Hugenoot Stoet' farm, but evident well before then, you'll indeed find this gneiss making a beautifully rounded dome so typical of granite and gneiss country (**geosite 6, map 17**) (GPS S 23° 17.215', E 29° 18.978'). After that, and also quite conspicuous for a while to the right of your direction of travel, is an elongate ridge with its highest peak quite close to the road. It is made up of resistant rocks including magnetite quartzite, amphibolite and calc-silicate, and is the most westerly, strongly attenuated part of the Rhenosterkoppies Greenstone Belt.

Few, if any, exposures of angular unconformities can compare with this one between the steeply dipping Blouberg Formation and the subhorizontal Waterberg Group. Geologists might detour to see this, turning off the R521 at Dendron and passing through the village of Bochum to GPS point S 23° 09.231', E 28° 42.147', for parking, and S 23° 09.453', E 28° 42.115' to view the unconformity. The distance, all on tarred road, is approximately 77 km.

Soon you're in Polokwane. Looking back, you can reflect on the fascinating geological setting for an iconic World Heritage Site as well as on a range of interesting snapshots from the earliest days of our geological history. And the story of how the Limpopo got its valley would have done Rudyard Kipling proud.

You finish, as you started, with an archetypal bushveld scene: a beautifully rounded gneiss dome, this of Goudplaats-Hout River Gneiss.

12 N18: N12 to Botswana

GEOLOGICAL OVERVIEW

Leaving the N12 not far north of the historical diamond capital of the world, Kimberley, and finishing at the Botswana border post closest to the world's biggest diamond producer, Jwaneng Mine, this route is in diamond country from start to finish. With these two locations, Kimberley and Jwaneng, both owing their production to kimberlites, not to secondary or alluvial deposits, it's fair to say that the entire route is on the Kaapvaal Craton. With one or two far-away exceptions, diamond-bearing kimberlites have been erupted through the ancient, deep-seated, stable continental nuclei called cratons.

The condition of the ancient Ventersdorp and Transvaal Supergroups that you cross for most of the way on this route is almost as it was when these groupings were first formed. The only deformed and metamorphosed rocks you'll see are tiny slivers of the even more ancient Kraaipan Greenstone Terrain, which is part of the craton, and you'll travel between the dumps of the Kalgold Mine, located in one such fragment. You'll go through Taung, a celebrated locale in terms of South Africa's palaeoanthropology. A little further north you'll pass Tiger Kloof, an educational institution with beautiful buildings of local stone.

White tufa is prized as a raw material for cement manufacture, and also has the valuable property of entombing bones for later discovery, which was the case here at the Australopithecus *discovery site near Taung.*

Geology of the route

Warrenton to Vryburg

Warrenton, where the route starts, is situated on Ventersdorp lavas known as andesite. These rocks are of intermediate composition, as opposed to those that are acidic (e.g. rhyolite) or basic (e.g. basalt). Andesite is well represented in the entirely volcanic Andes ranges in South America, as it is in the Ventersdorp Supergroup.

Heading north on the N18 and after crossing the Vaal River on the low-level bridge (immediately upstream of the new bridge, still to be completed at the time of writing), there are outcrops on both sides of the road. These are by far the best you'll see in terrain that is mostly flat to very mildly undulating, with few road cuttings. The rocks are amygdaloidal, with agate and crystalline apple-green epidote most conspicuous in the amygdales. Though the rock is mostly grey, barely tinged with green, there are vaguely defined patches of outcrop where the groundmass, enriched with epidote, carries a strong suggestion of the characteristic bright green colour of that mineral **(geosite 1, map 18)** (GPS S 28° 03.873', E 24° 50.127'). After leaving the slight valley of the Vaal, you'll see scattered loose blocks of lava, some quite large, on the surface within the road reserve until you drop into the Harts River valley. These blocks are a sign that you're travelling over shallowly buried Ventersdorp volcanics, including some basalt. In fact, though there's nothing to see on the surface, the Ventersdorp suboutcrop persists from here to well after Taung.

The stratigraphic column at the beginning of the book shows that the predominantly volcanic Ventersdorp Supergroup is sandwiched between two of South Africa's most important sedimentary groupings, the Witwatersrand and the Transvaal Supergroups (with major unconformities between the elements in the 'sandwich'). It is the filling of the sandwich that is substantially the most extensive volcanic sequence on the Kaapvaal Craton.

MAP 18

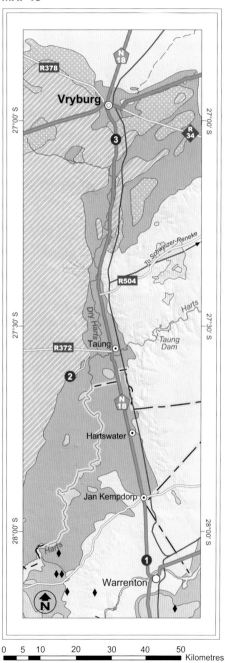

0 5 10   20   30   40   50
Kilometres

Andesite from the Ventersdorp Supergroup is often an unusual and attractive grass-green colour, derived from the mineral epidote, found in lavas and metamorphic rocks.

Heading north from Warrenton, keep an eye open for the canals bringing water from the Vaal River to the Vaal-Harts Scheme, one of the country's big irrigation projects, the first at marker plate N18-1: 2.2N, another at 16.0N. In the Harts valley you'll see orchard after orchard of pecan nut trees and smaller fields of other crops. The canal system distributes water from a weir in the Vaal River to the extensive and extremely level alluvial flats of its main local tributary, the Harts. Apart from the agricultural contribution of the valley, this wide river bed is a dramatic indicator of past climates that were very different from those of today. In wetter climes, the Harts and its junior tributary, the Dry Harts, must have comprised a powerful river system to have shaped a valley as mature as the one where the Vaal-Harts farms are now. Today the two rivers are mere shadows of anything that could have created flats like these.

You'll see the Harts River as you enter Taung. If there were alluvial (i.e. river-borne) gravels above the river level, it might be worth stopping to have a look, but all you would see is sand. At places up- and downstream, boulder and cobble gravels are visible above the water and it is easy to understand why this area has tempted diamond-diggers for many decades. As with any diamond-bearing river, there are beds of alluvial gravel at a distance from the present course of the Harts River – testifying to an ancient history when it meandered elsewhere. Not far upstream of Taung, the valley of the Harts River has been dammed, with areas of earlier diamond diggings now deep under water. Above the dam, towards Schweizer-Reneke, diggers still work the gravels. A 250-carat stone, about the size of a large pigeon's egg, has apparently been recovered quite recently from the Harts River not far above the dam.

But it is not for its diamonds that Taung is best known. In 1924, a skull from a limestone quarry **(geosite 2, map 18)** (GPS S 27° 37.142', E 24° 37.977') up the hill from the mining village of Buxton (subsequently Norlim), west of Taung, was sent to a professor at the University of the Witwatersrand (see text box on *The missing link*, p. 212).

The skull might have lain undiscovered were it not for the fact that the area was being mined for its limestone, in itself an interesting geological tale. Around Taung, the ground to the west of the Harts River valley forms a low but continuous escarpment – the Ghaap (Plateau) Escarpment. About 50 km due west of Taung, well onto the plateau, is the village of Reivilo after which the main formation underlying the plateau has been named. The Reivilo Formation (part of the Ghaap Group) consists mainly of dolomite, a magnesium-rich limestone of little interest to cement manufacturers, whose primary requirement is pure-calcium limestone. In a valley breaching the escarpment near Taung, though, the subterranean seepage during a wetter time in our past deposited significant quantities of the monomineralic rock called tufa. Forming a multilayered crust over the break of the scarp, it is pure calcium carbonate, highly desirable for the cement industry, and it formed the *raison d'être* of a thriving mining operation and community for many years. More important, though, it gave us the Taung skull.

This is the part of the Taung quarry where the skull was found that would soon make world history.

The missing link

Early in 1925, the name Taung leapt into the public domain, both via the scientific journal Nature and local daily newspapers. The fossil skull of a child had been found embedded in the bedrock of a lime quarry near the hitherto unknown village of Taung. It had been sent to Wits University anatomy professor, Raymond Dart, newly arrived from University College, London, who had shown interest in earlier material he had seen from Taung. He claimed that the skull had belonged to a species of proto-hominid he proposed be called Australopithecus africanus – austral *from the Latin for 'southern' and* pithecus *from the Greek for 'monkey' or 'ape'.*

The material he sent in support of his paper for Nature was shown by its editor to four respected specialists in London. Their reaction ranged from sceptical to cynical. However, Dart soon found he was not alone. He was joined in his excitement at the Taung find by fellow anatomy specialist and anthropologist, Dr Robert Broom, a medical doctor and avid palaeontologist who published prolifically in scientific journals. But the tide started to turn only in 1936 when fossil skulls similar to that from Taung were found by the two men and their students at and around Sterkfontein outside Johannesburg. A growing number of American and British palaeoanthropologists found the weight of evidence for australopithecines as ancestors of Homo species too compelling to question any longer. In 1947, 22 years after Dart's realization of the significance of the Taung discovery, Broom found and identified 'Mrs Ples', an adult version of the Taung child, in the Sterkfontein caves. Raymond Dart had been vindicated at last.

But let the last words on the subject be those of Dart's protégé, the revered Professor Phillip Tobias: '... Dart's Taung discovery and what he made of it, will be remembered as the most fundamental single breakthrough in the history of palaeoanthropology.' What a legacy! Drive slowly past Taung.

Dr Raymond Dart holds the skull that would rocket his name into headlines in South African newspapers and scientific journals worldwide.

Bruce Rubidge (Bernard Price Institute for Palaeontology, University of Witwatersrand)

The reason the limestone of tufa deposits such as those at Buxton/Norlim, Sterkfontein and Makapansgat could yield so many fossil treasures is that fossils form quickly. The very ancient primary limestone and dolomite found at all those localities are all from 2 500 million-year-old dolomite formations in the extensive Transvaal Supergroup. The limestone dissolves easily and formation of the secondary limestone when the calcium carbonate precipitates is fast enough to entomb fossils of a wide variety, including the vitally important australopithecines. That the secondary limestone is prized by cement manufacturers, who excavated the first remains, is pure serendipity.

After passing the Dry Harts siding – the railway line is close by to your right – you are off the Ventersdorp Supergroup and onto the overlying (i.e. younger) Ghaap Group of the Transvaal Supergroup, which forms a continuous line of hills to your right. The loose blocks on the surface near the road reserve fence are mostly dolomite, though some andesitic lava is also represented in this unit.

About 55 km north of Taung, look for the Tiger Kloof school **(geosite 3, map 18)** (GPS S 27° 03.126′, E 24° 45.362′). The complex of stone buildings is just behind the railway line, next to the road on the right. In the quarry in the valley behind the school are picturesque examples of the stromatolites so characteristic of Transvaal Supergroup dolomites. Many of the blocks of which the magnificent chapel on the school grounds is built contain small stromatolites, allowing one to view these organisms side-on, which is not always possible in the field. A geologist may have mixed feelings about seeing many of the blocks 'upside down', but how was a mason receiving building material from the quarry to know which way was up?

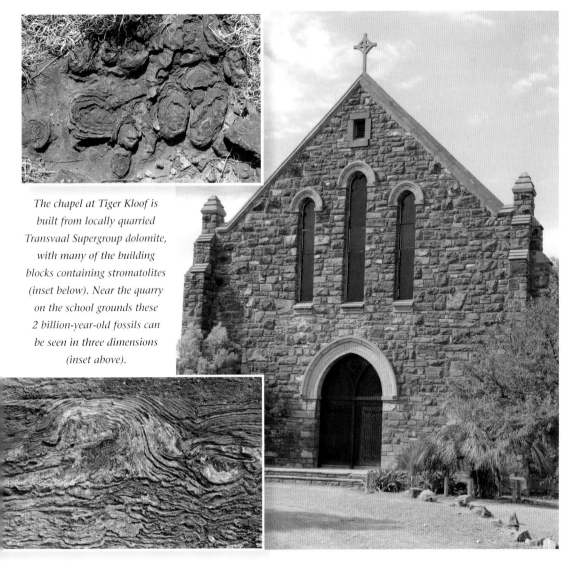

The chapel at Tiger Kloof is built from locally quarried Transvaal Supergroup dolomite, with many of the building blocks containing stromatolites (inset below). Near the quarry on the school grounds these 2 billion-year-old fossils can be seen in three dimensions (inset above).

Vryburg to Ramatlabama

As you approach Vryburg, the country starts to flatten out, and to the north of the town there are wide expanses where it is as flat as a billiard table. This very mature topography is quite common towards the Kalahari Basin. There are occasional low cuttings just south of Vryburg, one of which, after marker plate N18-3: 43.4, shows a good example of the quartzite interbedded with the dolomite **(geosite 1, map 19)** (GPS S 27° 00.313', E 24° 44.851'). Any loose blocks of andesite you might see are from flows of this lava interlayered with sediments of the Transvaal Supergroup. After Vryburg you're going down in the stratigraphy and are on the Ventersdorp Supergroup again, with loose andesite on the surface.

Approaching the next town after Vryburg, Stella, you catch a glimpse of quite a large flat-floored pan to the right of the road. Such pans are a common feature in the mature topography in the interior of South Africa, particularly in the drier parts (for a description of the

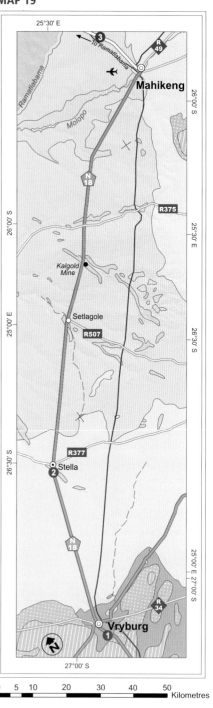

MAP 19

LEFT *Most of the Transvaal Supergroup sediments in these parts are dolomite, but cross-bedded sandstone may also be seen.*

The blocks of BIF (see inset), dramatically banded, show the rotation that took place during creep down the slope that formed during faulting.

formation of pans, see p. 237 in *Geological Journeys*). In the first cutting as you enter Stella, close to the pan, you can see a spectacular example of a fault scarp breccia. The fragments it contains are of strikingly banded iron formation, the banding demonstrating the randomized orientation of the blocks in the most dramatic fashion. Make sure you stop at this cutting, with the N18-4: 45.6N marker plate at the end of it **(geosite 2, map 19)** (GPS S 26° 34.400', E 24° 51.719'). The breccia is part of the first of two thin belts of Archaean 'greenstone' (comprising a range of sedimentary and volcanic rocks) that protrude through the Ventersdorp lavas from here to Mahikeng.

You get a hint of the second greenstone cordon as you breast a rise 36 km north of Stella. Not far ahead is the village of Setlagole, and in the far distance and just to the right of your direction of travel is the unmistakable flat top of a low mine dump. But before you move onto this so-called Kraaipan Greenstone Belt, be aware that Setlagole itself may at some time in the future have its own claim to fame – see text box on p. 216.

The oldest impact structure on Earth?

A recent geophysical survey between Mahikeng and Vryburg showed a conspicuous magnetic feature centred about 15 km southeast of Setlagole. By itself, it would have mystified geophysicists and geologists. However, coupled with some extraordinary rock outcrops just northwest of the village, interpretation of the magnetic structure as an astrobleme impact crater became tantalizing. The rock in the outcrops, described as a megabreccia, was noted by geologist Alexander du Toit in 1906. His interpretation was that it had been caused by a major thrust fault, but this view could not be corroborated. Keep in mind that he did not have access to geophysical data captured by aerial surveys using modern technology. The relatively common occurrence of impact structures was furthermore not known at the time. Even today the proposal that the structure near Setlagole may be impact-related raises some questions, but they may be answered in due course. If it were to be confirmed as an impact crater – subsequently planed by several phases of erosion – the Setlagole structure may arguably be the oldest impact structure on Earth. The megabreccia outcrop nearest to the N18 is more than a short walk, so you'll have to make do with a photograph.

Dr Carl Anhaeusser

It is easy to see why the great Alexander du Toit described this as a megabreccia. The scale of the fragments is ...well ... mega!

*It is difficult to imagine this pit at the Kalgold Mine (north of Setlagole) going
much deeper, but new additions to the ore-body are still being opened up.*

After the 50.0N marker plate, with two dumps now looming large, you see a low ridge to the right of the road: this is the outcrop of the greenstone belt that Harmony Gold has opened up in the Kalgold Mine right alongside the N18. The road from the N18 to the mine was never tarred, evidently because when it was built in 1996, it was intended for a mine with a life of around three years. However, mining here is now a major project straddling the national road, with no end in sight. Such is the nature of greenstone belt gold mines – they often have longevity far beyond the miners' wildest expectations. Kalgold is no exception.

Soon you're in the extended peri-urban sprawl of Mahikeng. To your left as you pass the N18-6: 34.0N marker plate you will see a very large dam. In fact there are two dams, both large and both on the Molopo River. This is the only place from where you'll see this river, unless you should travel the N10 to Namibia. Although not perennial, with a length of 960 km it is one of the main rivers in southern Africa. It forms the border between Botswana and South Africa for much of its length. To the south of the Kgalagadi Transfrontier Park it swings southwards to join the Orange River just below the Augrabies Falls.

By the time you reach Mahikeng, you are on the edge of the Kalahari with its conspicuous red sand so typical of that vast region. So, too, is the white calcrete (surface limestone) hardpan that characterizes the subsurface, and more rarely the surface, in the Kalahari. You will see plenty of both as you head northwards from Mahikeng to the border with Botswana at Ramatlabama. Just after passing the turn-off to the right marked 'Six Hundred', and with the N18-7: 16.0E marker plate visible ahead, you'll see a large road metal (crushed or broken stone for road building) quarry to your left **(geosite 3, map 19)** (GPS S 25° 43.570', E 25° 36.090'). Here you get a rare glimpse of some bedrock, mostly weathered, and in places intensely cleaved. However, there are fresh exposures where you'll see that it is a dark grey-green, coarsely crystalline igneous rock, interpreted as a metamorphosed norite. In its fresh, unmetamorphosed state, norite is the rock mostly used for tombstones today.

Ahead lies Ramatlabama and, not far beyond, the great wide Kalahari with its oceans of sand, its idyllic savanna and its wildlife. Behind you lies a short stretch of great geological experiences, from gold deposits formed billions of years ago to a skull so comparatively young and yet unimaginably old. Cherish the memory.

On the edge of the Kalahari you don't have to scratch too deeply to find the bedrock below. Further north, it won't be so easy.

13 The Richtersveld

GEOLOGICAL OVERVIEW

We need to start this chapter with a cautionary note: some of the sites recommended can only be reached by minor tracks, with no boards or signposts to guide you. **However, all turn-off points are indicated in the text that follows by GPS co-ordinates, so it is vital both for the purpose of using this book and for your own safety that you travel with a reliable GPS instrument suitable for off-road navigation.**

The area covered in this chapter incorporates the eastern, more accessible part of the Richtersveld and the adjacent stretch of Namaqualand traversed by the N7, bypassing Springbok and ending at the Vioolsdrif border post with Namibia. Geologically it consists of four main components, three of basement and one of sedimentary cover rocks, which overlie the basement in large patches across the area.

The divisions of the three-part basement are a roughly north-south line towards the west of the area, and an east-west line dividing the eastern sector into north and south domains. The divisions between the different parts consist of major

These dipping beds of Nama Group sediments are seen as one comes into Helskloof, near the edge of the Gariep Belt of folded rocks, and reflect the dying phases of Gariep tectonism. Mostly they are horizontal, or very nearly so.

structural breaks. The dividing line running north-south is a major fault that has thrust the Gariep Supergroup of late Proterozoic (771–550 million-year-old) rocks from the west over their eastern and older neighbour, the Namaqua-Natal Province (NNP). The NNP ranges in age from 2 000–1 100 million years. In the NNP the more northerly Richtersveld Subprovince has been thrust over the Bushmanland Terrane to the south of it. The fourth unit is the mostly horizontal Nama Group, which at approximately 540 million years, is only just younger than the uppermost Gariep Supergroup. It occurs as large fragments up and down the length of the region.

The focus of the trip is the Gariep Belt, where a rift basin opened as an ancient supercontinent split apart, leaving time enough for the basin thus formed to accumulate sediment and then close again in an episode of mountain-building, or orogeny.

The area is geologically so distinct from anything we've covered elsewhere that it calls for a review of the geological unfolding of the area.

In the beginning ...

In the beginning, and in the central and eastern parts of South Africa, the Kaapvaal Craton was consolidated from greenstone belts and granite plutons as a stable and deep-rooted landmass. Along its southern and western edges was accreted, or plastered on, the entire Namaqua-Natal Province, in various stages and with varying degrees of metamorphism and tectonism. This addition was completed around a billion years ago. Now there was a land mass much greater than the Kaapvaal Craton (although the added portion was not as deep-rooted), sometimes referred to as the Kalahari Craton, and part of a pre-Gondwana supercontinent called Rodinia.

Some time after the accretion of the NNP had been completed – some 800 million years ago – the newly collided crust started a process of extension and thinning as Rodinia prepared to break apart. A new ocean, the Adamastor Ocean, opened to the west of that part of Rodinia called Ur. Much later the Adamastor Ocean would close and Ur would be incorporated into a new supercontinent, Pangaea, that would later split into Laurasia and Gondwana, which would themselves subsequently divide into the continents we know today.

The crustal thinning prior to and during the break-up of Gondwana gave us the basalts of the Drakensberg and the Karoo dolerites; the Rodinia dismemberment was preceded by the intrusion of a line of granitoid (granite-like) plutons (including Rooiberg, which you'll see at close quarters) and a lesser quantity of lava.

Soon after this igneous precursor to break-up, the Stinkfontein Rift started to open, and then widen into the Adamastor Ocean, akin to the rift formed prior to the Atlantic Ocean opening up. In time to come (in tens

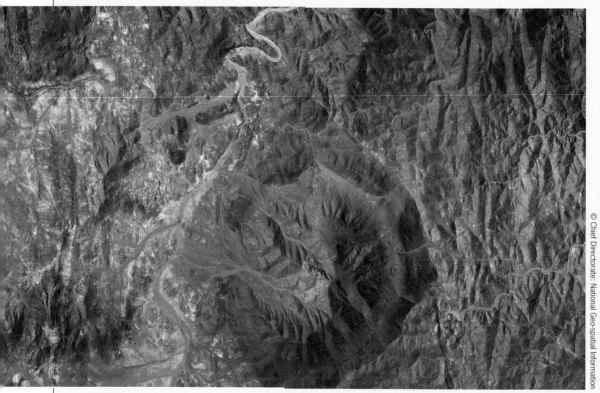

The aerial view of Rooiberg shows dramatically the intrusive, plug-like, nature of the massif, as well as – less dramatically – the concentric layering derived from its 'ring complex' origins, intruded in multiple phases.

– maybe hundreds – of millions of years) the same will happen along today's East African Rift valley. Down the towering west-facing slopes of the Stinkfontein Rift high-energy rivers flowed, depositing coarse conglomerates in alluvial fans, and sandstones across wide river plains. Magmas surging up the rift fractures fed volcanoes that blew out thin layers of lava and ash to settle within the sediments. The feeder dykes intruding the rift fractures were preserved as the Gannakouriep dyke swarm, which you will see along this route. Continued rifting caused the Adamastor Ocean to fill the wide trough, and the shallow marine limestones and shales of the Hilda Subgroup were deposited. The sequence also includes two glacial deposits.

The Kalahari Craton finally ruptured and new basaltic oceanic crust was formed. As forces in the mantle changed direction, as they do, crustal extension gave way to compression at around 550 Ma. The Adamastor Ocean basin closed, and continent-to-continent collision commenced. This was the Gariep orogeny, and gave rise to the Gariep Belt, within which was formed the Gariep Supergroup. The weight of the new deep-seated mountain chain caused the crust ahead of the Gariep Belt to flex downwards, forming a 'peripheral foreland basin' into which the Nama Group was deposited. Soon after the collision of the continents, a string of mostly granitic rocks intruded along a northeast-trending line, the so-called Kuboes-Bremen line.

The effect of the orogenic mountain-building extended geographically beyond the recently formed Gariep Belt sediments and volcanic rocks into the older rocks that were their basement and surrounding hinterland. The gneisses of the so-called West Coast Belt of the more ancient NNP adjacent to the sedimentary trough were tectonized together with the sediments and lavas.

The crystal faces on the staurolite crystals in this schist show they had time to grow in a slow-cooling wet and steamy environment.

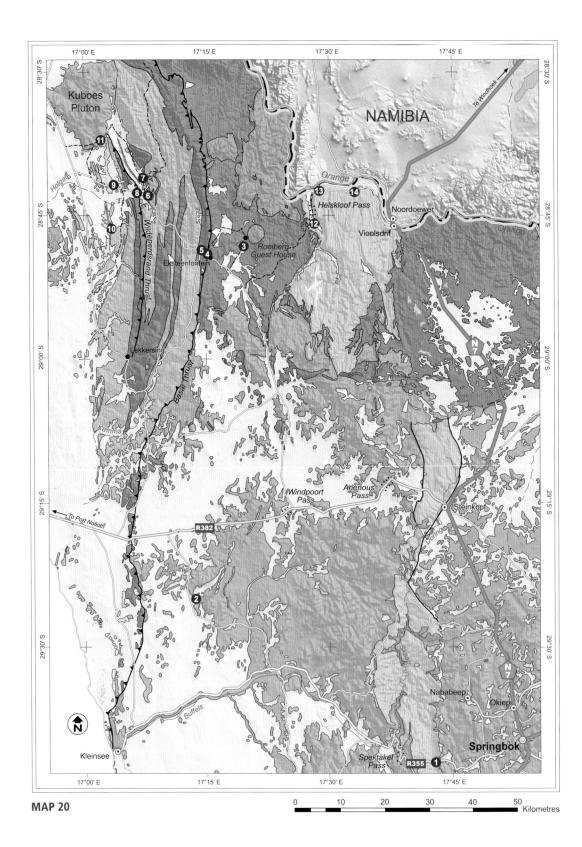

MAP 20

224   Geology off the beaten track

LEGEND

SEDIMENTARY AND VOLCANIC ROCKS

INTRUSIVE ROCKS

	FORMATION	SUBGROUP/GROUP	SUPERGROUP

65 Ma–Present

Superficial deposits

850 Ma–500 Ma

Nama

Holgat

Numees

Hilda

Kaigas

Gariep

Vredefontein — Stinkfontein

Lekkersing

Kuboes pluton

Richtersveld Suite

2000 Ma–1000 Ma

TERRANE / SUBPROVINCE

Bushmanland

Namaqua-Natal Province

Richtersveld

▲▲ Thrust

——— Fault

(Ma = millions of years)

The contact between well-bedded sandstone (towards the top of the image) and massive granitic gneiss (below it) is very clear as one descends Spektakel Pass, the gentle dip reflecting the dying phases of the nearby Gariep Belt tectonism.

From close up, the contrast between the massive granite and the overlying bedded sandstone is quite striking.

Geology of the route

Springbok to Vioolsdrif

You start the journey by leaving the N7 in Springbok and driving westwards on the R355 towards the Kleinsee diamond mining area on the coast. In Springbok and to the west of it you are in the Bushmanland Terrane of the NNP, consisting of high-grade metamorphic rocks from 1–2 billion years old, intruded by somewhat younger granite and associated intrusives.

You see the first rocks that are younger than these as you prepare to drop down to the lower coastal plain via the Spektakel Pass: they are subhorizontal Nama Group sediments, in fact the youngest rocks you'll see on this route. The unconformity between the old granitic gneiss and the lowest Nama sediments is clearly visible from around the 18 km (from Springbok) distance marker. These lowermost beds (**geosite 1, map 20**) (GPS S 29° 41.669', E 17° 42.878') are sandstones and conglomerates, strongly siliceous and quite resistant. Pale pink and grey shales overlie the basal coarser-grained sediments and these pass upwards into reddish impure sandstone, although you won't see these from the road.

Soon after reaching the bottom of the pass you see an excavation into the side of the slope on your right, and a little further ahead the old slimes dam of the Spektakel Copper Mine. These are reminders of the days when the town of Springbok lay near the centre of the copper mining district of Okiep and Nababeep, when Okiep Copper Company (OCC) mines were the mainstay of the Namaqualand economy. The Spektakel Mine is barely behind you when there's more evidence of substantial earth-moving, this time to your left (GPS S 29° 36.191', E 17° 28.637'). Large low hills – clearly artificial – just across a conspicuous dry river bed bear testimony to the other string to Namaqualand's mining bow: diamonds. This is the old Buffelsbank Mine, once an important producer, when mines along the Atlantic coast and inland, along the present Orange River and its previous courses (such as the Buffelsrivier), were important contributors to the vast South African diamond industry. The mounds you see are rehabilitated waste dumps, which fill – overfill, in fact – the old excavations from which the diamonds were recovered.

Soon after this you see a secondary road off to the right (GPS S 29° 32′ 13.62″, E 17° 23′ 02.19″), which you take and follow for about 27 km. It is corrugated, but not too badly, and should present no problems. At GPS S 29° 25.164′, E 17° 13.017′ turn off to the right (east) and after the farm gate, drive on a track for about a kilometre until you see a low rocky ridge just to the right of the track, which is what you've come to see (**geosite 2, map 20**) (GPS S 29° 24.702′, E 17° 14.040′).

Although it's still part of the Bushmanland Terrane you have been travelling over for a while, what you'll see here are nothing like the gneisses there. This is because they are part of the 'West Coast Belt', that strip of the NNP referred to above and which has been affected by metamorphism related to the Gariep orogeny, or mountain-building.

The rocks you have come to see here were NNP gneisses (approximately 1 000 million years old), which were 'overprinted', or subjected to retrograde metamorphism, during the Gariep orogeny (545 Ma). This gave them a texture and an assemblage of minerals not usually seen in NNP rocks. What you see here are staurolite-kyanite-almandine (garnet) schists, the staurolite forming well to perfectly shaped dark red-brown orthorhombic crystals, the other minerals much finer-grained.

Although the Buffelsbank Diamond Mine has been rehabilitated following its years of large-scale mining, there are still stones to be recovered from the tailings.

Although more rugged terrain lies ahead, here there are still reminders that you are on the edge of the Kalahari, famously flat, and in the south conspicuously red from the minor amounts of iron oxide in the sand.

Metamorphism

Metamorphism, such as was imposed on the rocks around and west of Springbok, is triggered by an increase in the temperature of rocks. It may happen with a concomitant increase in pressure, during orogeny or mountain-building (regional metamorphism), or it may be caused by the intrusion of hot magma adjacent to the rocks concerned, or near them (thermal or contact metamorphism). New minerals are formed which are in equilibrium with the elevated temperature and pressure. Usually the process is not accompanied by significant quantities of fluids, and as temperatures rise volatiles are lost; in other words the rocks become 'drier'.

A less common type of metamorphism is retrograde metamorphism, where the environment contains solutions mostly consisting of superheated water or steam. Again, new minerals may be formed, but more hydrous than those from which they formed. You'll see some retrograde metamorphic rocks at geosite 2, map 20.

Red-weathering syenite (quartz-poor, alkali feldspar-rich granitoid)
forms the outer hills of Rooiberg (Red Mountain), whence the name.

Note that they were not part of the Gariep sequence of rocks, which were directly involved in the Gariep orogeny. The overprinting of these *nearby* NNP gneisses resulted from the somewhat elevated temperatures and pressures and the hydrous environment that prevailed *across the region* during the orogeny.

Returning via the farm track to the road (remembering to close the gate on your way through), you continue north for some 11 km, joining the R382 linking Steinkopf and Port Nolloth, where you turn right towards Steinkopf. On either side of the highway there is a thin (up to about 1 m) blanket of Kalahari sand quite widespread in these parts, easily recognizable by its bright red colour. You see occasional exposures of gneiss in the road cuttings, these more like typical NNP metamorphic rocks, with none of the overprinting evident at the last locality. Some 25 km east of where you joined the tar road you turn left off it (GPS S 29° 15.644', E 17° 25.678'), now travelling north again.

There is not much geology to see at close quarters as you travel over these undulating plains and through the hills. After 60 km you're in the little hamlet of Eksteenfontein (GPS S 28° 49.384', E 17° 15.444'). (If you're planning to stay at the Rooiberg Guest House, not far east of the village, you may need to collect a key.) The village was formerly called Stinkfontein after the 'rotten eggs' odour imparted to the water by dissolved hydrogen sulphide.

Assuming you overnight at Rooiberg and particularly if you're there in the late afternoon, you'll see where the massif of hills got its name: both the syenites, which make the outer rings of the ring complex, and the granites in the core have a definite reddish hue (**geosite 3, map 20**) (GPS S 28° 47.108', E 17° 19.774'). You wouldn't know, seeing it from ground level, that it's a ring complex, but from the air – or on Google Earth – the rings are clearer. Bear in mind that, by their very nature, ring complexes are usually more perfectly circular than simple plutons, which are commonly somewhat irregular in shape. Remember that this is one of the four intrusives that resulted from the thinning of the crust *prior to the opening* of the Stinkfontein Rift. The four are known as the Richtersveld Suite.

The thick cross-beds in this fluvial sandstone near the base of the Lekkersing Formation are easy to pick out.

After leaving Rooiberg, you return to Eksteenfontein and then continue north-westwards, soon crossing the easternmost thrust of the Gariep Thrust Front (the Gemsbokvlei Thrust). You have crossed a regional geological divide, from the NNP into the Gariep Belt (occupied by the Gariep Supergroup). Soon after leaving Eksteenfontein you get into rugged terrain, where you start to see by far the most common rock type in the east of the belt, micaceous quartzite of the Lekkersing Formation that has been quarried as strikingly attractive, silvery grey, hard-wearing paving stones and floor tiles. This is the oldest part of the Port Nolloth Group, which makes up the main (southern) part of the Gariep Belt. The first striking exposure as one enters a narrow defile soon after leaving Eksteenfontein shows a good example of a thick cross-bed set of the sort typically seen in river-borne sandstone (**geosite 4, map 20**) (GPS S 28° 49.491′, E 17° 14.687′).

FIGURE 15   **GARIEP STRATIGRAPHY**

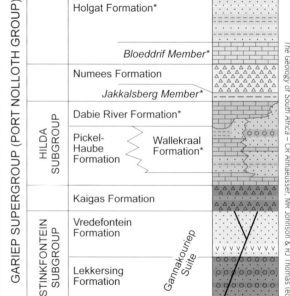

This simplified stratigraphic column is given for easy cross reference to a number of units you will not see outside the Richtersveld and so will not have come across before.

After this, as one winds across rocky uplands and later down a dramatic pass to the lower coastal plains, the Lekkersing Formation you see is made up almost entirely of conspicuously flaggy beige quartzitic sandstone. The village that gave the unit its name is 25 km south of here. The origin of such perfectly rhythmically layered sandstone is interpreted as deposition in still water, possibly a lake, from sand blown over the water. Some clay would have blown in, probably seasonally (accounting for the regularity of the bedding), which would have been converted to mica during the tectonism and facilitated the movement between the beds of sandstone as they were folded. Although you don't see them on this route, conglomerates are an important component of this formation, telling of steep headwater topography and brief periods of tectonic instability breaking the generally calm conditions.

At GPS S 28° 49.034', E 17° 13.204' **(geosite 5, map 20)** you should stop to have a look at a good example of the volcanics, which make their first appearance in the Vredefontein Formation, the unit that overlies the Lekkersing Formation. The outcrop is conspicuous, being almost black – a stark contrast after the very pale sandstones. If you think of Africa's famed volcanoes in the East African Rift Valley and remember that here you're in a similar rifting environment, the presence of volcanic rocks shouldn't surprise you.

Soon after this you reach the pass through the Stinkfontein mountains. You're dropping from higher ground to the interior edge of the coastal plain, which stretches to the Atlantic coast. You are mainly surrounded by steeply dipping flaggy quartzitic sandstone, in one of the

The very dark volcanics of the Vredefontein Formation make a strong contrast with the predominantly pale sandstone.

The dropstones in this outcrop as well as the massive nature of this Kaigas sandstone are the clue that its derivation is at least partly glacial.

most impressive packages of this rock type you're likely ever to see. However, at GPS position S 28° 46.653', E 17° 10.082' you'll find one of the so-called Gannakouriep dykes (here conformable with the bedding, so strictly a sill) that are also conspicuously dark. An integral part of the Gariep geological history, this is one of a dyke swarm more than 300 km long. For much of that length these dykes cut across geological boundaries, so it is correct to refer to the phenomenon in its entirety as a dyke swarm. Their main significance is that they illustrate unambiguously that the crust was being pulled apart by forces in the mantle below, which would lead to formation of the rift basin.

Emerging from the mountain pass, with the valley floor widening and wide plains visible ahead, you cannot help noticing a group of low hills off to the left of the road. They are strikingly different from the conspicuously bedded cream-coloured rocks you have been seeing for a long time, being darker and massive (unbedded). It's worth stopping and walking over to the outcrop to see the mostly fine- to medium-grained sandstone, its distinctive feature being the pebble- to cobble-sized 'dropstones' scattered through the rock. This is part of the Kaigas Formation, which overlies

The unsorted appearance of this Kaigas diamictite is convincingly suggestive of its glacial origin.

Stratigraphically above – so younger than – the diamictite is this dolomitic limestone of the Pickelhaube Formation, not far to the west of the diamictite.

High-strain basement in thrust zone

Lekkersing Formation

Vredefontein Formation

Quartz veins

The Wildeperdsrand thrust zone lies at the base of the resistant rocky 'reef' that makes the peak of the ridge, with the western slope following the bedding of the Lekkersing Formation, and the slope facing you a slice of much older basement rock.

the Vredefontein Formation and consists mainly of diamictite, at least part of which is attributable to a glacial origin **(geosite 6, map 20)** (GPS S 28° 43.924', E 17° 07.931').

Stratigraphically above the Kaigas Formation, the next unit in the sequence – and which you will encounter – is the Pickelhaube Formation (of the Hilda Subgroup of the Port Nolloth Group). To see the basal part of this younger formation you follow a track to the right (north) off this road at GPS S 28° 43.600', E 17° 07.741', where there is a board showing 'Welcome to the Richtersveld Community Conservancy'. Take this road, turning right after 2.3 km and following the road for approximately 2.7 km. The GPS point you are heading for has co-ordinates S 28° 41.215', E 17° 07.910' **(geosite 7, map 20)**. Here you are in the valley of the Kook River and, just across the river on the southern bank is an exposure that may look familiar. It is dark grey and massive like the last outcrop you saw, so you might have guessed that it is from the Kaigas Formation, which would be correct. This time, though, it is true diamictite, with a fairly liberal spread of small pebbles through the blue-grey matrix. Looking westwards down the valley, you'll note that it passes up into well-bedded rocks, which are sandstones of the Kaigas.

Turning here and heading back (now westwards) down the valley, stop before the road leaves the river

The conspicuously unsorted Numees diamictite near the main road is a reminder of the inability of glaciation to sort material in the way that water and wind can.

bed and have a look at the outcrops on the southern side of the river. Among the finely foliated phyllites you will see a bed with the diagnostic 'elephant-skin' weathering that characterizes limestone, in this case dolomitic limestone (carbonate of roughly equal amounts of calcium and magnesium). These are low down in the Pickelhaube Formation and carbon isotopes from the dolomite tell us there was a dramatic warming of climate soon after the partially glacial Kaigas diamictite was formed. Note that, like the bedded sandstones above the diamictite you've just seen, these sediments dip westwards, so that as you travel in that direction you can expect to see younger and younger units, the westerly dip consistent with the fact that the tectonism arising from the continental collision from the west gives rise to fold axial planes and thrusts that dip to the west.

As you get back to the main road off which you branched, and continue westwards, look to the south of the road for the end of a prominent ridge that stretches away southwards **(geosite 8, map 20)** (GPS S 28° 43.220', E 17° 06.171'). This is the Wildeperdsrand – almost certainly named after zebras in the area rather than wild horses – and is important because it marks a major thrust zone that takes its name from the ridge and duplicates the stratigraphy, as thrusts commonly do. The more prominent rocks that form the crest of the ridge and its western slope are quartzites of the Lekkersing

Formation. At the foot of the ridge the rocks directly below the quartzites are strongly sheared Vioolsdrif granitoids (granite-like intrusive rocks) of the Namaqua Metamorphic Province. Below them a fairly prominent spur separates them from the rocks that make up most of the ridge end. The spur marks the Wildeperdsrand Thrust, which continues up the slope (see image opposite, top). Below it the rocks have been subjected to very high levels of strain by the thrusting and have lost their primary identity altogether. Note that this thrust, like all thrusts, reflects the compressional regime that followed the tension-derived rifting, millions of years earlier.

To the right of the road, not far ahead, you see the first of several ridges made up of another diamictite unit **(geosite 9, map 20)** (GPS S 28° 42.656', E 17° 03.435'), this of the Numees Formation, which overlies the Hilda Subgroup. So if you recall what you have seen since entering the hills just west of Eksteenfontein, you have passed from the Lekkersing flaggy quartzites to the Vredefontein feldspathic sandstones to the Kaigas diamictite to the Pickelhaube phyllites and dolomite, and

Essentially the same rock as in the picture opposite, this diamictite has had its original texture completely overprinted during folding and thrusting, leading to its sheared character. Its dark colour reflects enrichment in iron, but without exposure to the atmosphere, and so remaining unoxidized.

Snowball Earth

The best known glacial formation in South Africa, the Dwyka tillite, formed about 300 million years ago at a time when Gondwana straddled the South Pole, before moving back to the lower latitudes where the mammal-like reptiles would roam – and leave their rich palaeontological heritage. A legacy of another kind lies in the diamictite of the Numees Formation, a tale so bizarre as to have been widely ridiculed when it was first aired. Years later the body of evidence in its support is substantial enough for it to be accepted by most geologists.

In the 1940s, a young geologist called Brian Harland proposed that the presence of dropstones was evidence that ice had spread over every continent, right across the tropics to the Equator itself, creating a 'snowball Earth'. The almost immediate response to this hypothesis was that if that had been the case, Earth would never have emerged from this 'total freeze'. It was argued that a 'tipping point' would have been reached where the white ice (in contrast to dark oceans and continents in their unfrozen state) would have reflected more than half the solar heat required to warm the planet. Earth would have got progressively icier until the end of time. In addition, mechanisms other than melting ice were proposed to explain the dropstones deposited in the equatorial belt. Snowball Earth still looked ludicrous.

The clue to the apparent impasse came from the realization that whatever was happening at Earth's surface was irrelevant when compared with the incomprehensibly huge store of heat in its core and mantle. The normal forces that have given us volcanoes from the beginning of Earth's history until today would have continued without a major break through the global ice age. As always, they would have pumped carbon dioxide (CO_2) into the atmosphere. But if Earth was covered with ice, there would have been nothing to extract the atmospheric CO_2, as stromatolites in the early oceans had done – in exchange for oxygen – since the Archaean. The theory's proponents argued that a tipping point of another kind would have been reached, when the accumulated CO_2 would have been sufficient to produce a greenhouse effect and the ice would have started melting. Evaporation of exposed patches of ocean would have brought rain, which, mixed with the CO_2, would have fallen as dilute carbonic acid, dissolving huge amounts of calcium from the increasingly exposed land. Combining with the CO_2, this would have created limestone, the so-called 'cap carbonate' found lying directly above snowball Earth tillite.

The last clue in confirmation of the hypothesis came from drastically anachronistic banded iron formation, or BIF, that formed while the ocean and atmosphere were insulated from each other by ice.

This 'cap carbonate' rock is characterized by elephant-skin weathering typical of limestone (geosite 10, map 20).

The sheared appearance of the dark diamictite, coupled with the equally striking white vein quartz cutting across the shear direction, tells that strain was extreme but temperatures not high enough to melt the rocks, and thereby reconstitute them entirely.

now onto the Numees diamictite. You have been going steadily up in the succession, from older to younger, across sediments dipping consistently to the west. The Numees diamictite, where you are now, is more like a conventional tillite, the glacial origin of which is beyond doubt. Its main significance, at least as far as you are concerned, is that its late Neoproterozoic or Vendian age (650–540 million years) consigns it to a period when the Varangian glaciation took place, giving rise to the 'snowball Earth' hypothesis (see text box opposite).

You'll see the Numees diamictite again. A little way ahead you're going to turn south and head along a rough track to see a remarkable piece of geology. (There are various tracks that will get you there across the plains and between low ranges, but the suggested route follows the best tracks, even if it's not the most direct route.) The distance to the hills where the outcrops occur is a little over 12 km (**geosite 10, map 20**) (GPS S 28° 47.213', E 17° 03.032').

Once there, climb up into the hills and see rocks you're unlikely to see again anywhere else: tillite with an iron formation (BIF) matrix and inorganic carbonates (the 'cap carbonates', devoid of any association with early life) associated with tillite. Remember that the two rock types – tillite and carbonate – are normally at opposite ends of the temperature range, coldest and hottest respectively. Here they are side by side – thanks to the snowball Earth event.

When you have savoured this rare treat find your way back to where you turned off the main road and cross it, now heading north. You're on your way to the most northwesterly stop on the journey, where you'll see truly awe-inspiring rock faces even if they're not geologically as unusual as the last stop. In the far distance, almost due north of where you cross the main road, is a massif that towers above any hills nearby. It is the Kuboes pluton or batholith, the biggest of nine intrusives that were intruded at the end of tectonism along the 270 km-long Kuboes-Bremen line.

In certain geomorphological environments granite may form steep-sided massifs, such as the dramatic granite massif of the Kuboes pluton at Tierkloof (geosite 11) – reminiscent of Rio de Janeiro's iconic 'Sugar Loaf'. (For more on the weathering of granite see pp. 31 and 33.)

To get to it, take the track northwards. After about 5 km the road curves to the right around the end of a north-south ridge; another 750 m on, you cross a dry river bed, then half a kilometre further on, go left at the intersection of two tracks; after a further kilometre turn right, and 700 m on, the granite rock-face is looming over you; another 200 m takes you to the camping site at Tierkloof **(geosite 11, map 20)** (GPS S 28° 38.104', E 17° 00.768'). You won't see more imposing granite cliffs this side of Rio de Janeiro's Sugar Loaf! It's worth the drive. This is a beautiful coarse-grained equigranular rock made up of perthite (an intergrowth of potassic and sodic feldspars) and quartz with minor plagioclase (feldspar with both sodium and calcium) and the dark mica biotite. After this you will have seen a good cross section of the Port Nolloth Zone of the Gariep Belt.

Before you leave these parts, though, you should see the sedimentary Nama Group. Together with the batholith you've just been to, it closes the chapter of end-Proterozoic/early Cambrian events in this corner of South Africa. This last part of the Richtersveld excursion takes you from Rooiberg (or Eksteenfontein) via a southerly detour northeastwards towards Vioolsdrif on the Orange River.

To begin with, crossing the upland plains between scattered higher-standing hills and groups of hills, you are mostly on the more-or-less tectonized granodiorite and volcanic rocks of the NNP. You cross a small outcrop of lavas of the Orange River Group before starting the descent down the Helskloof Pass, though these are best displayed in another outcrop just after you've reached the foot of the pass. Soon after you're on the flat floor of the Helskloof valley (itself a tributary

Down in the Helskloof valley, approaching the Orange River, look back and see the dark lines of the Gannakouriep dyke swarm. These dykes, which crossed the entire Gariep Belt and into the surrounding terrain, are the legacy of hot magma surging up through fissures in the crust, which was being stretched during continental rifting. The parallel dykes are a reflection of the stress patterns during evolution of the Gariep Belt.

Apart from the fault so clearly shown, this cliff section beautifully illustrates the effect of fluctuating sea level in the sedimentary record: the brown-weathering carbonate beds (limestone, partially dolomitized) reflect higher sea level with no clastic input, and the interbedded darker grey sandstone and mudrock (composed of land-derived detritus) indicate formation nearer the shoreline when sea level was lower.

valley of the Orange River valley), stop and look back for a moment **(geosite 12, map 20)** (GPS S 28° 46.382', E 17° 27.817'). You will see clear dark traces of the Gannakouriep dyke swarm, a powerful reminder that the Gariep Belt – with its flagstones and their interlayered sills – which seems a world away is, in fact, not so far away at all.

Then you're into the tilted basal sediments of the Nama Group. Their alternating harder dark sandstones and soft pale shales swirl in graceful curves up to high skylines near you. However, along the scarp of the Neint Nababeep Plateau that forms the imposing eastern wall to Helskloof they're all but horizontal, as the fold amplitude decreases eastwards. The tilting you see in this western part of the Nama basin is another reminder of the tectonism that closed the Gariep narrative. In fact, the Nama sediments themselves are an integral part of that story. It was loading of the asthenosphere by the Gariep orogeny and the resulting downwarping that formed the basin in which the Nama sediments accumulated.

Grey to black limestone is an important component of the Nama succession, and occurs at different levels, most conspicuously at the top of this particular sequence. Being quite soft and easily marked, the large fallen blocks strewn over the plains at the foot of the Neint Nababeep Plateau formed an ideal palette on which San artists could express themselves. Their paintings can be seen at various places along Helskloof (GPS S 28° 44.043', E 17° 27.913'), though, sadly, none appear to have escaped the ravages of mindless graffiti.

Where Helskloof joins the Orange River you are faced by magnificent krantzes of limestone, sandstone and shale on the Namibian side, with an excellent example of a fault just east of the confluence of the valleys **(geosite 13, map 20)** (GPS S 28° 42.201', E 17° 28.709'). The above photograph of the fault shows the various Nama Group lithologies in a text-book example of how different rock types express themselves differently. In the hills behind the road on the South African side of the river the sediments show the folding found adjacent to the Gariep tectonic belt, and which is conspicuously absent to the north of you.

And finally, as you head towards the N7, stop and look at the onion-like stromatolite domes in a limestone outcrop next to the road **(geosite 14, map 20)** (GPS S 28° 42.487′, E 17° 32.824′), showing that half a billion years ago photosynthesis was in full swing, the effects of snowball Earth consigned to the pages of history.

It is serendipitous, on this final journey 'off the beaten track', to have seen a simple but grand geological process so beautifully illustrated. The Gariep Belt has shown you a classical example of a basin that opened, was filled again, and ended with a mountain-building event. No place offers a better synopsis of Earth's history – via this unfolding sequence of evolutionary stages – than the Richtersveld. It is a fitting climax to your journeys.

On your way out of the Richtersveld you should stop and see some unusually large stromatolites in Nama limestone. The inset shows stromatolites that are nearly two billion years older, from the Transvaal Supergroup, and are a more usual size.

Glossary

accretion: process by which rigid cratons expand over geological time, as orogenic (mobile) belts become 'welded' onto craton margins

acid: applied to rocks – generally igneous – containing more than 67% silica (SiO_2)

aeolianite: sandstone derived from windblown sand

African Land Surface: land surface formed after commencement of the split-up of Gondwana, ending approximately 18 million years ago

agate: variegated quartz, usually concentrically banded and commonly found in basalt

agglomerate: pyroclastic rock (qv) with cobble-sized (more than 32 mm in diameter) fragments

alkaline: applied to rocks relatively deficient in silica (SiO_2) and rich in sodium and/or potassium

alluvial: describes detrital deposits, usually relatively recently formed, and usually found along the course of streams and rivers, though also applied to coastal deposits

alumina: aluminium oxide (Al_2O_3)

aluminosilicate: describes the common minerals in which alumina (Al_2O_3) and silica (SiO_2) are important components

amphibole: family of generally dark, common rock-forming (i.e. aluminosilicate) minerals, rich in magnesium, iron, calcium and/or sodium

amphibolite: metamorphic rock comprising mainly amphibole and feldspar, with little or no quartz

amygdale: small gas bubble in lava, filled with a secondary mineral such as quartz or calcite (see vesicle)

amygdaloidal: describes a lava containing amygdales

anastomose: tendency of a mature, low-energy, flat-gradient stream or river to form a net-like pattern

andalusite: metamorphic mineral with the composition Al_2SiO_5

andesite: volcanic rock of intermediate – between acid (or felsic) and basic (or mafic) – composition

anoxic: devoid of oxygen

anticline: convex-upward fold

anticlinorium: composite series of smaller synclinal and anticlinal folds that together form a larger downward-opening fold structure; (see anticline, synclinorium)

Archaean: the oldest rocks of the Precambrian, older than 2 500 million years

arkose: sandstone containing more than 25% feldspar

artesian: commonly applied to a spring that comes to the surface from an underground aquifer that lies topographically above it

asthenosphere: layer of the Earth of undefined thickness below the rigid crust and upper mantle where plastic movement takes place

astrobleme: meteorite impact crater usually leveled by one or more phases of erosion

augen: used when a mineral or collection of minerals in metamorphic rocks forms an eye-shaped unit that is conspicuously larger than the groundmass it is set in

australopithecine: related to the hominid genus *Australopithecus*

base metal: comprising mainly copper, lead, zinc and nickel

basement: applied to the floor onto which a sequence of rocks was deposited; commonly applied to Archaean formations

bauxite: weathered rock composed of hydrated alumina – the ore of alumina, from which aluminium is derived

bed: smallest unit in a sedimentary series, separated from units above and below by a clear bedding plane

bedding: characteristic given to a sequence of sediments by its beds

biomat: thin layer of accumulated algal remains formed on the primitive ocean floor

biotite: common, rock-forming mica, generally dark brown

bivalve: mollusk with two-part shells, such as mussels, clams, oysters, etc.

breccia: rock comprising angular fragments, most commonly created during faulting, occasionally by volcanism. A fault-scarp breccia is one formed at the surface where material broken from the upthrown block of a fault moves gravitationally down the fault surface

calc-silicate (rock): rock composed of calc-silicate minerals, which are rock-forming silicate minerals in which calcium is an important component

calcite: common mineral form of $CaCO_3$, translucent in individual crystals; where finely crystalline, it appears white

calcrete: secondary rock consisting mainly of calcium carbonate, and formed over a long time at or near the ground surface by the movement through the soil of upward-moving ground water; also called 'surface limestone' (see silcrete)

carbonatite: an unsusual carbonate-rich rock of igneous origin, often associated with alkaline igneous rocks

chert: extremely fine-grained silica rock, commonly found with limestone or dolomite, but conspicuously harder than either of those rocks; commonly grey

chrysocolla: blue-green, usually pale, hydrated copper silicate

clast: individual constituent of sedimentary, less commonly volcaniclastic, rocks

clastic: applied to a rock composed of clasts, commonly used synonymously with 'sedimentary'

competence: property of rocks that defines how they behave during tectonism, e.g. sandstone is more competent than shale or schist, and does not show the cleavage they do

complex: generally, an assemblage of rocks of any age or origin that has been folded or metamorphosed together

concretion: nodule formed by the concentration about a central nucleus of soluble constituents of sedimentary rocks

conglomerate: most commonly applied to a sedimentary rock containing rounded or semi-rounded clasts as large as or larger than pebbles

craton: fragment of the earliest part of the Earth's crust, comprising the most ancient sedimentary and volcanic rocks and the granites that intruded them

crinoids: marine animals more closely resembling plants, which have been plentiful in seas since the Palaeozoic

crocidolite: blue asbestos, a fibrous form of sodium-rich amphibole

cross-bedding: internal bedding within a single bed and oblique to the bedding planes that define it; formed by air or water currents active during deposition

cryptocrystalline: so finely crystalline that the crystals cannot be seen with a magnifying lens

delta front (sandstone): sandstone formed at the distal (open water) end of coastal deltas

diabase: shallow intrusive equivalent of basalt; in South Africa used of rocks older than the formation of the Karoo Supergroup, whose diabase-composition intrusives are called dolerite

diamictite: sedimentary rock that consists of a wide range of unsorted to poorly sorted clasts that are suspended in a sand or mud matrix

diatreme: near-surface part of a volcanic pipe

differentiation: process whereby an originally homogeneous magma separates into different fractions, as some minerals crystallise and settle, leaving magma of composition different from the original

dip: attitude of a tabular body of rock, usually a bed or assemblage of beds

dip slope: topographic feature formed when an inclined unit, usually a sedimentary bed, is hard enough to resist the weathering that has removed overlying material

dolerite: igneous rock of basaltic composition intruded into rock below Earth's surface

dolomite: limestone that contains a substantial amount of magnesium carbonate in addition to calcium carbonate

dome: upward-convex roughly circular feature, often meaning basement over which younger formations were draped and have been partially removed

dropstone: single, large (pebble- to boulder-size) clast set in a sandstone or finer-grained sedimentary rock, assumed to have fallen from a floating ice sheet into normal clastic sediment as it was forming

dune rock: see aeolianite

duricrust: hard crust formed at or near the surface of the ground as a result of the upward migration and evaporation of mineral-bearing ground water

Dwyka: river in the southern Karoo where the tillite that resulted from the Gondwana glaciation, the lowermost formation of the Karoo Basin, was first described; the name of the Group that contains tillite and allied sediments

dyke: near-vertical tabular intrusive body

Ecca: river and pass in the Eastern Cape, where the generally fine-grained sediments that form the second major sedimentary grouping in the Karoo

Supergroup were first described; the name given to this extensive Group of sediments

eon: the most fundamental division of geological time

epidote: calcium-rich silicate mineral of metamorphic origin, commonly conspicuously grass-green

exfoliation dome: dome formed when the weathered outer material of a usually igneous rock has been removed

fault: fracture where one block of the Earth's crust, of any size and in a brittle, i.e. non-fluid, state, has moved relative to adjacent crust

feldspar: one of the commonest rock-forming minerals in igneous and metamorphic rocks, consisting of aluminosilicate of sodium, potassium and/or calcium; also found in some sedimentary rocks

feldspathic: containing feldspar as a principal ingredient

ferricrete: iron-rich duricrust

ferruginous: iron-rich

flaggy: applied to sandstone, usually quite fine-grained and somewhat micaceous and of very constant thickness, from 10 to 100 mm, that breaks into large 'flags' or slabs.

float: detached rock material lying on the ground surface

fluvial: pertaining to rivers and river flow

fold belt: elongate zone of folding, typical of an orogeny

fold closure: part of the fold immediately around its axis, i.e. the hinge zone

fold plunge: dip of a fold structure; strictly the dip of the fold axis

foliation: structure resulting from the separation of minerals into different layers parallel to the schistosity

formation: assemblage of rocks that share broadly the same age and environment of origin

gabbro: the more common plutonic igneous rock of mafic composition, usually dark grey

garnet: any one of a complex group of rock-forming minerals usually rich in iron, calcium and manganese; mostly found in metamorphic rocks and in kimberlite

glacial till: sediment left behind when ice sheets or glaciers melt

gneiss: metamorphic rock with bands of granular and micaceous minerals

Gondwana: the Southern Hemisphere supercontinent whose break-up gave rise to Africa, South America, Australia, Antarctica, India and numerous islands

graben: generally elongate block of the Earth's crust dropped down between faults during extensional tectonics

grain: the direction of splitting in rock

granitized: describing rocks subjected to such high temperatures and pressures that melting has occurred and the recrystallized rock has the appearance, texture and mineral composition of granite

granitoid: granite-like, sometimes applied to a body of such rock

greenstone: old term used to describe basic volcanic rocks, usually in Archaean 'greenstone belts', where low-grade metamorphism has converted the original mafic minerals mainly into the dark green metamorphic mineral chlorite, often with some greenish hornblende and grass-green epidote

greywacke: massive, poorly sorted, dark grey sandstone with angular grains, generally including rock fragments; usually formed during periods of crustal instability

group: major unit of stratigraphy comprising more than one formation, formed in a period and environment where crustal conditions were broadly constant

haematite: common iron oxide mineral (Fe_2O_3)

heavy minerals: minerals that are dense enough to be naturally concentrated by wind action

hornblende: most common member of the amphibole family of rock-forming minerals; generally blackish and found in granite, gneiss and amphibolite

hornfels: fine-grained contact metamorphic rock, hardened by the heat of a nearby intrusion

hydrocarbons: materials formed by decay of marine organisms that may accumulate to form commercially exploitable oil and gas

igneous: describes a rock solidified from molten material called magma

igneous contact: contact where an igneous rock is intruded into an older rock; useful in dating rocks

inclusion: crystal, rock fragment or small bubble of liquid or gas, enclosed in a bigger crystal

inlier: 'window' of older rock completely enclosed by younger rocks, either a high-standing part of the floor of a sedimentary basin, or formed when a small area of the younger formation has been removed by erosion to expose the floor

inselberg: isolated hill or mountain dominating the surrounding plains

intermediate: grouping of igneous rocks between acid and mafic

intrusion: body of igneous rock that penetrates an older rock, or the process of such penetration; gives rise to terms 'intrusive' and 'intruded'

isoclinal: used to describe a fold whose limbs are parallel

isotope: one of two or more subtly differing forms of a chemical element

jasper: extremely finely crystalline quartz, coloured red by intermixing with iron oxide

jaspilite: rock composed of fine alternating bands of red jasper and black iron oxide

joint: fracture plane separating adjacent blocks of rock between which there has been no movement

kaolin: a rock composed essentially of kaolinite, a hydrous aluminium silicate, resulting from the decomposition of aluminous minerals like feldspar

kaolinization: process in which some rock-forming minerals, mainly feldspar, are converted – usually to the clay mineral kaolin, a hydrated aluminium silicate; also applied to the weathering of granite

kimberlite: ultramafic intrusive rock, dark when fresh and yellow when weathered; the primary ore of diamonds, though most kimberlites are effectively barren

kimberlite pipe: carrot-shaped intrusion in which kimberlite is commonly found

kinzigite: coarse-grained metamorphic rock consisting principally of garnet and biotite

koffieklip: the informal name given by farmers and artisans to ferricrete (qv)

komatiite: group of ultramafic volcanic rocks, having a distinctive chemical composition, representing hot, magnesium-rich magmas that erupted on Earth's early crust; named after the type area where they were originally found in the Komati valley, near Barberton

lapilli: small fragments blasted out of volcanoes

laterite: hard iron-rich layer within the soil, formed in humid tropical conditions from iron-rich bedrock

layering: phenomenon seen in sequences of beds or strata of contrasting appearance

Liesegang banding: colour-banding resulting from rhythmic precipitation of material from solutions passing through sedimentary rocks

limestone: bedded sediment consisting chiefly of calcium carbonate ($CaCO_3$), but in dolomitic limestone or dolomite, with roughly equal amounts of calcium

and magnesium carbonate malachite: common secondary or oxide mineral of copper, a hydrated carbonate, well-known for its brilliant colour

lithification: process of conversion – usually of long duration – of a newly deposited sediment into a rock

lunette dunes: crescent-shaped dunes along the downwind rim of pans, formed by dust and sand blown off the pans

Ma: abbreviation for millions of years

mafic: applied to generally dark rocks and minerals relatively rich in magnesium and poor in silica

magma: molten or partly molten phase of igneous rocks, which cools and solidifies to form such rocks

magmatic: rock or mineral deposit derived from a magma

magnetite: common blackish iron oxide mineral, Fe_3O_4, magnetic, giving rocks that contain it their magnetic property

mantle: one of the zones of the interior of the Earth, between the innermost core and the outer crust

marble: metamorphosed and recrystallized equivalent of a sedimentary carbonate rock, such as limestone or dolomite, often used as a decorative or monumental stone

marker: usually thin and easily recognised rock unit occurring at a more or less constant position within a larger formation, used to determine geological position

massif: mass of conspicuous hills or mountains not forming part of a range

massive: descriptive term for a rock unit having a homogeneous structure, without obvious bedding, layering or banding

megabreccia: the name given to a large area of breccia containing very large fragments

megacryst: relatively large crystal or mineral grain in an igneous or metamorphic rock that is easily visible with the unaided eye

melilitite: mafic rock containing a high content of the mineral melilite, a calcium magnesium silicate

member: distinctive subdivision of a formation that merits separate description because of distinct character

mesa: isolated, steep-sided, flat-topped mountain

metamorphic: applies to minerals, rocks, processes and regions resulting from metamorphism (qv)

metamorphism: the process whereby a rock is transformed in the solid state to a rock with different mineral composition and texture by the increase of temperature and pressure

metapelite: a metamorphic rock which was originally a pelite, or mudrock

metasediment(s): metamorphosed sediments

metavolcanics: metamorphosed lavas

meteorite: solid piece of debris from such sources as asteroids or comets originating in outer space that survives impact with the Earth's surface

methane: chemical compound with the formula CH_4, a gas in its natural state and commonly used in the manufacture of fuel

mica: common rock-forming hydrated silicate mineral characterized by its flakiness

microcline: whitish rock-forming mineral of the feldspar family, made up of silica (SiO_2), alumina (Al_2O_3) and potassium, and closely related to orthoclase

mobile belt: large linear geological region where rock formations are characterized by strong metamorphism and structural deformation, partly surrounding or between older stable craton(s)

monoclinal: sharp downward flexure or fold structure made of strata dipping in only one direction

moraine: material deposited by a glacier or large ice sheet

mudrock: rock formed by the lithification of muddy sediment

muscovite: the most common mica, white or pale in colour, occurring in granite, schists, phyllites and associated rocks

Neoproterozoic: the younger part of the Proterozoic era, from the end of the Mesoproterozoic until the beginning of the Cambrian and dating from 1 billion to 540 million years ago

norite: plutonic igneous rock of mafic composition, usually dark grey and when fresh favoured for tombstones

ochre: powdery oxide mineral, usually mustard-yellow or red, used for pigment

olifantsklip: rough pattern resembling elephant skin shown on weathered dolomite, the result of slow chemical weathering

olivine: silicate mineral composed of silica (SiO_2), and magnesium and iron oxides (MgO, FeO), common in ultramafic and some mafic rocks

open fold: fold structure in which the angle between the fold limbs is generally more than 70°

orogen: belt of deformed rocks, commonly used to describe a specific belt, e.g. the Damara(n) Orogen

orogenic zone: geologically deformed region reflecting large-scale folding and faulting, typical of a long-lived period of mountain-building, or orogeny

orogeny: mountain-building, usually by folding and thrusting. Orogeny may be used to describe a specific event, e.g. the Damaran Orogeny

orthogneiss: term applied to gneiss derived from rocks of igneous origin, in contrast to paragneiss which denotes gneiss of sedimentary origin

outlier: isolated occurrence of younger rocks entirely surrounded by outcrops of older rocks, or a detached remnant of younger rocks found on older rocks (see inlier)

pahoehoe: Hawaiian word for usually basaltic lava, or a flow of this lava, having a smooth, lobe-like or ropey, wrinkled surface indicating solidification from a very fluid lava stream

palaeoanthropology: the science of Early Man or all prehistoric hominids

palaeontology: the science of life of past geological ages, and of fossil remains

Palaeoproterozoic: The oldest part of the Proterozoic, lasting from the end of the Archaean to the beginning of the Mesoproterozoic and dating from 2.5 to 1.6 billion years ago

palaeosurface: the surface of a bed that remained uncovered for long enough for any imprints on it, such as animal tracks or ripples left by flowing water, to become hardened and to remain, as ensuing beds were deposited, and later stripped off by erosion

paragneiss: term applied to gneiss derived from rocks of sedimentary origin (see orthogneiss)

pegmatite: vein-like intrusion of very coarse-grained, crystalline, typically granitic minerals, such as quartz, feldspar and mica, and occasionally small amounts of tourmaline, beryl, topaz and other rarer minerals, formed during the final stage of granite formation

pegmatoid: pegmatite-like

peneplain: extensive land surface of flat to very gentle relief formed by the long-lived erosion of land to its base level

petroglyph: prehistoric rock engraving made by the San people on smooth rock surfaces

phenocryst: large and usually conspicuous crystal in an igneous rock, usually volcanic, that formed and grew before the groundmass started to grow

phyllite: low-grade metamorphic rock in which micaceous minerals have tended to form parallel to the foliation, but not to the extent seen in a schist

pillow structure: structure formed when some mafic lavas are erupted under water, resembling a mass of pillows

piracy (of rivers): process whereby the headwaters of a river are intersected by another river cutting back in a deeper valley

placer: alluvial deposit containing valuable minerals, usually gold or diamonds

Placoderm: class of primitive jawed fish found in Devonian to Permian sediments

plagioclase: group of common rock-forming minerals of the feldspar family, containing calcium and sodium oxides (Na_2O and CaO), silica (SiO_2) and alumina (Al_2O_3)

planation: the act of planing, or levelling

plastic: applied to deformation where the deformed material does not return to its pre-deformation state when the deforming pressure is released, as opposed to elastic deformation, which leaves no permanent effect

pluton: discrete, usually granite intrusions of generally rounded shape and of relatively limited size that form from a larger, deeper granitic magma

plutonic: applies to igneous bodies intruded at considerable depth

porphyry: hypabyssal or extrusive igneous rock in which relatively large conspicuous crystals (or phenocrysts) are set in a finer-grained or glassy matrix

Proterozoic: The geological eon spanning the period after photosynthesis commenced on a large scale, oxygenating the atmosphere, and immediately preceding the proliferation of complex life-forms (2 500 to 540 ma).

proto-crust: informal term used to describe the first crust-like material to form in the early Earth

province: region showing broadly similar rock types, level of metamorphism, structural history and geological age

pumice: highly porous or vesicular volcanic rock that floats on water

pyrite(s): most common iron sulphide mineral (FeS_2), brassy-looking when fresh and commonly known as 'fool's gold'

pyroclastic: poorly bedded volcanic rock composed of angular fragments of erupted material of variable size, formed during volcanic explosions; also volcaniclastic

pyroxene: family of common silicate minerals found in igneous rocks and rich in magnesium, iron and calcium

pyroxenite: medium- to coarse-grained igneous rock consisting mainly of pyroxene

quartz: commonest form of silica (SiO_2) and one of the most abundant minerals in the Earth's crust

quartzite: common metamorphic rock composed essentially of quartz grains, formed by the complete recrystallization of quartz-rich sandstone

reef: refers to a vein (usually gold-bearing quartz) of extractable minerals; in South Africa it is also used for the thin, gold-rich conglomerates of the Witwatersrand

regression: period of time during the life of a sedimentary basin when sea level recedes and newly formed sediments are exposed to the air (see transgression)

residual mountain: mountain that originates because all the surrounding high-standing material has been eroded and washed away

rheomorphism: process associated with deep burial and very high-grade metamorphism, whereby gneissic rocks and migmatites eventually begin to melt and flow

rhombohedral: of minerals that crystallize or cleave in rhombohedrons; the latter term refers to crystals that show faces having the shape of a rhombus, or an oblique parallelogram, such as certain calcite crystals

sandstone: consolidated sedimentary rock made up of sand-sized grains (clearly visible), usually predominantly of quartz and lesser feldspar, cemented together by silica, clay minerals or carbonate

scarp: plateau edge, vertical or nearly so

schist: metamorphic rock in which platy or flaky minerals (micas in particular) lie parallel to each other, to give the rock conspicuous foliation, along which it may be easily broken

schistose: having the appearance and texture of a schist where it lies on a rock surface that is usually much older than the sediments (see igneous contact)

sericitic: very fine-grained aggregate of white mica (muscovite), invariably the alteration or weathering product of feldspar

series: term formerly applied to a unit of stratigraphy approximately equivalent to a formation in today's terminology, several of which made up a system

serpentinite: fairly soft rock composed largely of the serpentine group of minerals, and generally formed by the alteration of ultramafic rocks, rich in olivine

shale: fine-grained, layered, sedimentary rock made of deposits of clay-like sediment or fine silt and mud

sheet: in igneous geology, this refers to a shallow, more or less tabular intrusion that cuts through the intruded rock strata at a fairly shallow angle (see dyke); it may also refer to a layer of extrusive lava

silcrete: hard layer of secondary cherty rock formed by the upward movement of silica in solution and its deposition near-surface under dry conditions (also called 'surface quartzite') (see calcrete)

silica: applies to quartz and other mineral forms with the formula SiO_2

silicate: mineral with the SiO_2 radical forming a major part, including most of the rock-forming minerals

sill: shallow, tabular intrusion that intrudes parallel to the bedding of the intruded sedimentary rock strata (see sheet)

sillimanite: high-grade metamorphic mineral, aluminium silicate

siltstone: sediment composed mainly of silt-sized clasts, coarser-grained than mudstone, finer than sandstone

spinifex (texture): spiky texture in komatiite, formed by an interlocking 'mat' of bladed olivine crystals

stratigraphic column: idealized graphical section, or column, of geological strata or formations, youngest at the top and oldest at the bottom

stratigraphy: branch of geology dealing with aspects of stratified rocks

ABOVE LEFT: *Ghaap Group dolomitic limestone near Prieska.* **ABOVE RIGHT:** *Sand ridges in the western lee of pebbles on the Woody Cape beach (Eastern Cape) show the prevailing easterly wind at the time the photo was taken.*

stratum: layer of sedimentary rock that shows its own specific character and is distinct from the layers above and below it

stromatolites: finely layered, concentric, mound-like structures found in dolomite and formed by microscopic algal organisms

structure: arrangement of deformed rocks as seen today

subaerial: formed on land ('under air' as opposed to under deep water)

subaqueous: formed under semi-permanent water, commonly deep

subduction: process whereby one crustal plate moves beneath another, along a subduction zone, causing earthquakes and generating new magma

subhorizontal: nearly horizontal

subvertical: nearly vertical

suite: used in igneous intrusive and high-grade metamorphic geology as the collective grouping of related rocks; equivalent to 'group' in sedimentary classification

supergroup: largest grouping used in the classification of geological units, made up of more than one group

supracrustal: applied to relatively younger sedimentary and volcanic rocks, and their metamorphic equivalents, that overlie rocks of the crystalline basement, usually granitic gneisses

syenite: plutonic igneous rock less acid and more alkaline than granite

syncline: concave-upward fold

synclinorium: composite series of smaller synclinal and anticlinal folds that together form a larger upward-opening fold structure (see also anticlinorium)

syntaxis zone: used to describe the zone around Cape Town where the western and southern branches of the Cape Fold Belt meet, and where folding is not conspicuous

system: term formerly used to describe a group or series (qv), where Group and Supergroup are used today

tailings: in metallurgical usage the usually fine-grained material that is discarded or rejected after the extraction of valuable minerals from ore, e.g. gold or diamonds

talus: rocky material on hill slopes fallen from higher levels

tantalite: ore of tantalum metal, valuable mineral found in some pegmatites

tectonism: deformation of the Earth's crust by means of folding, thrusting and faulting

terrane: geological setting or type of geology in a general sense; may also be spelled 'terrain'

terroir: the whole ecology of a vineyard

thrust fault: fault produced by low-angle or near-horizontal compression in which the upper block is moved obliquely over the lower block

thrusting: process giving rise to thrust faults, with considerable lateral movement relative to vertical displacement

tidalite: sediment formed in the intertidal zone of an ocean or sea

tiger's eye: yellowish-brown ornamental stone formed by the replacement of blue asbestos by silica

tight fold: fold structure in which the angle between the fold limbs is generally less than 30°

tillite: accumulated glacial debris that has turned into rock, comprising a jumbled mix of boulders, pebbles, gravel and sand set in a matrix of glacial flour

tonalite: sodium-rich granitoid (qv)

tor: small, bouldery, granite hill, the remnant left after the erosion of the surrounding granite

trachyte: the extrusive equivalent of syenite (qv)

transform (fracture zone): fault where the relative movement of blocks is lateral (horizontal) rather than vertical

transgression: period of time during the life of a sedimentary basin when sea level rises and deposition spreads over older sediments and extends further inland, creating an unconformity (see regression)

trough cross-bedding: bedding seen in fluvial sandstone where discrete troughs of bedded sandstone overlie and overlap one another

tufa: chemical sedimentary rock composed of calcium carbonate or silica, deposited from solution in the water of a spring or percolating ground water

tuff: fine-grained pyroclastic rock formed from the deposition, usually in water, of volcanic ash, the result of faraway explosive volcanic activity

turbidite: sedimentary rock made of coarse sediment of shallow-water origin that was redeposited under deeper-water conditions down-slope by a denser current called a turbidity current

ultramafic: igneous rock containing an exceptionally low silica (SiO_2) content, and consisting almost entirely of magnesium- and iron-rich minerals, comprising rocks such as peridotite and kimberlite

unconformity: contact in a sedimentary assemblage that reflects a break during sedimentation, of some considerable duration, during which erosion and possibly tilting of the older sediments may have occurred

uplift: elevation of the land surface relative to sea level

vesicle: small cavity within a volcanic rock formed by the expansion of a bubble of gas or steam during its solidification, giving rocks that are vesicular (when filled with many cavities), and forming amygdales when filled with secondary mineral

xenolith: foreign rock fragment within an igneous rock, generally unrelated to the magma; comparable to but larger than a xenocryst

Bibliography

Anderson, JM (ed.). 2001. *Towards Gondwana Alive: Promoting biodiversity & stemming the sixth extinction*, Vol. 1. National Herbarium, National Botanical Institute, Pretoria.

Cairncross, B & Dixon, R. 1995. *Minerals of South Africa*. The Geological Society of South Africa, Johannesburg.

Cluver, MA. 1978. *Fossil Reptiles of the South African Karoo*. South African Museum, Cape Town.

Curror, WD. 2002. *Golden Memories of Barberton*, revised and enlarged by Hans Bornman. African Pioneer Mining (Pty) Ltd, Barberton.

Deacon, HJ & Deacon, J. 1999. *Human Beginnings in South Africa: Uncovering the Stone Age*. David Philip, Cape Town.

Dingle, RV, Siesser, WG & Newton, R. 1980. *Mesozoic and Tertiary Geology of Southern Africa*. AA Balkema, Rotterdam.

Directorate: Mineral Economics. *South Africa's Mineral Industry 2002/2003*. Department of Minerals and Energy, Republic of South Africa.

Drennan, MR. [no date.] *Gogga Brown: The life story of Alfred Brown, South Africa's hermit-naturalist: told from his journal*. Maskew Miller Ltd, Cape Town.

Eales, HV. 2001. *A First Introduction to the Geology of the Bushveld Complex*. The Council for Geoscience as Popular Geoscience Series #2.

Hartzer, FJ, Johnson, MR & Eglington, BM. 1998. *Stratigraphic Table of South Africa*. The Council for Geoscience, Pretoria.

Haughton, SH. 1969. *Geological History of Southern Africa*. The Geological Society of South Africa, Johannesburg.

Joubert, P & Johnson, MR. 1998. *Abridged Lexicon of South African Stratigraphy*. South African Committee for Stratigraphy, The Council for Geoscience, Pretoria.

King, LC. 1951. *South African Scenery: A textbook of geomorphology*, 2nd edn, revised. Oliver and Boyd, London.

MacRae, C. 1999. *Life Etched in Stone: Fossils of South Africa*. The Geological Society of South Africa, Johannesburg.

McCarthy, T & Rubidge, B (eds). 2005. *The Story of Earth & Life: A southern African perspective on a 4.6-billion-year journey*. Struik Nature, Cape Town.

Meredith, M. 2011. *Born in Africa: The quest for the origins of human life*. Simon & Schuster Ltd, London.

Norman, N & Whitfield, G. 2006. *Geological Journeys: A traveller's guide to South Africa's rocks and landforms*. Struik Nature, Cape Town.

South African Committee for Stratigraphy (compiler LE Kent). 1980. *Stratigraphy of South Africa*. Handbook 8, Part 1. Geological Survey of South Africa.

Taljaard, MS. 1949. *A Glimpse of South Africa*. The University Publishers and Booksellers (Pty) Ltd, Stellenbosch.

Tankard, AJ, Jackson, MPA, Erikson, KA, Hobday, DK, Hunter, DR & Minter, WEL. 1982. *Crustal Evolution of Southern Africa: 3.8 billion years of earth history*. Springer-Verlag, New York.

The Automobile Association of South Africa. 1987. *Off the Beaten Track – selected day drives in southern Africa*. The Motorist Publications (Pty) Ltd.

Viljoen, MJ & Reimold, WU. 1999. *An Introduction to South Africa's Geological and Mining Heritage*. Mintek in association with The Geological Society of South Africa, Johannesburg.

Wagner, PA. 1914. *The Diamond Fields of Southern Africa*, 1st edn, The Transvaal Leader, Johannesburg; 2nd impression (1971), C. Struik, Cape Town.

Wannenburgh, A & Dickson, JR. 1987. *The Natural Wonder of Southern Africa*. C. Struik, Cape Town.

Wilson, JE. 1998. *Terroir: The role of geology, climate and culture in the making of French wines*. University of California Press, Berkeley, California.

Wilson, MGC & Anhaeusser, CR (eds). 1999. *The Mineral Resources of South Africa*, 6th edn. Handbook 16. The Council for Geoscience, Pretoria.

Different weathering patterns of Beaufort mudrock (below) and dolerite (above) near Cradock.

Index

Turbidite sandstone over shale in the Tankwa Karoo.

'You may have come to the end of this book, but the open road stretches ahead invitingly ...'